NO PLACE FOR CHIVALRY

No Place For Chivalry

RAF night fighters defend the East of England
against the German air force in two world wars

Alastair Goodrum

GRUB STREET · LONDON

Published by
Grub Street
4 Rainham Close
London
SW11 6SS

British Library Cataloguing in Publication Data
Goodrum, Alastair
  No place for chivalry : RAF night fighters defend the East
  of England against the German air force in two world wars
  1. Great Britain. Royal Air Force – History – 1939-1945
  2. World War, 1939-1945 – Aerial operations, British
  3. Air defences – Great Britain – History – 20th century
  4. Night fighting (Military science) 5. Night fighter planes
  I. Title
  940.5′44941

ISBN 1 904943 22 5

Typeset by Pearl Graphics, Hemel Hempstead
Printed and bound by Biddles, King's Lynn

Contents

Acknowledgements   7

Chapter 1   Dangerous Moonlight   8
Chapter 2   Zeppelin!   25
Chapter 3   Fighter Nights   41
Chapter 4   Patrolling the Blue Lines   64
Chapter 5   Airborne Searchlights   83
Chapter 6   Night Hawks   101
Chapter 7   Mosquitoes Bite and Beaufighters Punch   124
Chapter 8   Steinbock, Gisela and Buzz-bombs   146

Appendix 1   Imperial German Naval Zeppelin incursions over
             the Midlands region in WW1   165
Appendix 2   Interceptions made by aircraft of Wittering
             and Digby sector night fighter squadrons in WW2   168
Appendix 3   Explanatory notes and diagram for AI Mk IV   172
Appendix 4   Comparative ranks   174
Appendix 5   Maps showing Group and Sector boundaries
             in WW2   175
Appendix 6   Map showing locations of Fg Off R P Stevens'
             air victories   177
Appendix 7   Map showing the distribution of interceptions
             made by Digby and Wittering night fighter
             squadrons in WW2   178
Appendix 8   Abbreviations used in text   179

Bibliography   182

Index   185

In memory of Jack and Mike

"... night fighter pilots are individualists who do not want very much
to be disciplined. For them night is more free than day,
free space for the expression of a feud. They find raiders in the moon
above low cloud, as shadows in the flare of ack-ack and searchlight
and above the flickering glare of ground fires."

H E Bates

Acknowledgements

I would like to thank Ian Blackamore and Dave Stubley of the Lincolnshire Aircraft Recovery Group, Bill Welbourne of the Fenland and West Norfolk Aircraft Preservation Society, Nick Squires of 23 Squadron, Peter Montgomery and Simon Parry, all of whom have provided details that have enhanced the technical and human interest elements of a number of the incidents mentioned. I am grateful to C R Salewski MA, archivist of the Deutches Museum fur Luftschiffahrt und Marinefliegerei in Nordholz, Germany, for information and illustrations relating to WW1 Naval Zeppelin operations. Illustrations have come from many sources but I appreciate particular help received from Roy Bonser, Alec Brew, Peter Brooks, Robin Duke-Woolley, Ron Durand, Ken Ellis, Chris Goss, Peter Green, Mike Kelsey, Simon Parry, Winston Ramsey, Wilhelm Ratuszynski and E A Walker. However, the original ownership of some photographs remains obscure or has been unable to be established and I apologise for any credit omitted for this reason. Extracts from official documents appear by permission of the Controller HMSO and Crown copyright is acknowledged. Quotes from Bill Norman's article in the December 2000 issue of *Flypast* are reproduced by permission of Key Publishing Ltd. Finally I am most grateful to John Davies and Louise Stanley of Grub Street, for giving me the opportunity to bring my project to life.

Author's note: Some combat reports consulted have been found to state range distances in yards while others have expressed them in feet. Although range measurements in feet appear in many reports where AI interceptions are involved, this practice is only evident in such reports from 1942 onwards. In the interests of consistency, in the narrative of this book range distances have been expressed in yards.

CHAPTER 1

Dangerous Moonlight

Peering through the cockpit canopy of a Junkers Ju88, Luftwaffe Unteroffizier Heinrich Beul shifted uneasily, gripped his MG15 machine gun more tightly and tried to scan the blackness of the night sky with his eyes. Peering intently at two flickering cathode-ray tubes, Pilot Officer Yeomans, Royal Air Force, seated in the rear cockpit of a Beaufighter, was piercing that same blackness with his airborne radar. On a midsummer night in 1941 each had a scent of the other; each one was seeking a kill.

In World War 2 the counties of Lincolnshire, Norfolk and Cambridgeshire, clustered round The Wash, were littered with airfields that made juicy targets for Luftwaffe raiders. For the Luftwaffe, the night fighter unit that evolved into Nachtjagdgeschwader 2 (NJG2) bore the brunt of the first phase of intruder missions that lasted until late 1941, scoring a considerable measure of success against operational units, while also disrupting the flying training programme on the RAF's home territory. Furthermore, when the Luftwaffe's daylight offensive in the south and east of England was finally broken, its attention turned to mounting a night bombing blitz across the United Kingdom that increased its intensity from September 1940. Thus, in addition to being an arena for night fighter versus intruder encounters, this three-dimensional corridor into the heart of England also became an aerial crossroads for elements of the German night bombing offensive directed, for example, against the industrial Midlands and North. It soon became apparent that the watery expanse of The Wash, pointing like a signpost to the heart of England, together with its sparsely populated fenlands, was a one hundred-mile passageway through which the Luftwaffe expected to fly with little interference into the industrial heartland – and indeed beyond. No doubt this same philosophy also appealed to RAF Bomber Command planners when they plotted routes into the German homeland across the Zuider Zee in Holland. Both combatants found, to their cost, that what began as a quiet back-door route became, instead, a killing ground for the night fighters of RAF Wittering and Digby Sectors.

A clue to the Luftwaffe's intentions was first discovered in the form of a navigational radio beam, oriented from east to west near Spalding, by the Wireless Intelligence Development Unit (WIDU), a special signals flight commanded by Sqn Ldr R Blucke, based at RAF Wyton on the southern edge of the region. Documents recovered from downed enemy aircraft, together with intercepted radio traffic, suggested the existence of such beams and WIDU was hastily established to conduct a detailed search of the airwaves. Equipped with radio receivers capable of monitoring signals around the 30-33 megacycle wavelength, the unit had three Avro Ansons to carry the sets and a team of specialist wireless operators to do the job. Success came quickly, for on June 21 1940, after only a handful of sorties, Anson pilot Flt Lt Hal Bufton and his Y-service radio operator Corporal Dennis Mackey located signals with the dot, dash and continuous tone characteristics of the German Lorenz blind-landing system, passing east/west one mile south of Spalding. Following the beam allowed them to detect a second beam intersecting the first at Beeston – right on track for the Rolls-Royce aero-engine factories in Derby! Later it was established that the first beam was being transmitted from Kleves on the Dutch border, while the second was believed to have originated in Bredstedt on the German-Danish border. Together they were part of a German air radio-navigation system used to guide bombers to their targets that became known by the code name Knickebein (Crooked Leg). The subsequent electronics war is the fascinating in-depth subject of several books and it is not intended to re-examine it here.

This, then, was the stage on which the battle for control of the English night sky in World War 2 was acted out. Now we'll take a look at some of the players in this deadly game in their various guises, to show what happened when the hunter got to grips with the hunted.

Air cover against possible night bombing raids was spread thinly in the Midland region at the beginning of 1940 and it seemed as if the lessons of the last war had been forgotten. In order to appreciate how events unfold in this story, yet avoid becoming bogged down with the complexity of trying to follow operations by all the night fighter squadrons throughout the whole of the UK, the exploits of one unit – 23 Squadron – will be taken as representative of this particular period of the night air war. Night fighter squadrons, in the area of the country covered by this narrative, came under the control of 12 Group of Fighter Command, whose patch stretched across the heartland of England from The Wash to the Mersey and York to Birmingham. 23 Squadron was in RAF Wittering Sector.

23, equipped with the Bristol Blenheim Mk I, had moved to RAF Wittering from RAF Northolt in May 1938 and thence to Collyweston, Wittering's adjacent satellite field, also known as K3, from where, at the end of March 1940, it began night patrols. Initially five Blenheims were converted to Mark IF (fighter) version by the addition of a bolt-on under-belly tray containing four .303 inch calibre machine guns. This was in addition to a single forward-firing .303 machine gun fitted as standard in the wing root plus the dorsal turret gun.

Right from the onset of war, a small number of 23 Squadron's Blenheims, first one, then later two sections at a time, were detached to

RAF Digby for a week in rotation, carrying out night readiness duty, standing patrols and searchlight cooperation sorties in that sector. Between October 1939 and January 1940, however, the Digby detachments had just two night scrambles, both of which proved fruitless.

Early in 1940 the eminent scientist Dr E G 'Taffy' Bowen CBE FRS worked not only on the development and construction of the first practical airborne radar sets – generally referred to as Airborne Interception and abbreviated to AI – but, due to his direct involvement over several years, was also in a unique position to give much thought to the elementary theory of air interception tactics. His analysis showed that first:

> ... a pursuing night fighter must have a speed advantage over its target. If the fighter were no faster than the target it would never catch it... if it went too fast it would overshoot. The optimum overtaking speed was about 20 to 25% greater than the aircraft being chased.

Secondly:

> In order to have a reasonable chance of completing an interception, the night fighter must be placed within a cone of about 40 or 50° behind the raider and heading on a track not more than 30° different from the target. This presented a formidable task to the ground control as it existed at that time and was not solved until the appearance of special GCI equipment towards the end of 1940.

While in approximate terms the maximum speed of a Blenheim was said to be as good as or better than its opponents – with the exception of the Junkers Ju88 – in reality, it had neither the sort of speed margin nor weight of firepower to deal with its opponents with ease. So, as will become apparent from many of the sorties described in this narrative, the Blenheim was often at a disadvantage. During those early days few airborne radar sets were available to install in Blenheims and it was not until late July 1940 that the first AI-assisted kill was achieved in the south of England. It was a slow old business though, with only eight enemy aircraft being claimed as shot down by AI-assisted Blenheims between August and November 1940.

In the meantime 23 Squadron, having ended its detachments to Digby, was to meet with some small success over the Fenlands in June 1940. This was not without losses that in themselves highlight not only the tenacity and skill of the aircrews, but also the shortcomings of the Blenheim in this role.

The night of June 18/19 1940 was a clear example of this, when the Luftwaffe mounted its first large scale night raid of the war on mainland British targets and over seventy enemy aircraft (E/A) struck at several towns, cities, airfields and rail targets across eastern and southern England, in addition to raids in other parts of the country.

From its base at Collyweston, 23 Squadron was in action that night, deploying seven Blenheim Mk IF aircraft on night fighter patrols in the vicinity of The Wash. Similar patrols had been flown every night that month to date without sighting the enemy but this occasion was going to be a hot one. What transpired is an excellent illustration of night fighter operations based on 'eyeball Mark One' technology, prior to the advent of practical airborne radar – which itself was later made more effective by precision Ground Controlled Interception (GCI) techniques. The limitation of the human eye in such situations was summarised by a former AI operator, Sqn Ldr Lewis Brandon DSO DFC:

> On an average dark night the range at which a pilot could expect to see the bomber was between 1,000 and 1,500 feet. On a very dark night, without the benefit of starlight he might have to close in to 600 or 800 feet before the vital visual. Of course there were nights when visibility was exceptionally good and one might obtain a visual at 3,000 to 4,000 feet. This was usually in conditions of bright moonlight.

The engagement by 23 Squadron illustrates – and certainly not for the last time – how confused a tactical situation could become, with several units and numerous individual aircraft all trying to tackle enemy aircraft in the dark. Furthermore, analysis of official documentation covering this action – and indeed various interpretations of it in a number of books and press articles in which it is mentioned – contain what can only be described as a trying amount of anomalies!

Involved from the Thames to the Humber on this particular night for the RAF were 23, 29 and 604 Squadrons with Blenheims and 19, 66 and 74 Squadrons with Spitfires. The overall Luftwaffe raiding force was composed of Gruppen from Kampfgeschwader 4 (KG4) and KG27, but as the focus here is on 23 Squadron's action around The Wash it would be the aircraft of KG4, operating from Merville and Lille-Roubaix, for whom places such as RAF Mildenhall, RAF Honington and RAF Marham were the primary objectives, that would clash with 23 Squadron that night.

According to the Squadron Operational Record Book (RAF Form 540) Squadron Leader Joseph 'Spike' O'Brien in L8687, YP-X was the first aircraft away from Collyweston at 22.30 hours. Interestingly, his combat report is annotated – in different handwriting – that he left the ground at 00.30 hrs and there is a curious difference between his original take-off time and of those aircraft that followed. Tonight though, seated at his shoulder in the normally unoccupied navigator's position was Pilot Officer Cuthbert King-Clarke, a new pilot being shown the ropes by his CO. Back in the turret was air gunner Corporal David Little. One explanation for the timing anomaly might be that since the sortie was primarily a familiarisation flight for King-Clarke it was combined with the regular evening standing patrol and that he probably returned to Wittering, possibly to refuel, before taking off again at 00.30 hours to join the action. While it is quite usual for a combat report to note time of take-off for the action being described, this does not mean that an ORB will necessarily reflect every event, nor guarantee its accuracy.

However, once the raiders' intentions became clearer, fighters across the east of England appear to have been ordered aloft from about 23.30 hours onwards. Six other Blenheims of A and B Flights left for their patrol lines at ten minute intervals. Sgt Alan Close, pilot, with his gunner LAC Laurence Karasek in L1458, YP-S, went off at 23.35, followed by Plt Off Aberconway Pattinson and air gunner Cpl William McAdam, in YP-U. Next up was Flt Lt Raymond Duke-Woolley in YP-L with AC2 Derek Bell in the turret. Plt Off Derek Willans, Flt Lt Roland Knight and Fg Off Nelson Harding flew the remaining Blenheims. It is interesting to note that the ranks of the non-commissioned air gunners, ranging from AC2 to Sgt, are typical of that period and that it was not until later that few operational RAF aircrew held a rank below that of sergeant.

Patrol lines were taken up on bearings fanning out eastwards from Wittering and it was Sgt Close who made the first interception in the vicinity of King's Lynn. Searchlights in The Wash belt picked out some of the raiders and initially this helped the Blenheim crews. Caught in the beam of one searchlight was a Heinkel He111.

It should not be overlooked that searchlights played an important role in support of night fighter operations – as well as AA guns – by not only locating enemy aircraft, indicating their courses and allowing their altitude to be judged, but also by providing this visual information instantly. While it is clear from some combat reports that night fighter crews occasionally cursed overzealous searchlights, in the main the searchlights and fighters worked effectively together. Realisation of their true value to the fighters brought a reorganisation at the start of 1942, when searchlights were placed in geographical 'boxes' patrolled by night fighters.

Close and Karasek exchanged gunfire with the enemy aircraft but the Blenheim lacked both the speed and firepower to kill at a relatively safe distance. Their Blenheim too was lit up by the searchlight glare and it was the enemy gunners who got the better of this exchange. A burst of gunfire from the Heinkel shattered the cockpit, probably wounding or even killing Sgt Close because the aircraft immediately dived out of control and crashed into Chapel Road, Terrington St Clement. LAC Karasek was fortunate indeed to bale out and landed safely nearby. Away to his north Sqn Ldr O'Brien saw an aircraft fall in flames in the vicinity of King's Lynn – Close's aircraft – and further confirmation of the incident is noted in the RAF Sutton Bridge ORB – at that time home to 6 OTU – which reads as follows.

Air raid warning red at 23.37. Observed an air action against E/A at 01.30 [sic] in the east. An aircraft was seen to fall in flames.

Transport rushed to the scene at Terrington St Clement and found Blenheim L1458. The two airmen were brought to Sutton Bridge, the air gunner going to the sickbay at 03.00 and the pilot being found dead at 03.45. A guard was mounted over the wreckage, which was scattered over a 1,000 yard area. The 'all clear' sounded at 03.44 hours.

First blood to the Luftwaffe – but then the situation changed. Flt Lt Duke-Woolley's patrol line took him towards Sutton Bridge from where he, too, saw this searchlight activity and spotted the two aircraft involved. He gave chase at full throttle and his combat report takes up the story:

Time 00.45. Observed a ball of fire, which I took to be a Blenheim fighter in flames, break away from behind the tail of the E/A. I climbed to engage this E/A and attacked from below the tail after the searchlights were extinguished. I closed to a range of fifty yards and opened fire. E/A returned fire and appeared to throttle back suddenly. My own speed was 130-140mph and I estimate the E/A slowed to 110mph. I delivered five attacks with front guns and during these my air gunner fired seven bursts at various ranges. After the last front gun attack my air gunner reported that the E/A's port engine was on fire. As my starboard engine was now u/s, I broke off the engagement and returned to base, where several bullet holes were found in the wings and fuselage, including cannon strikes in the starboard wing and rear fuselage.

Spirited return gunfire from the Heinkel caused no significant damage to the Blenheim, although Derek Bell realised he had had a lucky escape when he found a bullet had pierced and lodged in his parachute pack! Airspeeds mentioned here may seem quite slow but it will be seen that, certainly in the era of the Blenheim and Defiant, rarely did night combats involve speeds above 200mph.

Duke-Woolley claimed the Heinkel as a probable but later that day (19th) an RAF intelligence report stated a Heinkel He111 H-4 had crash-landed in the shallows of Blakeney Creek on the north Norfolk coast. As the gruppenkommandeur of II/KG4, Major Dietrich Freiherr von Massenbach, his lead pilot Oberleutnant Ulrich Jordan and radio operator Ofw Max Leimer from Heinkel He111, 5J+DM, waded ashore into captivity carrying their wounded flight engineer Fw Karl Amberger, they would have had plenty of time to wonder where their planning went wrong. When interrogated they confirmed shooting down one fighter and then being attacked themselves almost immediately afterwards and having to force-land as a result.

Honours were now even but the night's action was not over yet. Sqn Ldr O'Brien's own search line took him south from Wittering where, at about 01.25, searchlights coned another Heinkel He111 which he intercepted at

12,000 feet about ten miles from Newmarket. O'Brien's combat report takes up the story:

> Opened fire at E/A with rear [turret] gun from below and in front as it was held by searchlights. The E/A turned to port and dived. I gave him several long bursts with the front guns from fifty to one hundred yards range and saw clouds of smoke from the target's starboard engine and a lesser amount from the port engine. I overshot the E/A and passed very close below and in front of him. My rear gunner put a burst into the cockpit at close range and the E/A disappeared in a diving turn apparently out of control. I suddenly lost control of my own aircraft, which spun violently to the left. Failing to recover from the spin I ordered my crew to abandon the aircraft and I followed the navigator [sic] out of the hatch.

This latter was not an easy undertaking.

Interviewed by the writer Trevor Grove for a *Daily Mail* feature about the Battle of Britain, Raymond Duke-Woolley recalled what Sqn Ldr O'Brien had told him about that eventful night. He said:

> In the gunfight the Heinkel went down then Spike's Blenheim went out of control in a spin. At that time, popular opinion among pilots was that no pilot had ever got out of a spinning Blenheim alive, because the only way out was through the top sliding hatch and you then fell through one or other of the airscrews! The new boy probably didn't know that but nevertheless he froze and Spike had to get him out. He undid his seat belt, unplugged his oxygen and pushed him up out of the top hatch while holding his parachute ripcord. He told me afterwards that he felt sick when the lad fell through the airscrew. Spike then had to get out himself. He grasped the wireless aerial behind the hatch, pulled himself up by it and then turned round so that his feet were on the side of the fuselage. Then he kicked outwards as hard as he could. He felt what he thought was the tip of an airscrew blade tap him on his helmet earpiece but luck was with him that night.

Raymond Duke-Woolley then went on to recount the rest of the tale, which may or may not have been simply a good RAF line-shoot, but nevertheless is a story that sums up Spike O'Brien's character.

> He parachuted down safely on the outskirts of a village and went to the nearest pub to ring Wittering and ask for transport to fetch him home. He bought a pint and sat down to await transport and began chatting idly to another chap in uniform who was in the room when he arrived. After a while, thinking the chap's dress was a bit unusual, O'Brien asked him if he was a Pole or a Czech. 'Oh no,' replied his

companion in impeccable English, 'I'm a German pilot actually. Just been shot down by one of your chaps.' At this point – so the story goes – O'Brien sprang to his feet and said, 'I arrest you in the name of the King. Anyway where did you learn English?' To which the German replied, 'That's all right. I won't try to get away. In fact I studied for three years at Cambridge, just down the road. My shout, what's yours?' So that's just what they did: sat and had a drink.

A Heinkel He111P of KG4, coded 5J+AM, had indeed crashed at Fleam Dyke near the quaintly-named village of Six Mile Bottom. Sqn Ldr O'Brien filed a claim for the kill and a telexed intelligence report said he thought the cause of his own crash was that he was shot down by AA fire. At 01:30 his Blenheim L8687 crashed and exploded, scattering wreckage over a wide area of Warren Hill, Newmarket and sadly his air gunner, Cpl Little, perished in the crash.

But hold on a minute, what about the Spitfire? What Spitfire, you may ask? Well, in the darkness and confusion of this running battle a fighter pilot from 19 Squadron, Fg Off G W 'John' Petre flying Spitfire L1032, also attacked this same Heinkel at the same time as Sqn Ldr O'Brien. Petre's account of the combat told of how he opened fire with his eight machine guns but had to sheer off hard to one side to avoid colliding with an aeroplane that simultaneously opened fire alongside him. In that split second he recognised it as a Blenheim firing at *his* target. Hundreds of bullets from all sides sprayed the bomber, killing one gunner, but when searchlights illuminated the Spitfire others of the crew manning gun positions gave back as good as they got. Now their explosive bullets hit the Spitfire's fuel tank and set it on fire. Suffering burns to his face and hands Fg Off Petre was forced to dive away from the battle and bale out.

Riddled with bullets, losing altitude and with both engines on fire the Heinkel, too, was mortally hit. Instinctively trying to shake off his attacker(s), pilot Feldwebel Willi Maier dived westwards and jettisoned the bomb load, most of it falling on Warren Hill on the outskirts of Newmarket. This must have been about the time that things went pear-shaped for O'Brien because when the Heinkel "…disappeared in a diving turn apparently out of control [he] suddenly lost control of [his] aircraft", and the Blenheim also crashed at Warren Hill. With no chance of staying in the air, Maier baled out with those of his crew left alive. Flight engineer Fw Karl Hauck, observer (and aircraft commander), Oblt Joachim von Arnim and Fw Maier landed safely but radio operator, Fw Paul Gersch, was killed.

When the RAF claims for this combat were submitted – quite separately – Sqn Ldr O'Brien was credited with a probable and Fg Off Petre a confirmed kill. Overall that night the RAF claimed to have destroyed seven bombers and probably three others but the Luftwaffe actually lost five aircraft and their crews. Four RAF fighters had been shot down with the loss of five airmen killed.

Writing after the war, Flt Lt Duke-Woolley expressed the opinion that:

... in the early days, aircrew were totally unbriefed about the best way to shoot down enemy aircraft. They were told to aim for the fuselage but this was pretty ineffective, since bullets often hit crewmen rather than doing much damage to the aeroplane. When interrogated, one of the German pilots brought down that night [June 18/19], made it clear that his aircraft came down because all his instruments had been shot away rather than the aircraft itself not operating. The pilot had a seat with armour plating so he was reasonably well protected against attack from the stern. Later strategies were to go for the fuel tank, engines or a frontal attack on the pilot.

It would not be right to bring this incident to a close without making reference to the earlier tale of the German airman in the pub who was said to have been up at Cambridge before the war. Somehow the tale seems to have been embellished in the telling and trying to unravel such pieces of information is the bane of research. The reader can reach his/her own conclusion. I have not been able to confirm it, as well as finding similar tales – the truth is elusive.

First there is Sqn Ldr O'Brien's version as attributed to Flt Lt Duke-Woolley above – of which it might be said 23 Squadron's own historian has expressed some scepticism. Then there is a more succinct version in the book *Air Raid!* – also felt by that author to be dubious. Finally there are another two similar incidents recounted in an article entitled 'First of Many' that may have had some influence on the tale. The latter states that Oblt Ulrich Jordan, from 5J+DM which crashed at Blakeney, on being captured was taken to an army field dressing station where he met and recognised an army chaplain who was cox of a British rowing crew that won a 1936 Olympics race that Jordan had watched in Germany. A little later the same article states that Oblt von Arnim, from 5J+AM which crashed at Fleam Dyke, was taken to RAF Duxford after capture and entertained in the 19 Squadron mess, being looked after by Flt Lt Brian Lane. Lane's wife apparently joined them in the mess and she and von Arnim recognised each other immediately from motor racing meetings they had both attended before the war. It's a small world!

Having survived this violent engagement Sqn Ldr O'Brien, posted from 23 to 234 Squadron to fly single-seat fighters, was killed in action over Kent on September 7 1940. Karasek did not survive much longer than his former skipper either for, having been promoted to sergeant, he died in an air accident on September 25 of that same year. During its operations from Wittering and Digby, air accidents also accounted for the loss of Flt Lt Percy Walker and AC2 Benjamin France (attached from 229 Sqn) when L1452 crashed near Gainsborough on November 4 1939. Air gunner, LAC Chrystall, escaped by baling out and said he thought the crash was due to his pilot being dazzled by a searchlight. In January 1940, Plt Off Roy Barritt and Cpl Ronald Wilson died when L1466 crashed at Helpston for unknown reasons and Plt Off Charles Cardnell and Sgt Cyril Stevens were killed when L1448 crashed at Peterborough on August 8 1940, shortly after taking off for a night patrol.

By the end of September 23 Squadron moved out of Wittering for intruder duties based on the south coast and towards the end of November 1940, 25 Squadron arrived from RAF Debden to take their place in the sector and to be re-equipped with the Beaufighter.

By way of contrast, another aspect of the night air war – that of the German intruder – will now be illustrated.

Skegness, on the coast at the northern corner of The Wash, features in this narrative from time to time for several reasons, not least of which is that it was often one of the first friendly landfalls for RAF bombers returning from raids on northern Germany. For crews on these long-duration operations (some sorties lasted twelve hours or more), when it came to hazards in the harsh autumn and winter of 1940, if storms, fog or fatigue didn't get you then a marauding Luftwaffe intruder just might. The story of one such incident begins in Skegness, not in wartime but on a sunny Sunday in September 1992.

It was just another quiet seaside afternoon that coincided with one of the lowest tides of the year. Returning to station after a routine exercise with the Mablethorpe inshore rescue boat, in the gentle swell two hundred yards off the end of the pier, crewmen of the *Lincolnshire Poacher* lifeboat saw a glint of sunlight reflecting from a piece of metal. Recognisable as the tip of a propeller blade they marked the spot with a buoy. Returning at low water next day it was hauled from the seabed with the aid of the lifeboat launch tractor.

Cleaned up, that three-bladed propeller, complete with hub and reduction gear, now stands in the lifeboat station with a simple plaque on which is stated the aircraft type, date of crash and location. Behind that simple legend, however, lies a drama enacted one pitch-dark autumn night more than half a century earlier.

In the early hours of October 28 1940, Handley Page Hampden X3027 of 49 Squadron, based at RAF Scampton, made the long haul back from a minelaying sortie off the French port of Lorient, with Fg Off John Bufton in command. One of the early successes of the Luftwaffe intruder campaign, X3027 now fell victim to a Junkers Ju88 flown by Leutnant Heinz Völker of I/NJG2.

Although the bomber hit the sea at 02.00, it was not until 02.50 that the lifeboat could be launched to search for the aircraft and its crew. This delay was said by locals to be due to soldiers being reluctant to open barbed wire barricading the beach. Despite the darkness, Sgt Frederick Bichard, wireless operator/air gunner (WOp/AG), was found and pulled from the water at 05.00, but sadly died later in hospital. Speaking afterwards, members of the public believed they heard cries for help offshore and once, a searchlight even picked out men in the water before orders came to douse the light owing to the presence of hostile aircraft.

Lifeboatmen did not give up the search until the grey morning light confirmed nothing more could be done. The bodies of Fg Off Bufton and WOp/AG Sgt Bob Robertson were found on the beach but of navigator, Plt Off Konstantine Ballas-Andersen, nothing was found.

This was Lt Völker's first success as an intruder pilot. During the next nine months he was credited with seven claims until on July 22 1941 he too ran out of luck, killed in a mid-air collision with his eighth intended victim, a Wellington from 11 OTU Bassingbourn.

Night combats, though, would not always involve multi-engine aeroplanes and of the many pilots guarding the way to Midlands targets, some worked best alone in a single-seat fighter. One such man was Richard Playne Stevens. Over thirty years of age when he joined the RAF, this pre-war flyer was old by the fighter pilot standards of the day. After a spell with army cooperation he was posted to 6 OTU at RAF Sutton Bridge from October 29 to November 26 1940, to undergo a Hurricane conversion course. Former Battle of Britain pilot Flt Lt Bill Whitty was an instructor at 6 OTU between November 1940 and August 1941 and he recalled: "We had 'Cat's Eyes' Stevens as a pupil, he was desperate to get onto night fighters as his parents [sic] had been killed in a bombing raid."

Since his next posting was to 151 Squadron at Wittering he would arrive with at least a little familiarity with the area around The Wash. Ever the loner, all his air victories (fourteen confirmed destroyed) were achieved in a Hurricane fighter, without on-board radar and all while flying air defence sorties with 151 Squadron based at RAF Wittering. Popular myths have grown up about this legendary pilot, some of which suggest he wandered the night sky like a demon sniffing out the enemy by some superhuman process but this seems – like all myths – to stretch the truth somewhat. It was rumoured that he was driven by revenge for the death of his wife and/or children in an air raid on Manchester and that this accounted for his aggressive approach to night operations. This latter could infer that his contemporaries somehow acted differently or were less driven to get to grips with the enemy but that would do them an injustice.

Like his contemporaries, Stevens was an excellent flyer under night conditions – perhaps better than most – but he had had the benefit of pre-war commercial night flying experience. He was therefore at home in the night sky but as for 'wandering' about the sky, let's remember these were all disciplined airmen who were despatched on orders and placed in or near potential combat areas, by an efficient ground control organisation. After that, naturally, they had the freedom for any action and aggression that the job demanded, wherever it might take them, for there were no rules once combat was joined. In the chapters that follow, an examination of night sorties originating or terminating in Wittering and Digby sectors, will show that defending night fighter pilots engaged the enemy across a vast area of England. They were limited only by their own fuel and ammunition supply.

Cold and calculating perhaps but it was no place for the hot-headed, as the following sortie carried out by Plt Off Stevens himself illustrates.

On April 8/9 1941 Coventry was still being hammered as the Blitz moved towards its zenith. Nine Hurricane and Defiant fighters were sent off by 151 Squadron, with orders to orbit Coventry on Fighter Night patrols. Flying Hawker Hurricane V6934, Plt Off Stevens took off from Wittering at 00.52 on the 9th and reached Coventry at his patrol altitude of 19,000 feet, well above the AA gun level. About fifteen minutes later he saw a Heinkel He111 below him, silhouetted against a cloud layer. Keeping the bandit in sight, a curving dive took him down 4,000 feet and brought him neatly into a quarter position just below the bomber's stern, where at a range of only seventy-five yards he eased up the Hurricane's nose and opened fire. The first burst hit the belly of the bomber causing a large explosion (seen by another 151 pilot nearby) and the bomber dived with flames streaming from the port engine. He put another burst into the fuselage, which brought more flames as it went into the cloud layer at 5,000 feet. Stevens followed and saw the Heinkel emerge ahead of him, still blazing and with the appearance of bombs and incendiaries exploding, it crashed to earth. Resuming his patrol just above the AA layer at 12,000 feet over the north-east part of the city, Plt Off Stevens saw another Heinkel He111 slightly above him travelling east. He tailed this one until he was within 200 yards when the ventral gunner spotted him and started firing at the Hurricane. Stevens dived underneath, fired a deflection burst at the nose and centre section from a hundred yards range then pulled up on the port side, gave it another burst and the ventral gunner stopped firing. At this point the dorsal gunner sent some accurate bursts of machine-gun fire at the Hurricane, hitting it several times and making Stevens drop back a little.

Another firing pass from astern set the bomber's starboard engine on fire, from which streaming glycol covered the Hurricane windscreen and obscured Stevens' view. Once more he dropped back, slid back the cockpit hood and wiped the screen clear with his glove before closing to a hundred yards where, buffeted by the slipstream, he hit the Heinkel with another burst. With both engines on fire now, the bomber dived steeply towards the cloud layer with Plt Off Stevens catching it with a final burst as he followed it down. The stricken bomber went through the cloud but having lost sight of it, he headed back to Wittering. In a sortie lasting just sixty-six minutes he had only twenty-five rounds left in each of seven guns, the eighth gun having jammed early in the fight. His claim for two Heinkels destroyed was later confirmed. The first Heinkel was identified as 1G+FK from I/KG27, which crashed near Wellesbourne in Warwickshire, and the second was G1+DL from I/KG55 that crashed near Desford, Leicestershire. This was the second time Plt Off Stevens had brought down two enemy aircraft in one night.

Night fighter air gunners – and for that matter, AI operators – tend to be overlooked by many writers (but not, I am sure, by their own pilots!) when it comes to handing out credit for shooting down enemy aeroplanes. Let it be made absolutely clear then that, in the world of two-seat night fighters, success in the air was due to teamwork, with the end result coming down to the shooting ability of an air gunner or the keen eye and mental agility of an AI radar operator, just as much as to those same qualities in the pilot of a night fighter. No better example can be found to illustrate the part played by an air gunner than by looking at the following typical Defiant Fighter Night sortie.

On the same night that Richard Stevens flew the sortie mentioned above, 151 Squadron also sent several of its Defiant aircraft to patrol Coventry. Flt Lt Desmond McMullen with air gunner Sgt Sam Fairweather was one of these, leaving Wittering at 00.50 on April 9 to circle the city at his allotted altitude of 17,000 feet. It was an uneventful patrol and as the end of his hour approached without a sniff of the enemy, McMullen received the call to return to base. He circled the city one more time, losing altitude to 13,000 feet ready to head back to Wittering. Suddenly, silhouetted against bright moonlight, he saw the shape of a Heinkel He111 going south, crossing his track about 400 yards ahead. McMullen brought the Defiant in under the port wing of the bomber and at seventy-five yards range Sgt Fairweather let go a three-second burst into the fuselage, followed by a long five-second burst into the cockpit area as the Defiant overshot. Keeping the range to between fifty and a hundred yards McMullen clung to the Heinkel as it twisted and turned, making for a cloud layer down at 6,000 feet. Now handicapped by a reflector sight that kept jumping from fully-dim to fully-bright and with one of his four .303 guns jammed, Fairweather managed to fire a two-second burst into the bomber's belly before it disappeared into cloud south of Coventry, going down vertically with smoke pouring from both engines. Since Fairweather was having problems with his weapons, McMullen did not hang about and landed back at Wittering at 02.04. It seems that the 600 rounds expended may, with the possible intervention of AA fire for good measure, have contributed to the demise of Heinkel He111 G1+LS from III/KG55 which crashed in Windsor Great Park about twenty-five minutes later.

In just one year since that chaotic air battle of June 18/19 1940 the night air war over England had developed dramatically. By June 1941 the process of interception had become, by necessity, a technological war run by men working flickering black boxes, operating within an integrated air/ground system. Here is an example of just how much things had changed.

At fifteen minutes past midnight on Sunday June 22 1941, an all-black Junkers Ju88C-2 night fighter, coded R4+JH, werk nummer 0827, of the Luftwaffe's specialist night intruder unit, Nachtjagdgeschwader 2 (NJG2), took off from its base at Gilze-Rijen, in Holland, for a mission over England. For the crew, Oberfeldwebel Otto Weise (pilot), Gefreiter Hermann Mandel (flight engineer) and Unteroffizier Heinrich Beul (radio operator/gunner), it was the latest of many such sorties, which had made them old hands at their deadly game of hide and seek.

The Junkers pilot is an example of an experienced airman – just like RAF aircrew at the start of the war – trained over many years in a peacetime situation. Aged nineteen, Otto Weise had joined the pre-war German flying service in July 1933, training at various locations as the embryo Luftwaffe evolved into its wartime shape. His first operational posting was to the Zerstörerstaffel of Kampfgeschwader 30 (Z/KG30) in February 1940, based at Stavanger during the Norwegian campaign. It was with this unit that he filed his only kill, a Wellington – claimed but unsubstantiated – as shot down into the North Sea on July 23 1940 (just before he was posted to I/NJG2 on July 28 1940). Otto was awarded the Iron Cross (First Class) in May 1941.

The Ju88 crew's task that night was to roam above the airfields of Lincolnshire, seeking out unwary RAF aircraft and sending them to their doom. RAF inspectors were later to find that the armament installed for this purpose on this particular aircraft was concentrated in the 'solid' nose and consisted of one MG FF (a drum-fed 20mm cannon), and three belt-fed MG17, 7.92mm machine guns. Four drums each containing sixty rounds of 20mm ammunition were found on board. In addition, the Junkers carried two MG15 (7.92mm) guns in the crew compartment and eight 50kg bombs plus a small quantity of incendiaries, the latter to plaster over any aerodrome foolish enough to show a gleam of light. On this fateful night, however, it was to be the German crew that would be despatched from the Fenland sky, to meet a fiery end at the hands of one of the RAF's most successful night fighter squadrons.

Unteroffizier Beul, on his ninth sortie over England, became the sole survivor from the Junkers crew and as he recalled many years later, anti-aircraft guns and searchlights, normally active when they were detected crossing the English coast, were unusually quiet that night – an ominous sign that RAF night fighters were probably lurking in wait for incoming raiders.

Just before midnight that same night, Flying Officer Michael Herrick, a New Zealand pilot with 25 Squadron, together with his radar operator Pilot Officer Yeomans, was lining up R2277, a Merlin-engined Beaufighter II, call-sign 'Cockle 22', on the long runway at RAF Wittering. Less than two hours later they would be locked in a battle for survival in the dark sky above the south Lincolnshire village of Market Deeping.

Fg Off Herrick, also a seasoned campaigner in his deadly trade, was already credited with the destruction of four enemy aeroplanes in night actions, including two in one sortie, in the nine months since the Blitz had begun. For this success, achieved in slow, poorly-armed Blenheims and without the aid of radar, he had been awarded the Distinguished Flying Cross.

Instructed to patrol at 12,000 feet, north of The Wash, he eased open the throttles of his twin Merlins and thundered off into the starlit night. Once airborne, control of the Beaufighter was handed over to Orby GCI, an installation located a few miles west of Skegness, equipped with Air Ministry Experimental Station (AMES) intermediate type 8 radar apparatus. After an uneventful hour and a half, Herrick was given several course changes towards the general direction of Wittering and told to reduce altitude to 9,000 feet as there was some trade in the vicinity. At 01.10, while losing height, Plt Off Yeomans picked up a target trace on the twin display tubes of his Mark IV Airborne Interception radar set (AI Mk IV) and Herrick set off in chase. Their target was heading inland from the direction of The Wash. A four-minute, AI-guided chase and there it was – an aircraft flying south at 9,000 feet, dead ahead and a couple of hundred feet below, with the Beaufighter in a perfect attacking position. Herrick at once turned to port to bleed off speed then approached the target, which was travelling at about 180mph, from below and behind. Closing gently now to one hundred yards range, Fg Off Herrick, without the aid of any moonlight, believed his bandit was a Heinkel He111. Being uncertain though and unable to manoeuvre to get it silhouetted against any northern light, with a calmness for which he was renowned, he slowly overtook the aircraft and drew alongside at about one hundred yards abeam. In the cold light of morning, events would confirm the bandit as a Ju88 but with just a silhouette, a single fin and four exhaust flames to go on – and the prospect of being hit by machine-gun fire at any second – Herrick was confident enough just to confirm it as a hostile to his controller and drop back to his attacking position.

All this time – although only a few minutes in reality – the Beaufighter remained undetected by the enemy, but at the instant Herrick opened fire with his four 20mm cannon, the enemy plunged into a diving turn to starboard. Beul had spotted something but his shouted warning to the pilot came too late to save them. Herrick clung tenaciously to the German's tail. Throwing caution to the wind and spurning the reflector sight in order to keep his prey in view, he pressed the firing button again, this time holding it down, in his own words "...using the guns like a hosepipe". Flashes of cannon strikes could be seen exploding all over the enemy aircraft and fuel tanks in the starboard wing were ruptured and caught fire. Otto dived to try to subdue the flames but to no avail. Having dropped to 7,000 feet, the Junkers was rocked by a fierce explosion inside the fuselage. Circling, it continued to burn and as Herrick was about to put in a decisive burst of gunfire, another explosion jolted the stricken machine. At this point it plunged to earth in a fiery spiral, crashing into a wheat field on Haines Farm, Backgate, Deeping St James, not far from the village church. Although heavily censored, local newspapers carried sensational, jingoistic accounts of the combat itself.

> Residents in several villages gathered in the roads in the warm night and in the clear starlit sky had a thrilling view... a terrific dogfight, witnessed by hundreds of people, many of whom had dashed from their houses in their night attire ... ...when the enemy fighter went

down, the British fighter performed the victory roll.

There was no time for rejoicing in the sky though and Herrick and Yeomans continued their patrol, but with no more contacts they returned to Wittering at 02:45 hours.

This was the first occasion on which 25 Squadron had used a Merlin-engine Beaufighter with success, but in his combat report Fg Off Herrick commented: "the extra engine power and speed is not considered beneficial at the heights flown during this particular engagement." He fired a total of 181 rounds of 20mm ammunition to despatch this Ju88. Beaufighter Mk II, R2277, had been allocated to the squadron for operational evaluation but was struck off charge on June 26 after a month's trial and no further examples of this mark appeared on the squadron strength.

Meanwhile, inside that burning Junkers, Beul and his companion, Mandel, tried in vain to extinguish the flames. Otto Weise, no longer able to control the aircraft in its headlong dive towards the ground, gave the order to bale out. In the frantic seconds that followed, Beul jettisoned the cockpit hood, stood on his seat and dived out. His parachute cracked open with a jerk and he floated safely to earth. Mandel was all but engulfed by flames and his parachute caught fire. When he jumped out of the aircraft the tattered, burning canopy failed to support him and he fell to his death. Pilot Otto Weise perished in the wreckage of his aeroplane.

Looking about him as he fell, Beul could see the Welland river glinting below and even had the presence of mind to inflate his lifejacket because he thought he might land in the water! In the event the wind carried him well past the river and he came down on the outskirts of Northborough village, as did the unfortunate Mandel. While he was still about a hundred feet in the air he saw a group of people converging on him and a member of the Home Guard captured him just as soon as his feet touched the ground. According to the local newspaper report, Beul offered no resistance and walked quietly with his captors to the Home Guard's house nearby, where he was offered food. He refused everything except a glass of water and would only drink that after he had seen the soldier taste it first then, after some first aid on an injured arm, he was driven off into custody at RAF Wittering.

It was during this stage of his captivity that the final act of this ferocious combat was played out. Beul, by now feeling the effect of his ghastly experience, was unable to eat any food offered by his captors. It can only be imagined what thoughts passed through his mind when the door of his cell opened and he was introduced to Fg Off Herrick, his recent tormentor. What were Herrick's thoughts too, on coming face to face with his vanquished foe, a fellow flyer?

Beul went on his way later, to an interrogation centre and thence to POW camp. Michael James Herrick flew more night fighter patrols, received a bar to his DFC and advanced to the rank of squadron leader. He was killed on June 16 1944, shot down into the sea off Denmark, while flying with 302 Squadron on a Day Ranger sortie.

There is a sting in the tail of this story. The *Lincolnshire Free Press* of July 11 1989 carried a headline 'Bomb Found' under which was the story of bomb disposal officers – ironically also from RAF Wittering – being called out to deal with a 50kg World War 2 bomb. It had been discovered in a field at Haines Farm in Backgate, Deeping St James by a group of aviation archaeologists from RAF Henlow while they were in the process of recovering the remains of the Ju88 for preservation. The bomb was declared too unstable to move and after the few local residents nearby had been evacuated, it was blown up where it lay.

Immediately after the Junkers had crashed in 1941 an RAF intelligence team inspected the site, as was the custom, gleaning whatever information they could about the construction and performance of enemy aircraft by sifting through the wreckage. Their report, now open to public view, states that six 50kg bombs were recovered from the site and that at least one bomb may have exploded on impact. In 1989 another turned up, making a total of eight. Heinrich Beul has been quoted as stating eight 50kg bombs were loaded onto the Junkers that night – so perhaps that deadly cargo has been accounted for at long last.

The night sky in wartime was certainly no place for chivalry... ...but how did it all start?

CHAPTER 2

Zeppelin!

In World War 1, the night sky over England resounded not to the beat of Junkers, BMW or Daimler-Benz engines but to the menacing throb of Maybach engines propelling enormous Zeppelin airships through the darkness.

Initially reluctant to unleash his bombers, early in January 1915 Kaiser Wilhelm, under pressure from his Military High Command, at last authorised his navy – responsible for operating a large part of the German airship (Luftschiff) force – to mount air raids on Britain. At first ordering such attacks to be limited to coastal, dock and other military targets, the Kaiser stipulated none must be directed at central London. This strategy, soon revised to include the capital, was initially one of several factors that accounted for the Midlands being visited in one way or another by a relatively high proportion (20%) of German airship raids on England during that conflict.

Zeppelin! The very word itself struck fear into the hearts of the British population. In reality though, the people knew very little of such machines, instead from propaganda circulating since the outbreak of war, they had acquired a rather exaggerated perception of their effect. Since the turn of the century, while Count Ferdinand Von Zeppelin developed the rigid airships that bore his name for military as well as civil purposes, Britain lacked a comparable programme. Germany had quickly recognised the military potential of lighter-than-air craft as long-range reconnaissance machines and bombers. The British Government, on the other hand, subscribed to the view that heavier-than-air aeroplanes had more military value in a reconnaissance role, than for bombing on the limited scale then envisaged.

That Zeppelins were able to wander relatively freely through night-time British skies caused much consternation at the War Office. Soon it became evident, however, that air navigation at night for friend and foe alike, unless aided by good weather and moonlight, was open to considerable error. Radio direction finding equipment was unreliable and navigation relied on nautical dead reckoning techniques which, given the poor meteorological information available to flyers, is another factor that resulted in incursions into provincial airspace accessible from around The Wash.

Prior to this Zeppelin problem becoming a stark reality, two respected

British airmen (among many others) whose names are familiar from the pre-war powered flying and ballooning era, were called upon to help assess the feasibility of enemy airships being able to locate targets in England at night. B C Hucks, a renowned pre-WW1 pioneering aviator commissioned as 2nd Lieutenant in the Royal Flying Corps (RFC) in August 1914 and N F Usborne, a former balloon pilot, later to be Wing Commander, Royal Naval Air Service (RNAS), separately undertook some of this test work. The findings of this investigative flying during the months immediately following the outbreak of war included the opinion that, on dark nights, or in fog, or cloudy conditions, it was only possible to locate major, blacked-out conurbations by flying strict compass courses from an identified way-point. It might also be possible to follow prominent rivers if these, too, could be seen and identified. Furthermore, it was considered that bombing under such conditions and from the altitudes anticipated would be very inaccurate. In practice these opinions seem to be borne out by the methods and failures of subsequent Zeppelin raids. The British War Office was probably lulled into a false sense of security by this evidence, as nearly two years elapsed before the increasing frequency and size of enemy air raids eventually forced a reorganisation of British night air defence.

At this point it is worth clarifying the German airship numbering scheme that will be appearing from time to time in this text. Rigid, aluminium-framed airships produced by the Zeppelin organisation were known as Luftschiff Zeppelin and given the factory abbreviation LZ followed by a sequential Arabic number. Although these machines were used both by the German Navy and the German Army it is the former that conducted the majority of airship raids on England and the Midland region in particular and therefore will feature most prominently in this story. Upon allocation to the German Navy, Zeppelins were marked with the letter L followed by their own Arabic, sequential naval distinguishing number. By contrast, army Zeppelins were marked with the letter Z (later changed to LZ) followed by Roman numerals. Popular usage has also turned the word Zeppelin itself into a generic name covering almost any rigid airship of that era, including the wooden-construction Schutte-Lanz types.

Furthermore, it will help the reader to appreciate the size of these naval airships in relation to aeroplanes by tabulating some basic dimensions:

Serial	Length	Diameter	Capacity Gas (Cu Ft)	Max Airspeed
L 3 (M-class)	518 feet	48 feet	790,000	53mph
L 10 (P-class)	536 feet	61 feet	1,120,000	60mph
L 30 (R-class)	650 feet	78 feet	1,950,000	64mph
L 53 (V-class)	740 feet	78 feet	2,420,000	67mph
L 70 (X-class)	690 feet	78 feet	2,200,000	81mph

It might also put things into perspective to realise these monsters were as long as two football pitches and as half as tall as Nelson's column!

Within ten days of the Kaiser's directive authorising attacks on England, being issued under pressure from his Military High Command, two German Naval Zeppelins – Luftschiff 3 (L3), and L4, left their base at Fuhlsbuttel, near Hamburg, at 11.00 on January 19 1915, bound for the English coast. Initially, Fuhlsbuttel was the headquarters of the Imperial German Navy Airship Division, but it would shortly relocate to Nordholtz. The principal target for future German airship attacks was to be London, mainly because it was the capital city of the British Empire, its seat of government, centre of economics and also as a huge centre of population there was a massive opportunity to affect civilian morale. The German High Command was confident this would turn the war in its favour. This first foray though was not without its problems and the effect of weather conditions brings to light yet another reason for German intrusions into skies around The Wash.

Intending to strike at targets in the Humber area, strong winds and a maximum airspeed of around 50mph resulted in the formation's navigation being hopelessly wide of the mark. After L6 (commanded by Kapitän-leutnant Horst Freiherr Treusch von Buttlar-Brandenfels), which joined the group from Nordholtz, near Cuxhafen, turned back early with engine trouble, the other two made landfall on the north Norfolk coast at Bacton near Cromer at 20.30, well south of the intended track. At this point L3, with Kapitänleutnant (Kptlt) Johann Fritze in command, turned southwards while L4 headed north and it is the latter's track we shall follow now.

Commanded by Kptlt Magnus von Platen-Hallermund, L4 followed the north Norfolk coast, reaching Hunstanton at the mouth of The Wash by 22.00. Leaving a calling card of bombs on the occasional village, (Heacham one, Snettisham one, Grimston one) this airship followed the coast road and gleaming railway tracks towards King's Lynn. Incidentally, von Platen-Hallermund believed himself to be near Grimsby and the Humber estuary!

Much public consternation and outrage was stirred up when it was announced in the press, after the event, that L4 had passed close to the royal residence of Sandringham House. Newspapers seemed to take it for granted that the King's residence was the objective of the Lynn district raid. Much joy was expressed, therefore, when it became known that the Royal Family, although in residence, had departed some twelve hours earlier. This is bound to invite the question: did the government know of the possibility of raiders in that district before the local towns knew, or was the King's departure merely a coincidence? In view of the German commander's later report stating an opinion of his whereabouts and in view of consistent gross navigational errors in subsequent raids, it seems most unlikely it was anything more than pure chance that took L4 near Sandringham that night. In fact, the nearest bomb fell on Snettisham church some four miles from the royal residence but close to those prominent navigational features of the coast, coast road and railway. This 'wanton act', however, made good propaganda and prompted an immediate influx of anti-aircraft guns to the district, with orders to fire at anything in the air having either the audacity or misfortune to approach Sandringham in future.

Reaching King's Lynn by 23.00, L4 claimed the first lives to be lost in the Fenland region to enemy air action. Approaching the town, the noise of L4's engines brought residents to their doors, unaware if the sound heralded friend or foe. Brilliant flashes resembling lightning lit the night sky, and three loud explosions following in quick succession soon settled any doubts. In all, seven bombs were dropped on the town. Falling in a line from The Walks to Alexandra Dock, this 'stick' killed Mrs Alice Maud Gazely and Percy Goate, aged fourteen, in Bentinck Street. Warning of a potential attack on King's Lynn had in fact reached the town earlier that evening. The question of instituting a blackout was left to individual town councils but in King's Lynn arrangements were made to hasten the switching off of street lamps that, of late, had been brought forward to 22.00 anyway. Blackout, however, was incomplete by the time the first bomb fell but hearing the explosions, the town engineer instantly shut off the current to the whole town. Circling King's Lynn for a while, L4 then headed off eastwards towards Norwich, recrossing the coast at Great Yarmouth where L3 had wrought havoc earlier, bound for its base at Fuhlsbuttel.

Chief of the German Admiralty staff in Berlin, Admiral Paul von Behnke, issued a communiqué stating his airships had attacked "fortified places between the Tyne and the Humber".

German newspapers eulogised over the apparent success of the raid that, in their eyes, was seen as "ending the legend of English invulnerability". Iron Cross medals were liberally distributed among the sixteen-man Zeppelin crews but retribution was not long in coming, for just one month later, both airships were wrecked in a storm over Denmark.

Night defences covering East Anglia's coastal region, based on RNAS Great Yarmouth, were pretty meagre at this time. Although willing to undertake their difficult task, the defenders, poorly equipped and inadequately informed about the progress of the raiders, were unable to mount an attack on L4. As it headed for London, a few RFC aeroplanes had a go at trying to find L3 but were equally unsuccessful in engaging the enemy. First round to the Zeppelins.

It was shortly after this raid that Monsieur Frantz Reichel was interviewed by the British press. Described as "a famous French aeronautical expert" he expressed an opinion that: "Zeppelins cannot possibly come over London or Paris as long as the aeroplane patrol service is well organised." With this confident remark he was not far from the truth, but it took some time before that confidence became a reality.

At this juncture, it will be of interest to touch upon some of the ways by which civil and military authorities were provided with information about enemy air activity over England. First indications of impending airship operations often came as a result of intercepted German radio signals traffic by British listening posts, such as the naval wireless station located at Hunstanton. Reports of air activity off the coast would most likely begin with observations by crews of lightships and lighthouses, these being reported by radio or telephone to navy or army command. The earliest system for detection and reporting of air activity over land began in 1914. In those days potential attacks on London were considered to pose the greatest danger and police forces were to telephone to report to the Admiralty (at that time responsible for defences) any aircraft seen or heard within a radius of sixty miles of the capital. In 1915 this system was extended to include East Anglia, Northamptonshire, Oxfordshire, Hampshire and the Isle of Wight, police reports being submitted by telegram. A year later the War Office took over responsibility for defences and in view of the extensive German air offensive, military reporting areas were introduced for thirty miles around major targets. The intensity, particularly in the south of England, of enemy aeroplane activity, coupled with increasing altitudes and speeds flown, made this latest system rather cumbersome. By mid 1918, responsibility for such reporting was returned to the police, supported by all the AA gun and searchlight sites, but due to the cessation of enemy air activity over England by that time, the effectiveness of the revised structure was never really tested. These various schemes can be regarded as the forerunners of the later Observer Corps system and the records kept also account for the availability of much of the information about the raiders' movements.

During the months that followed, German Army and Naval airships launched air raids directed principally at London and the Humber area. While both these targets were hit regularly, as a consequence of bad weather and poor navigation there were also sporadic attacks on east coast port targets situated between these two locations. However, the courses flown generally followed coastwise routes and there were no more incursions into this region until September 1915.

London was again the intended primary target for German Naval Zeppelins L13 (Kptlt Heinrich Mathy) and L14 (Kptlt Alois Böcker) on Tuesday, September 8. A third airship, L9, headed for the north-east coast in the Newcastle area.

L14 crossed the coast near Cromer, Norfolk, but developed engine trouble and returned to base early. It was 19.30 when Mathy in L13 turned north at Wells-next-the-sea, hugging the coast all the way into The Wash as far as King's Lynn. Taking his bearings from the prominent landmark of King's Lynn and guided by lights from un-blacked out towns and villages, he declined to leave a calling card on that fortunate town and set course directly for the distant glow that was London. Here he deposited his entire bomb load before retracing his course north for home. Altering direction to the east between Ely and Newmarket, Mathy re-crossed the coast at Great Yarmouth at 02:00, heading out across the North Sea to Zeppelin bases around Wilhelmshaven.

Once again, with just a handful of sorties flown from RNAS Great

Yarmouth, the air defences were ineffective. In mitigation it should be pointed out that the art of flying at night had never been considered a high priority by the military prior to this time. From Berlin, the enemy's version of events claimed good results against "great factories near Norwich and the Humber and ironworks at Middlesborough". The airships were said to have been fired upon very heavily by AA gunfire but all returned to base unharmed.

Just over a month later, Wednesday night October 13/14, Kptlt Mathy in L13 led five Zeppelins in the largest raid so far, against London. Inbound over the Norfolk coast, despite later navigational errors, this force kept clear of the Fens on this occasion. Official records suggest only airborne defenders around the capital mounted sorties in search of the raiders but the mere suspicion of the presence of Zeppelins, however, could cause defensive activity over a very wide area. In its first edition following this particular raid, the *Spalding Guardian* newspaper reported a strange occurrence that seems to indicate the RFC, even in the Fenland region, was airborne in search of these hostile machines.

A young farm labourer had an eerie experience at 4.00am on the morning after a Zeppelin raid which passed over Spalding. As he was out in the darkness rounding up horses on Mowbray's Farm, Surfleet (Gosberton) Fen, near Spalding, he saw a light near the Forty Foot river bank. Approaching cautiously, he was startled when the light rose into the air, accompanied by the clatter of an aeroplane engine. Later, as dawn broke, he found tyre tracks in the grass and several other people reported seeing aeroplanes in the area.

This was probably a pilot sent out on patrol during the night who, unable to find his home airfield, sensibly landed to await first light. Alternatively this may be the first known reference to the existence of the unlit landing ground, established for just this situation, less than a quarter mile from the South Forty Foot river in Gosberton Fen. Originally set up for emergency use by 38 HD (Home Defence) Squadron RFC based at Melton Mowbray, it was later used by elements of 90 (HD) Squadron, Buckminster.

Every Zeppelin raid mounted now was larger than its predecessor and the selection of targets was widened to include all major industrial areas. On this next raid, the first of 1916, nine Naval Zeppelins set out to bomb Liverpool on the night of January 31/February 1. Crossing the English coast randomly from 17.00 onwards between The Wash and the north Norfolk coast, their courses inland were quite erratic. Due to navigational errors and poor visibility in the bad weather, all were well south of their intended tracks and went nowhere near Liverpool. Zeppelin L11 had Kptlt Horst von Buttlar-Brandenfels in command but the head of the German Naval Airship Division, Korvettenkapitän Peter Strasser, was also on board that night. Von Buttlar, inbound down the centre of The Wash, turned north near Spalding, towards Lincoln. Meandering along the county border, unknowingly L11 reached the Scunthorpe/Grimsby area before leaving the coast without dropping any bombs, having been unable to identify a legitimate target. Meanwhile Kptlt Mathy, in L13, came in over Cromer and entered Fenland airspace in the vicinity of Downham Market. Turning north towards Sutton Bridge for a short time, then west, he exited the county at Grantham. Once again, L13's course was very erratic, wandering around the Midlands area as far as Burton (bombed), Stoke-on-Trent and Buxton, before returning to the east coast near Skegness.

Meandering was certainly the most appropriate term to describe L14's (Kptlt Böcker) progress. Making landfall at Wells-next-the-sea it set course across the southern Fenlands, passing west between Stamford and Grantham. Böcker penetrated as far west as Shrewsbury before returning equally erratically, bombing Derby on the way, to depart the English coast north of Skegness. Coming from the general direction of Cromer, L15 (Kptlt Joachim Breithaupt) flew towards Ely, turning north to skirt Wisbech, Spalding and Sleaford. Now Breithaupt changed course first towards Skegness, then Boston. From there he maintained a reasonably straight track across The Wash to King's Lynn and Norwich, finally leaving the coast at Lowestoft. Hunstanton was landfall for L16 with Oberleutnant-zur-See (Oblt-z-See) W Peterson in command but it avoided the Fens by swinging in an arc to the south-east across Norfolk and out over Lowestoft. L17 also remained over Norfolk, while L19 (Kptlt Odo Loewe) made a protracted inland flight.

On his flight from the Norfolk coast, Loewe took a westerly course roughly from Downham Market via Stamford, eventually to reach Wolverhampton, Kidderminster and Birmingham. Reversing his course from the heart of the Midlands, L19 was spotted near Ely and Norwich on its way to the coast at Happisburgh. It was 05.00 next morning before it departed, having been at large over Britain for nearly ten hours! That morning, however, was a fateful one for L19 for it was lost in the North Sea with all hands after engine failure and being holed by gunfire near the Dutch coast.

Kptlt Franz Stabbert (L20) followed a similar route to his force commander until, reaching the vicinity of Spalding he, too, ventured westwards towards the same areas of the Midlands blindly attacked by his compatriots. Finally, L21 (Kptlt Max Dietrich) inbound from Cromer in poor weather, crossed the Fens from east to west on its way to the Birmingham area. Returning, Dietrich passed over the southern Fens near Ely and left these shores at Lowestoft.

Fenland skies throbbed to the sound of Maybach engines for many hours that night. Unintentionally and blindly for the most part, Zeppelins had wandered freely and with impunity across not only the Fens but also over large tracts of the industrial Midlands.

Airship crews seemed to have had little idea of their true whereabouts and defenders little idea of how to find them. The British believed the intended target was London but none went closer than sixty miles of the capital. Subsequent German communiqués erroneously proclaimed the airships had struck Liverpool and Birkenhead Docks, Manchester, iron foundries in Nottingham and Sheffield and great industrial works on the Humber and near Great Yarmouth. The silencing of a gun battery on the Humber was also claimed.

Sixty-one people were killed that night and the horror of war from the air was suddenly brought to the public in districts that previously had found it hard to realise quite what all the fuss was about. This raid therefore can be considered a significant turning point in the nation's awareness of what airpower could mean.

There is no record of any anti-Zeppelin fighter patrols being launched specifically over the Midlands, although all but two of the marauders flew around and through the region for many hours.

The RFC and RNAS lost several aeroplanes and some lives that night carrying out abortive patrols in bad weather and in the wrong places. It was a fiasco for the defenders, precipitating a major reorganisation of the Home Air Defences in forthcoming months. Progress was, however, painfully slow and not without its share of mishaps.

As part of this reorganisation, 51 (HD) Squadron was formed with its HQ flight at Thetford and other flights based on airfields at Mattishall, Harling Road (south of Norwich), Marham/Narborough (west Norfolk) and Tydd St Mary (Lincs). Most of the Home Defence squadrons created were (under-!) equipped initially, with BE2 aircraft. However, in mid 1916 the single-seat BE12 and two-seat 'pusher' FE2b were being introduced. 51 Squadron began with a mix of BE2, BE12 and both single- and two-seat FE2b aeroplanes, standardising eventually on the latter type.

For several months the Midlands region was spared any incursion by the Zeppelin force. Practice sorties, by 51 Squadron, covering the region from the east, supported now by 38 Squadron at Buckminster (Leics), Stamford (the airfield was actually in the parish of Wittering) and Leadenham near Sleaford (Lincs) to the west, continued unabated. The latter unit was equipped initially with BE2s but had FE2bs by October 1916. Finally, to the north of the region was RNAS Cranwell, opened in April 1916. It had become clear that German airships would attack or traverse the Fens regularly and these squadrons were now – at least in theory – well placed all around The Wash to deal with such raids.

Although aeroplanes flying overhead had become commonplace, it was crashes that still captured the public's attention. That summer, however, only one accident on July 20 caught the eye of the local press. The flight of what may well have been an FE2b of 51 Squadron, from Thetford or Tydd St Mary, was interrupted when its engine stopped suddenly over Holbeach Marsh and began to emit smoke. Gliding to earth at once, the pilot landed at Leadenhall Farm. Unfortunately potato ridges, onto which he alighted, are not conducive to safe landings and the aeroplane overturned. The pilot was unhurt, but his observer sustained a few cuts in the process.

After this lull, eight German Naval Zeppelins reopened the night battle by attempting another attack on London on July 31. It was yet another failure. Adverse winds over the North Sea completely scattered the force and airships were seen as far apart as Kent and Skegness. Fog inland also added to their problems but it was equally unhelpful to the defenders and the airships kept coming during that murky Fenland night. From landfall at Skegness L16 (Kptlt Erich Summerfeldt) crossed the north of the region and penetrated unchallenged as far as Newark, while L14 (Hauptmann Kuno Manger) flew around the March area. All bombs dropped, believed to total about thirty-two in number, fell in open countryside. The only casualties reported were two cows!

It was September 1916 before the fledgling night defences began to turn the tide. Airship SL11, a wooden-framework design built by the Schutte-Lanz airship manufacturing company and operated by the German Army, was destroyed on the night of September 2/3, by Lt Leefe Robinson, falling at Cuffley to the north of London. His success, in shooting down the first airship to be brought down on British soil, marked a significant upturn in fortune for the Home Defences.

On this momentous night, the greatest airship fleet ever assembled concentrated over East Anglia to mount an attack on London. Once more, though, it failed in its primary objective. Official records show that although many bombs were dropped by the fifteen airships most of these fell harmlessly in open countryside. Poor weather, strong winds, heavy rain and icing were factors chiefly responsible for the failure. It was 22.00 when Naval Zeppelin L14 (Hptmn Kuno Manger) was recorded passing Wells-next-the-sea. Manger swung south over The Wash, near Hunstanton, heading for King's Lynn, which he circled an hour later. Reaching Downham Market by midnight L14 left the region south of Upwood and proceeded to undertake a grand tour of the Cambridgeshire, Essex and Suffolk countryside, scattering bombs as it tracked north to exit the coast at Mundesley after seven hours over British territory.

During the remainder of 1916 five more airships were destroyed over England. Apart from the natural dangers of adverse winds and bad weather, there had been little for the Zeppelins to fear from anti-aircraft (AA) gunfire or fighters in the early war years. Natural hazards were an ever-present danger but analysis of the airship fleet's performance told the War Office that enemy airships were still only operating at altitudes of 8,000 to 10,000 feet. At these heights it should be vulnerable to AA fire, searchlights and more significantly to fighters, if only the performance and disposition of all these components could be improved.

From mid 1916 this improvement had begun to materialise. In particular, fighter aeroplane design and performance was showing noticeable, if modest, changes. Another much more significant change, however, was the introduction of explosive/incendiary machine-gun ammunition, like the Brock or Pomeroy types, and incendiary ammunition such as the Buckingham or SPK types, with which fighters could now attack these potentially highly inflammable raiders. It was well understood that the hydrogen gas that filled the Zeppelins was inflammable but it needed to mix with oxygen to create that unstable state. Ordinary ball (solid) ammunition simply punched holes in the gas cells – allowing gas to escape and mix with ambient air – but there was nothing to ignite the mixture at the point of impact, where it would be at its most concentrated. Aircraft machine guns were now generally loaded with a blend of explosive and incendiary rounds and this was found to be a lethal combination. All that remained was to catch the blighters!

It was on the night of September 23/24 that explosions next rocked Fenland soil. Naval Zeppelin L13 (Kptlt Franz Georg Eichler) was one of twelve airships that crossed the English coast between The Wash and the Thames, seeking London and targets in the Midlands. Part of the London force comprised four new 'Super' class airships (L30/31/32/33). Measuring 640 feet in length and carried aloft by almost two million cubic feet of hydrogen gas, two of these giants were to meet a fiery end that night, proving the lethal effectiveness of the new incendiary ammunition. Meanwhile, back in rural Lincolnshire the calm of the night was being shattered too.

Interviewed in 1990, Cecil Haresign, farmer and lifelong resident of Surfleet Fen, near Spalding, recalled that night, seventy-four years earlier. His memory was crystal clear as the raid he said, "… was two days before the annual Spalding Horse Fair." This coincided with the date of the raid September 23/24 1916 and the track of L13. "Aeroplanes," he recalled, "had been using George Mowbray's field as a landing ground for some time." These are believed to have been from 38 Squadron, as mentioned earlier. "Often as many as nine machines could be counted at one time in the field, the centre of which was marked by a chalk circle about forty feet in diameter."

Mr Haresign and others were of the opinion that the field had a dual purpose of also acting as a decoy for Zeppelin bombs. During most days sheep were allowed to graze the field but a large pen was staked out into which they could be herded, presumably to allow aeroplanes to land by day or night. A small contingent of soldiers was housed in a hut in one corner of the field. In addition to being shepherds it was their task to set out a flare-path of oil pans, lit to give off a smoky, yellow glare at night. Although to the locals it may have seemed like a decoy device, in the circumstances it was probably a night as well as a day landing ground for the RFC. Popularity for the decoy theory would, no doubt, be gained when, on the night of September 23/24, the oil lamps were lit and apparently promptly attracted a rain of bombs as an airship slowly circled the village. Five bombs showered down at intervals, falling at Grange Farm (failed to explode), allotments near Second Drove (house tiles damaged), near the main Gosberton to Dowsby road at Fourth Drove, and on the bank of the Forty Foot river. Next morning a somewhat shaken Private Albert

Foulsham, one of the airfield contingent, had quite a tale to tell curious villagers. This dour Yorkshireman, out lighting oil lamps for the airfield flare-path, received the fright of his life when a loud whistling noise was terminated by a huge 'crump', which threw him to the ground and showered him with earth. The fifth bomb had gouged a large crater in the middle of his flare-path. Some accounts claim L13 was attacked that night by a 38 Squadron BE2c near Sleaford but this is unsubstantiated.

It was now autumn. Bad weather, fog and icing conditions conspired against the German airship force sent out on October 1/2 1916, once more targeting London and the Midlands. With losses now occurring on almost every raid it must have become apparent to these crews that the defences were getting the measure of the attackers. For their persistence under such difficult flying conditions, they are to be admired for the same qualities that WW2 aircrews displayed at night on both sides, knowing the odds were shortening with every sortie.

Seven Zeppelins made landfall on the Norfolk and Lincolnshire coasts either side of The Wash. Kptlt Mathy in L31 headed directly for London but met a fiery end over Potters Bar at the hands of 2/Lt W J Tempest. Of the other six airships, L14, L21 and Super class L34 all passed over the Fens, with L14 being chased around the Sleaford area, unsuccessfully, by a BE12 from 38 Squadron at Leadenham. This latter incident may well have been that which was confused with the previous raid. L34 tracked in from Cromer to Oundle and Corby, where coming under AA fire, Kplt Dietrich released seventeen HE bombs before heading for the Lincolnshire coast via Stamford.

Almost two months elapsed before the German Navy sent out another airship raid when ten Zeppelins left the Heligoland area on the night of November 27/28 1916, bound for Midland targets. This raid conformed to much the same pattern as its predecessors, with the raiders becoming dispersed, lost and generally off target. Furthermore, the defenders mounted a record level of sorties and enjoyed considerable success. Zeppelin L21 (Oblt-z-See Kurt Frankenberg), setting out from Nordholz, came in over the Yorkshire coast heading for Midland targets. In this respect Frankenberg appears to have been the most successful of his group. He tracked via Leeds and Sheffield to the Potteries (Birmingham) area which was bombed but with no serious effect. It was L21's homeward track, however, that led it into deep trouble.

Leading a charmed life, for a while Kurt Frankenberg steered L21 through the night sky above a string of RFC airfields. Turning east after his bombs were released, he passed south of Nottingham towards the Fens north of Peterborough. Entering 38 Squadron territory L21 flew perilously close to Buckminster, Leadenham and Stamford airfields then on into 51 Squadron's patch, as it headed for the Norfolk coast and home. First, 38 Squadron sent up five aeroplanes in pursuit, one of which, a BE2e flown by Capt G Birley, made contact with L21 east of Buckminster. After a long chase into the Fens, Birley had climbed to 11,000 feet before catching up with the airship. He fired off a full drum of ammunition at the target without any visible effect. The Zeppelin was by no means a sitting duck, for it appeared to manoeuvre continually, giving the impression of trying to avoid its attacker.

Eventually Birley lost sight of L21 but the chase was taken up by Second Lieutenant D Allan in a BE2e from Leadenham. Flying now in the general direction of Spalding at 12,000 feet altitude and with the 'Zepp' nearly 2,000 feet above him, the poor old BE2's performance was quite inadequate to allow Allan even to keep pace and he, too, lost his quarry. As L21 cruised high above the dark fenscape no other contacts were reported until it left the region. Then, forewarned, 51 Squadron put up an FE2b from Marham but the pilot, Lt Gayner, having struggled to come within sight of his target, was forced to land with engine trouble. The lucky (so far) L21 crossed the coast near Great Yarmouth where two BE2c aircraft from RNAS Great Yarmouth finally caught up with her in the cold light of dawn and this time there was to be no mistake. Flight Lieutenant Egbert Cadbury and Flight Sub-Lt Edward Pulling were jointly credited with shooting down L21, which crashed into the sea in flames, with the loss of all hands.

New Year 1917 brought a further slight change in air defence policy. The War Office believed the night Zeppelin menace and day bomber offensive (the latter mostly directed against south-east England) was, in the light of 1916's successes, now contained. Thoughts were therefore refocused on France and as a result 51 Squadron, for example, lost some of its FE2bs to help form the nucleus of a new night bomber squadron in France. There were even cuts in the home AA gun strength.

On the German side, leader of the airship fleet, Peter Strasser, was severely shaken by the reverses his airships had suffered, but he seemed determined to carry on the battle despite the mounting odds and convinced his masters to back him. As mentioned earlier, airship operating altitudes were generally up to 10-12,000 feet and British Home Defence fighters, although clearly stretched to reach that level, were achieving results. In addition AA guns, working in conjunction with searchlights, were also taking their toll. In an effort to avoid interception German strategy also took a new turn. A programme was begun in which new airships (called 'heightclimbers') were built and stripped of all excess weight to maximise their higher-flying capabilities. This new class of Zeppelin included L35, L36, L39, L40, L41, L42 and L47, which could now reach altitudes of between 16,000 and 20,000 feet. High-flying Zeppelin raids of early 1917 thus proved to be well beyond the altitude capability of most of the defending fighters. However, in other respects, the new class of airship suffered even more from weather-related problems, particularly the greater effects of adverse winds at the higher altitudes flown. Navigation, therefore, suffered and as a consequence bombing results were still generally ineffective.

The New Year also brought a substantial drop in the number of airship raids mounted against England, with only seven during the whole year compared to twenty-two in 1916 and twenty in 1915. Defences were just too good, and the Germans were bloodied. Apart from one unconfirmed report of a Zeppelin being seen near The Wash on September 24/25, it was not until October 19/20 1917, a full year since the last major incursion into the region's airspace, that Zeppelins returned in earnest – but yet again with poor results. This was the occasion of an attack, intended for the north of England, which subsequently became known as 'the Silent Raid'. Eleven airships set off for England, but encountering strong north winds at altitudes up to 20,000 feet they became lost and widely dispersed even before they crossed the English coast. Crews also suffered much discomfort from lack of oxygen and the biting, -30°F, cold. These undoubtedly brave men must have wondered if it was all really worth the effort, but discipline and leadership prevailed.

Boston came in for unusual attention as it was overflown by no less than four of these Naval Zeppelins, L44 (Kptlt Franz Stabbert), L47 (Kptlt Max von Freudenreich), L52 (Oblt-z-See Kurt Friemel) and L55 (Kptlt Hans-Kurt Flemming). Apparently, though, no bombs were dropped, probably due to dense cloud and fog obscuring the town itself. It was this same cloud layer which deadened engine sounds to those below, giving rise to the erroneous notion that engines were shut down to coast in silently – hence 'the Silent Raid'. Tracking down The Wash, L44 flew up the Witham Haven river before turning south to pick up the railway line to Spalding and Peterborough, on its way to Bedford, which was bombed. Cruising across the northern Home Counties, it left British territory behind at Folkestone, having dropped other bombs at intervals on the way. L47 crossed the Lincolnshire coast near Sutton-on-Sea, spotted Skegness on which it dropped one bomb, before making off for Boston. This airship also crossed Witham Haven, then the mouth of the Welland river but, thereafter, seemed to wander aimlessly, first in the direction of Holbeach, then back to Spalding and on to Stamford. Reaching the latter, L47 appeared to regain its bearings, setting a steady course to the village of Holme, near Peterborough (bombed), before leaving the Fens at Ramsey (bombed), en route to Ipswich and Harwich. Oberleutnant-zur-See Friemel, in L52, followed closely the route of L47, but identifying his own location from the Welland river and Witham river estuaries, he struck inland to attack Northampton. This Zeppelin, like L44, seems to have attempted to find London but instead, traversed the Home Counties and Kent to exit at Dungeness. The raiders roamed England from early evening to around midnight. L55 was, for example, reported in the Skegness area at 19.30 and at Hastings, on the south coast at 22.15. Kptlt Flemming took his craft towards Boston, then cruised across the Fens in the general direction of Cambridge. In the vicinity of Wisbech he probably spotted the glow of L47's calling cards exploding at Holme and Ramsey, prompting him to alter course towards those villages. Heading south again to London, L55 flew in an arc round the west of the capital, finally leaving these shores at Hastings.

In addition, L41 (Hptmn Manger) managed to find and bomb Birmingham and Northampton and L45 (Kptlt Waldemar Kolle), who came inbound through Yorkshire, may have been intercepted near Leicester by Lt Harrison in an FE2b from Stamford, as it was driven south to bomb London.

A large number of fighter sorties were flown that night, including BE2s from RNAS Cranwell and Freiston and FE2bs of 38 Squadron's C Flight at Stamford, 51 Squadron's B Flight at Tydd St Mary and C Flight at Marham. Of the fourteen night sorties launched by 38 and 51 Squadrons, Harrison was the only one who managed to actually fire – albeit ineffectually – at a Zepp that night, mainly due to the extreme altitudes at which the Zeppelins were flying. What the Home Defence fighters missed though, the weather and AA over France made up for. No less than five airships, nearly half the raiding force, were lost to one or the other cause.

The day – or rather the night – of the Zeppelin was almost over. Enemy air raids on England by day and increasingly by night were now in the hands of bomber aeroplanes. In the south of England, Gothas and Zeppelin-Staaken Giants were locked with British fighters in the first Battle of Britain. Peter Strasser and his decimated airship force were left to lick their wounds and it was March 1918 before the height-climbers were committed, though only in token numbers, once more.

Tydd St Mary airfield regained prominence for a fleeting moment for quite a different reason in April 1918. It was, in a way, almost as if the endless training flights, fruitless patrols and casualties discussed above, synthesised for a final fling with Germany's airship fleet. Adverse weather had played its usual role in frustrating two airship attacks on northern England in March 1918, neither of which had affected the Fenland region. It was the night of April 12/13 before five latest-design Zeppelins of the L60 class roamed across the area once again. High altitude winds scattered this force along the east coast, with L62 venturing across the Fens to thrust inland to Birmingham, while L63 and L64 unloaded their bombs into the rural pastures of mid Lincolnshire. L62 flew inland from Cromer at nearly 20,000 feet, setting course for Birmingham. This route took her directly over the RAF (since April 1) station Tydd St Mary that, due to this enemy presence, was busy putting up its FEs on patrol. Fighters are recorded as taking off from 22.00 at Tydd and no doubt as a result of showing lights for this purpose, L62 was drawn like a moth to a candle.

The airfield rocked to the explosions of a stick of three bombs as the Zeppelin droned overhead. Of the three fighters launched by 51 Squadron from Tydd that night, only one spotted L62 as it flew majestically above the airfield. Lt F Sergeant in FE2b A5753 had to struggle to reach even 15,000 feet and after more than an hour chasing the airship without closing the gap, gave up near Coventry, returning to base while he still had fuel to do so. Another FE2b fighter from 38 Squadron (B Flight) airfield at Buckminster, spotted L62 at 01.00 hours as it was heading home from Birmingham, but although struggling to 16,000 feet, the pilot Lt Noble-Campbell was still too low to engage it. Lt W Brown in A5578 from C Flight at Stamford, patrolling between Peterborough and Coventry, also tried in vain to intercept L62. He and several other pilots crash-landed with engine failure – which sadly was an all too regular outcome of these night defence sorties.

Hptmn Kuno Manger released the remainder of his bomb load ineffectually in the countryside around Coventry then headed back to the coast at Great Yarmouth, where bad weather for a change helped protect her from the unwelcome attention of the fighters.

By 1918 a significant change to defence equipment was taking place. In order to combat the altitude advantage now enjoyed by Zeppelin airships and Gotha and Zeppelin-Staaken 'Giant' aeroplanes, quantities of Sopwith Camel, DH4 and SE5 fighters were diverted to Home Defence squadrons. Furthermore, specialist night fighters, such as a variant of the Sopwith Dolphin, were being tested. However, German aeroplanes had almost entirely taken over as the main bomber threat to England and air action was by now concentrated in the south and south-east of the country. A portent of years to come.

The Zeppelin menace reached a final climax in what became the last airship raid on England of the war, August 5/6 1918. Obsessed by his desire to re-establish the strategic credibility of his airship fleet, Fregattenkapitän Peter Strasser led this raid aboard the pride of his fleet, L70 (Kptlt Johannes von Lossnitzer in command).

Departing Nordholz at 15.30, this desire seems to have turned to impatience, since Strasser unwisely appeared off the Norfolk coast before darkness fell. Spotted early, off Wells-next-the-sea, at 20.00, L70 and its companion craft L65 and L53 were attacked by DH4 and Sopwith Camel aircraft at 18,000 feet just offshore. Two DH4s, A8032 piloted by Major Egbert Cadbury with Capt Robert Leckie acting as gunner and A8039, Lt R Keys with Air Mechanic A Harman, both from Great Yarmouth air station, quite separately attacked L70. So enormous was this Zeppelin that these two fighters were apparently completely unaware of each other's attack. At 22.00 the effects of their incendiary ammunition had sealed the fate not only of the majestic airship but also of its crew of twenty-two men, including Strasser, who died along with his dream.

Primarily designed for bombing, the Great Yarmouth crews had found the two-seat DH4's performance, when powered by a 375hp RR Eagle engine, effective at the altitudes at which the latest Zeppelins operated and could meet them on equal terms at last. Among the twenty-nine aeroplanes launched against raiders that night, FE2bs of 51 Squadron were airborne over the region but as none of the airships ventured inland, they found no trade. One, however, Lt Drummond from Mattishall in A5732, was obliged to make a forced landing at Skegness, fortunately without injury.

Although officially recorded as having crashed at 53.01N, 01.04E, because of darkness and cloud the true position of L70's fiery plunge into the sea is unclear but appears to have been a few miles out to sea towards the mouth of The Wash. Next day major remains were found to have drifted onto sandbanks in The Wash in the vicinity of Skegness and Hunstanton. Witnessing from a distance the horrific end to L70, both companions turned tail for home and thus drew the night 'shooting' war in the region to a close.

It is not intended here to conduct a detailed analysis of WW1 air defence policy since other writers have dealt more than adequately with that subject. In the context of this account of one phase in the evolution of the night air defence of Britain, suffice it to say that airships represented German long-range bombing strategy of the time and the defenders were, for a long time, unable to contain them. They were thus, in theory, able to strike at any part of the British Isles. In practice, though, a degenerative cycle of circumstances brought about by factors such as: the sheer size of these weather-vane-like airships; perverse weather; poor navigation; limited radio aids and not least, intransigence among its leaders on the one side, opposed by steadily improving defensive aeroplanes, armament and searchlights on the other side – all severely curtailed the airship fleet's effectiveness and caused it in effect, to self-destruct.

Of the 115 Zeppelins built:

25 were lost to enemy air or ground attack over England and the continent
19 were damaged and wrecked on landing
26 were lost in accidents
22 were scrapped in service
7 were interned after being forced down
9 were handed over to the enemy at the end of the war
7 were 'scuttled' at the end of the war

About fifty crews were involved in German naval airship operations during the war and each crew could consist of up to eighteen airmen, so a total of no more than about 900 airmen made up the operational aircrew establishment, of whom about 400 lost their lives.

Just as in WW2, in this aspect of the enemy night offensive against England, the provinces outside the capital and the area around The Wash and Midlands in particular, saw a great deal more of the action than is generally appreciated. No less than eleven out of a total of fifty-four German airship raids on England (20%), directly or indirectly involved the region. Those particular eleven raids were mounted entirely by airships of the Imperial German Navy. Thus it has been shown here that the region felt the weight of this new form of warfare and aeroplanes based there played a small but important role in helping to defeat the menace. It will be seen next that, twenty-five years later, these provincial night skies would once more become a battleground – with a similar outcome for the protagonists.

CHAPTER 3

Fighter Nights

For night fighters in general, let alone in this region, the second half of 1940 was both a time of frustration and a time of change. Airborne radar was gradually being rolled out but like most electronic inventions, delivery was slow: it suffered teething problems; its air operators had to acquire a new skill that was largely self-taught and acquired 'on the job', and the aeroplane that carried it was not man enough for its task. Nevertheless, it was all that was available. Furthermore, according to E G Bowen, the man responsible for the government's airborne radar development programme, the very future of airborne radar was precarious. In his book *Radar Days* he states:

> As 1940 drew to a close, night fighters were simply not shooting down German aircraft at night and the very concept of using radar-equipped fighters for night interception came under criticism. The source of this criticism could not be clearly defined but it was undoubtedly fuelled by the nagging refrain from Lord Cherwell, who lost no opportunity of throwing spanners into the radar works. It gave rise to a whole host of competing ideas. One of these was the so-called Turbinlite... another was bombing the enemy from above; many other schemes were proposed... they were seldom thought through... and not one of them developed into a useful method of defence against night air attack.

As one of the efforts to plug the gap, in September 1940 Air Marshal Sholto Douglas, recently appointed C-in-C Fighter Command, ordered more use of single-engine fighters at night. In *Years of Command*, the second volume of his autobiography, he wrote:

> The defeat of the German night bomber was clearly my first responsibility. I was convinced, as Dowding had been, that this airborne radar, linked with radar on the ground, would provide the answer but it [AI] was still too unstable and unreliable and control from the ground had not been worked out. The enemy might not oblige by waiting until the new equipment was ready. For these reasons I could not put all my eggs in one basket and I had to pay attention to other means of coping with the night raiders. So strongly

had Dowding come to believe in his radar-equipped fighters that he had become a little blinded, I felt, to the more simple hit or miss, trial and error, use of single-engine fighters. I felt ... that the effort should be made and despite his strenuous protest Dowding was given instructions to make more use of his Hurricanes and Defiants at night.

Based at RAF Digby, the sector HQ airfield, Hawker Hurricane-equipped 151 Squadron was re-designated from day fighter to night fighter squadron on October 20 1940 and in this new role it was to operate from the Wellingore satellite landing ground. The squadron was ordered to provide one section of aircraft at readiness all night, and one section at readiness and another at fifteen minutes availability all day. Night readiness duty was to be carried out alternately by the squadron's two flights on a weekly rotation basis.

Night flying practice began immediately but the action – such as it was – was mostly in daylight scrambles (known colloquially as 'flaps') to investigate hostile aircraft. Although several pilots caught glimpses of the enemy, he usually escaped in cloud cover over the district. For example, Flt Lt Roddick Smith, (B Flight commander) attacked a Dornier Do17 or Do215 while on patrol at dusk on October 29 but only one of his cannon worked and this bomber, too, escaped into the cloud cover.

On October 2 though, just before this change of status, another Smith for 151 Squadron had better luck and incidentally displayed a streak of mettle that would lead him to command the squadron in less than eighteen months' time. Just as dusk was beginning to set in, New Zealander Plt Off Irving Smith, leading Red section on a local practice sortie, was ordered to intercept an outbound enemy aircraft heading towards The Wash. As Red 2 was not yet operational Smith instructed him to return to base and was himself vectored to the enemy. Climbing above the cloud layer, as soon as he emerged he spotted the enemy aircraft – a Heinkel He111 – dead ahead of him. Closing rapidly, Smith fired a single long burst of gunfire at his target, which promptly dived into the cloud cover with the Hurricane in hot pursuit. Firing the remainder of his ammunition at the fleeing Heinkel he was rewarded by seeing the port propeller windmill come to a stop. The Heinkel seemed able to maintain height and flew out to sea for about twenty miles with Plt Off Smith keeping station on it at a discrete distance. It soon became quite evident that it was beginning to lose height and it must have become apparent to its pilot that he was not going to make it back to base, because the bomber turned round and retraced its course towards the coast. Approaching the coast its starboard motor began to burn and the aircraft glided down to 'pancake' on the sea about two or three hundred yards from the beach at Chapel St Leonards, just north of Skegness. Circling his victim for a while he watched the crew swim ashore into captivity; Smith landed back at Digby at 18.50 hours. The story goes that when soldiers arrived on the scene the Heinkel was partially submerged in the shallows and its crew were standing on the wing calling out for a boat to bring them off. In no uncertain terms the shout went back, "Swim for it or b----y well drown!!" Having survived the ditching unharmed the crew, Oblt H Seidel, Ofws K Ziller, W Zickler and V Weidner together with Uffz A Kreuzer, took the cold plunge into captivity. Their Heinkel was later identified as He111H-5, wk nr 3554, coded A1+CH of I/KG53, out on a lone reconnaissance sortie when it was shot down.

Left where it crashed just offshore the bomber gradually succumbed to the ravages of the North Sea. Substantial components from this wreck, including both engines, were recovered in 1967 and displayed in the Lincolnshire Air Museum and Newark Air Museum. The large centre section structure remained embedded in the beach, laid bare by tidal action and proving to be something of a hazard until it, too, was removed after being blown up into smaller pieces by the navy in 1973.

On November 7, Flt Lt Kenneth Blair (A Flight commander) took off after a Heinkel 111 that had laid a stick of bombs across Digby and machine-gunned some parked Hurricanes but he, too, had to return without catching his quarry. A couple of days later though, Blair and Sgt Percy Copeland on a dawn patrol over The Wash intercepted a Dornier Do17 at 08.00 and claimed to have shot it down between them. As Red section they took off from Digby at 07.20 to patrol below cloud over Skegness and half an hour later Flt Lt Blair (Red 1) was warned of a bandit approaching from the north at 7,000 feet altitude. Blair wrote in his combat report:

I climbed up and suddenly above a layer of thin cloud a Do17 appeared flying south. I gave chase and fired my ammunition at it in six bursts from two to three hundred yards range as it flew in and out of a thin cloud layer. When at 5,000 feet the E/A half-rolled and dived towards the ground and I then called Red 2 [Copeland] to come in and shoot. I could see my explosive ammunition bursting on the E/A and thought I had damaged it. Red section returned to base, landing at 08.30.

Sgt Percy Copeland's own report noted that he could see the Heinkel's rear gunner returning fire as Blair went in and he himself put in a short burst from the other beam. When the Heinkel dived, Red 1 broke away but Copeland stayed with it long enough to close the range from 300 to 100 yards while firing two more bursts. By now the rear gunner had stopped firing but Copeland lost contact as the rapidly diving fight reached ground level.

Kenneth Blair claimed a probable jointly with Sgt Copeland, but both combat reports were endorsed, "Since confirmed as destroyed." Post-war research established however that, while sustaining battle damage, this Do17 actually made it back to base at Gilze-Rijen, in Holland, although two of the crew had been wounded during the action.

It was not until November 16 that 151 Squadron began flying night patrols in earnest and this task was actually carried out by sending a detachment of nine Hurricanes to RAF Wittering. At this time only seven pilots had been trained and passed for night ops but no action came their way before the end of the month.

December 1940 saw more organisational changes for 151. The squadron itself moved from Wellingore to RAF Bramcote in Warwickshire, but at the same time a whole flight was detached to Wittering for night operations. Initially that detachment was a composite unit made up of pilots drawn from both flights but it was intended, when all pilots were night-trained, to rotate A and B Flights for the detachments. The flight remaining at Bramcote would carry out daytime operational training and maintain daytime patrols. This dual role placed a strain both on the Hurricanes and their pilots and in mid-month the first seven, (of an expected complement of ten), Boulton Paul Defiants were taken on charge specifically for night operations. In addition the full complement of eighteen Hurricanes was to be retained for daytime ops. In the meantime Group also decreed that twelve aircraft – Hurricanes, because the Defiants were not yet ready – had to be sent on the Wittering detachment, causing their diarist to complain: "...that practically all the squadron is at RAF Wittering now."

In its efforts to bring the Luftwaffe to battle at night, RAF Command concocted many bright (!) ideas as alternatives to AI radar, or until it became more prolifically available and in mid December 151 Squadron became involved with one such scheme called 'Night Flying Curtains'. This technique involved stacking nine aircraft at intervals of 1,000 feet altitude, with the lowest at between 11,000 and 14,000 feet. The idea was to move these aircraft around the night sky in a block and thus "... to be sure of intercepting German night bombers." 151 practised this in clear daylight conditions and it worked without a hitch and was even considered to show great promise. This feeling did not persist though after more 'Curtain' practices, this time in cloudy conditions, caused problems to such an extent that it was agreed the technique would not be used in anything less than perfect weather.

Two days before Christmas 151 Squadron upped and moved entirely to RAF Wittering where as the year finally came to an end there was just a small amount of local night flying training carried out by the Defiant crews. For all squadron personnel it must have seemed during this period as if nothing was ever going to stay still long enough to concentrate on getting to grips with the Luftwaffe. Just to add to its woes, the squadron was ordered to donate five of its Hurricanes to the newly formed 71 (Eagle) Squadron at Kirton in Lindsey.

Even if 151 was not engaging the enemy, the enemy was taking potshots at 151! On December 21 one pilot was fired upon as he came into land after a night patrol while another was shot at during his patrol. Neither pilot saw his attacker but fortunately both emerged unscathed.

The New Year brought no sign of stability either, as three Hurricanes were detached on January 4 to RAF Kirton in Lindsey with their pilots: Flt

Lt Kenneth Blair, Plt Off Irving Smith and Plt Off Richard Stevens. On the same night Blair intercepted an enemy aircraft actually in the RAF Waddington circuit at 600 feet, but it got away again.

January 1941 saw 151 Squadron begin mounting the type of night sortie known as a 'Fighter Night'. These patrols were night flights involving pilots considered, by the squadron commander, to have acquired above average skills both in combat and flying at night. Fighter Nights were launched when raid activity threatened and/or there was a reasonable amount of light from the moon. Up to now many single-seat fighter pilots had little experience of night flying and could not simply be pitched into an environment and situation where they would be more danger to themselves than the enemy. Night flying training therefore began to increase on those squadrons affected. Individual single-seat or non-AI equipped fighters would be allocated to a city or part of, say, a large urban conurbation by their sector control and be despatched at intervals depending on the intensity of enemy activity. Proceeding to his designated area, he would commence patrolling at a pre-determined altitude and it was then up to the pilot to use signs offered by AA or searchlights, together with his own initiative to try to spot an enemy aircraft and bring it into combat. What happened thereafter was up to the pilot – and the enemy! 151 Squadron recorded that it used this technique for the first time on the night of January 9 1941 when nine Hurricanes were sent off from Wittering. Unfortunately they had to be recalled due to deteriorating weather so it was not possible to judge the merits of the technique on that occasion. There was a little consolation, though, when the AOC sent congratulations to the squadron for getting all nine aircraft airborne within the space of five minutes from receiving the signal. It seems reasonable to view subsequent Luftwaffe night fighter operations known as 'Wilde Sau' as similar in concept to Fighter Nights.

While training with the Defiants continued it fell to the Hurricanes to achieve the first real success at night. At this point, too, for the squadron and indeed the RAF in general, it seemed to mark a turning point in this phase of the night air campaign.

During a break in the awful January weather, that had curtailed operations by both attacker and defender alike, the first tangible success occurred when 151 Squadron launched four Hurricanes on January 15/16, namely Flt Lt Blair in P3813, Plt Off Irving Smith in V7222, Plt Off Richard Stevens in V6934 and Flt Lt Desmond McMullen in V7496. The squadron diarist began the entry for the day with: "Tonight we experienced our first success as night fighters."

The Luftwaffe was out in force between the Thames and Yorkshire. At 21.00 hours Des McMullen was patrolling a beat from The Wash to Cromer and Winterton at altitudes between 14,000 and 20,000 feet, logging this sortie as a 'freelance' rather than a Fighter Night patrol, the former type covering a more loose geographic area. Craning his neck to scan the sky he was quite astonished to find a Junkers Ju88 flying almost alongside, slightly below him. McMullen promptly attacked it, moving his fire from its left quarter across to the right. Closing to seventy-five yards, he saw his de Wilde ammunition bursting on the enemy's wings and centre section – stopping the rear gunner's fire – as it dived steeply to sea level where, in the vicinity of Cromer, he lost sight of it heading out to sea at wave-top height.

Next off was Kenneth Blair who spotted a Ju88 high over south Lincolnshire. His own freelance combat report conveys the flavour of the difficulties these pilots endured on high-level interceptions in those days.

Blair lifted Hurricane P3813 off Wittering's runway at 22.23 hours and headed for the patrol line covering most of the Norfolk coast between RAF Sutton Bridge, Sheringham and on to Winterton, near Great Yarmouth. Reaching the end of the beat at Winterton, ground control gave him a heading to take him back to Sutton Bridge. Taking a final look round as he turned for home, he spotted what he called "a smoke trail a long way behind me and very high." At this point he was at about 10,000 feet altitude when he turned onto an intercepting course. Blair reported:

I started to climb towards it but when it was level with me I was still 7,000 feet too low – so I pulled the plug on the engine [emergency boost] and climbed from dead behind – still gaining nothing at all. I increased the engine revs to 2,800 and began to catch up.

It took Blair until he reached the vicinity of Spalding before he could get into a firing position.

At 600 yards range I could clearly see the two trails from the engines [condensation trails?] and when I got to 400 yards I identified the aircraft as a Ju88. At 200 yards I opened fire while closing to 150 yards and after five short bursts of gunfire, flames came from the port side and black smoke from the port engine. Oil hitting my windscreen made it difficult to see the target so I fired nearly all my ammunition at the flames. These flames began to increase and more smoke and oil came from the port engine but at no time was there any return fire from the rear gunner.

Flt Lt Blair continued:

At the time I began the attack, 22.50 hours, I was at 27,000 feet and greatly affected by the severe cold, so having finished off my ammunition I decided to lose altitude and watch the E/A from below. Shortly afterwards, as far as I could see, the flames went out and the Ju88 itself began to lose height. As soon as it came lower, the smoke trail stopped and losing sight of it near Grantham, I returned to base where I landed at 00.09 hours.

Blair also commented that if he had been flying anything other than a

Hurricane – or a Spitfire – it would have been impossible to reach the enemy aircraft and even then his own Hurricane controls froze up. Flt Lt Blair claimed a damaged but although it was changed later to a probable, post-war research of Luftwaffe quartermaster returns (monthly reports on aircraft on strength) is unfortunately unable to corroborate either of the claims made by Flt Lts McMullen or Blair.

There was no doubt, however, about the two kills – the first for himself and the squadron in its night role – made on this same night by a third 151 pilot, the legendary Plt Off Richard Playne Stevens, who demonstrated his lethal potential during his own Fighter Night patrol. Wittering control sent him via the eastern approaches to London where, at 01.35 he shot down a Do17Z-2, 5K+DM, wk nr 3456 of II/KG3 near Brentwood. After tracking all the way back to Wittering to refuel and rearm, he took off again for the same area, this time on a freelance sortie and at 04.53 shot down Heinkel He111, A1+JK, wk nr 3638 of I/KG53, near Canvey Island, both aircraft being confirmed kills. Apart from appreciating the normal hazards associated with flying by night – such as navigation and actually spotting a target – one can begin to glean an indication of the personal qualities required as well as the physical difficulties under which such solo night sorties were made. Richard Stevens reported his first interception began at 20,000 feet altitude and increased to 30,000 feet while the second engagement was fought at around 19,000 feet. In addition Stevens used the normal reflector gunsight fully dimmed for the first combat but when he fired his first burst, vibration from the guns turned the sight light-source out so he had to revert to the external bead foresight, which he also used during the second engagement. Furthermore two of the Hurricane's eight guns would not fire during the second combat. Upon his return Richard Stevens was magnanimous enough to praise his colleagues on the ground, writing in his combat report: "I consider Wittering control very instrumental in the success of these interceptions."

On the night's down side, at 06:00 Sqn Ldr Adams ran out of fuel during one of the final patrols and had to bale out of his Hurricane. In doing so he was injured when his leg struck the tailplane. He was carted off to Stamford hospital for treatment but did not miss much as bad weather for the rest of the month prevented the squadron doing any operational flying.

On January 30, 151 Squadron was reorganised into three flights, two of Defiants and one of Hurricanes, the objective being – according to the ORB – "to prove the Hurricane is a better night fighter than the Defiant." As will be seen, that aim was never achieved and even the most biased person would consider the real outcome an honourable draw.

From the beginning of February, 151 Squadron mounted night patrols with both Hurricanes and Defiants and the latter achieved success early in the month when, during a Fighter Night patrol on the evening of February 4, pilot Sgt Henry Bodien and Sgt D E O Jonas (air gunner) in Defiant N3387 intercepted a Dornier Do17.

Waiting at readiness, at 20.30 hours Bodien was given the order to

'scramble' by Wittering control and soon had the Defiant climbing hard
into a clear moonlit sky towards Birmingham. By the time they reached
12,000 feet altitude showers of incendiaries could be seen in the distance
falling to the south of the city, but despite several changes of course no
interceptions were made. Bodien was told to return to Wittering and orbit
base where he was then given a possible target north-east of the airfield at
ten miles range. Settling on that course and losing height a little Sgt
Bodien, now flying at 10,000 feet altitude, spotted an aircraft in front of
him heading in the opposite direction. While keeping the pale yellow glow
of the target's exhaust flames in sight Bodien hauled the Defiant round in a
tight left-hand turn and came in from slightly below the other aeroplane. At
200 yards range he and Jonas agreed it was a Dornier Do17Z. Matching the
Dornier's speed of 130mph Bodien eased out to its starboard beam and Sgt
Jonas, aiming at the centre-section between the wings, opened fire on the
unsuspecting enemy with a two-second burst from his four machine guns at
less than seventy yards range. The Dornier pilot reacted like a startled
rabbit, breaking upwards and left to get away from his attacker. Bodien
clung to him in the climbing turn and when the target levelled out he found
himself ideally positioned just ten yards below the Dornier's starboard
wing tip and twenty-five yards out. At point blank range Sgt Jonas let fly
with another three-second burst from his turret guns into the Dornier's
fuselage and wing and again it turned away – but this time gently and with
flames licking from its belly. It had been hit fatally and the turn tightened
into a spiral until it crashed into the ground, exploding at Cawthwick
Lodge, Weldon, (near Corby) at 21.45 hours.

Bodien and Jonas's victim was found to be a Dornier Do17Z-3, wk nr
2907, U5+AR from III/KG2 whose pilot, Oblt H Krisch and his crew, Uffz
Kliem and Fws Bahr and Uehlemann, died in the wreckage. They were
believed to be part of a raid on Derby. It took only 750 rounds of ball and
armour-piercing .303 ammunition to despatch this bomber, and South
African Henry Bodien had now begun to carve out his own reputation as a
distinguished night fighter pilot. We will hear more of him later.

In its new role as a night fighter, the oft-maligned Boulton Paul Defiant will
feature regularly in this story from now on and will be seen to be a very
effective weapon, so it is appropriate at this point to put in a few
explanatory words on its behalf. According to one former Defiant pilot,
Peter Montgomery, it handled:

> ...much like the Hurricane, except that the effect of its turret
> weighing three-quarters of a ton considerably reduced its rate of roll!
> In straight and level flight the aeroplane was given to shuddering
> somewhat when the gunner rotated the turret guns from side to side,
> which could be a bit disconcerting until the pilot got used to it. This
> effect was caused by the gun barrels and associated movements of
> the turret fairing, disturbing air flowing over the tail surfaces. Space

for the gunner in the turret was very tight so instead of a seat or chest-type parachute, most Defiant gunners wore a combined denim smock and parachute called a 'parasuit'. The parachute canopy was packed in a large, slim pouch to form a two-inch thick padded back cushion and by all accounts was most efficient in allowing a rapid exit from the turret when needed.

In fact it can be argued that, during 1941, the Defiant actually came into its own as a night fighter/bomber-destroyer and the flexibility of its turret guns – not least with their upward-firing capability – made it ideal for that role. Later in the war an upward-firing arrangement, code-named 'schrage-musik', would be adopted by the Luftwaffe to devastating effect against RAF bombers. Peter Montgomery summed it up thus:

> In the darkness the Defiant could approach unseen beneath a Heinkel or Dornier and, using a wing or engine nacelle of the bomber as cover against the eyes of the German gunners, close in to 'formate' on the enemy in his blind spot. From this position the four .303 Brownings of the turret, each fed with 600 rounds per gun, could pour up to 2,400 rounds at the rate of 4,800 per minute into the target as the gunner fired up and across in a no-deflection, point-blank shot.

Some historians are at odds with Air Intelligence records over the actual location of the crash of Junkers Ju88A-5, 0580, V4+AT. Leutnant Heinz Gibbens and his crew from III/KG1 went missing in action on the night of February 9/10 and this Ju88 appears to be the only aircraft shot down that night. From his combat report, it seems highly probable that Sgt Alan Wagner of 151 Squadron, flying a Hurricane, was responsible for Gibbens' demise near RAF Mildenhall rather than in the Birmingham area as some have suggested. An extract from Wagner's combat report reads as follows.

Type of Enemy Aircraft:	Unidentified
Time Attack was delivered:	About 03.10
Place Attack was delivered:	Near Mildenhall
Enemy Casualties:	One damaged

Sgt Wagner took off from Wittering in a Hurricane at 02.20 (on the 10th). He was ordered onto a course of 140°, later amended to 120°, with instructions to intercept enemy aircraft at 3,000 feet travelling south-east. A little later he was ordered to increase speed, as the E/A was a short distance ahead. Soon after this when he was at 3,000 feet he observed twin exhaust flames below him on his starboard side. The target was travelling at about 200mph on a 140° course, and losing height. Alan Wagner 'pulled the plug', closed to fifty yards and fired a two-second burst from directly astern and aiming between the exhaust flames. A nearly full moon gave good visibility but 8/10ths cloud at 1,500 feet partly obscured it so identification was impossible against the dark background and with the altitude then being a mere fifty feet. Sgt Wagner pulled up immediately to avoid collision and turned in a tight circle. He did not sight the other aircraft again but noticed a number of burning fragments on the ground covering a wide area. There was no return fire, no searchlights and no AA fire and he landed back at Wittering at 03.25 hours.

Wagner fired 550 rounds at his target and was clearly experienced enough not to rely on his reflector sight at night, as it was noted that he used the bead foresight with tape stuck on his windscreen as a backsight. Wagner's two courses would put him in the vicinity of Mildenhall at least and, while Lt Gibbens' objective was Birmingham, it is quite feasible that his route either to or from Birmingham could have brought him close to Wagner's, too. In fact since Wagner states his target was heading south-east this suggests the target was returning to its base. Another interesting point is that anti-aircraft defences in the Birmingham area submitted claims for destroying three bombers during this raid. It might be considered curious that Wagner's target was "at 3,000 feet and losing height" and at the time he opened fire it was "then only fifty feet" which is hardly a healthy altitude at which to cross England! Is it possible, then, that Gibbens' Ju88 was hit by AA over Birmingham and may have been credited to them, but he was actually struggling to get back to base and losing the battle to keep airborne when the coup-de-grâce was delivered by Sgt Wagner?

For the remainder of February there was little flying due to 'duff' weather but a break in the gloom on the 23rd/24th brought a few enemy aircraft over the region. 151 put up some night patrols, including Sgt James Hopewell in Defiant N3388 but he ran out of fuel over Norfolk and although he managed to bale out safely, his air gunner Sgt Jack Wallace died when his parachute became snagged by the tailplane as the aircraft crashed near RAF Watton. Another Defiant crew, Sgt Percy Copeland, (having converted from Hurricanes) and his air gunner Sgt Lynas, in N1794, intercepted a Heinkel He111 but lost sight of it before it could be engaged. Two nights later Sgt Copeland's luck was no better when, this time in Defiant N3317, he intercepted a Ju88, but the turret guns jammed and the Junkers got clean away. The squadron's run of bad luck continued with the loss of a Defiant crew in the late afternoon of March 4, not far from the airfield. Piloted by Fg Off Peter Gordon-Dean, he and his air gunner Sgt George Worledge died when their Defiant N1794 crashed at Ketton, near Stamford, as a result of a section of wing covering peeling off while the aircraft was in a steep dive. This aeroplane had had a new clear vision panel fitted and was being air-tested when the accident happened.

As the weather improved in March, the Luftwaffe made more frequent night incursions into the region's airspace, mainly bombers on the way to, or from, juicier industrial targets, but also in the form of intruder missions nosing around the large quantity of airfields in the region. This increased activity caused six of 151 Squadron's Hurricanes to be detached from Wittering to RAF Digby early in the month for Fighter Night ops and is evidence that detachments of fighter aircraft were being moved around like pawns in a chess game. Squadron pilots also ranged far and wide during these night patrols, so that squadron combats – and not just 151 Squadron – are actually recorded as occurring across a large segment of England between London and Manchester, The Wash and the West Midlands. The weather was sufficiently improved on the night of March 10/11 to bring a force of Luftwaffe bombers out in strength to attack Plymouth. Roaming further north, in the clear moonlit sky over the East Midlands, were about eight intruder aircraft. For the crew of one of these, Luftwaffe intruder expert Oblt Kurt Herrmann, Uffz Engelbert Böttner and Fw Wilhelm Rüppel, it would be their last night as free men. Flying in Junkers Ju88C, wk nr 0343, R4+CH, of I/NJG2, their belly-landing just before midnight on the 10th, although causing considerable damage to the starboard wing and centre section and fuselage, brought the first example of a relatively intact night fighter to fall in this country. An official intelligence report at the time classified this aircraft as an A-5, which is incorrect since – in view of the engines being identified as Jumo211B – it was actually a C-2. In general terms the A-series was the bomber version and the C-series was the solid-nose night fighter development. The following extract from the Intelligence examination report gives a useful description of the sort of armament carried by these intruders.

One belt-fed MG151 [a 15mm cannon that occasionally supplanted the drum-fed MG FF 20mm cannon on some aircraft] was installed below three MG17 [7.92mm] machine guns, all belt-fed by lengthy and apparently complicated ammunition tracks. All four weapons are fixed to fire forwards through a cowling covering what would normally be the bomb-aimer position. They are all fired by one press-button on the pilot's control column. There is an 11mm-thick armour bulkhead in the nose immediately in front of the ammunition containers and the pilot's feet. This bulkhead is slotted to allow the gun barrels to pass through. The ammunition feed for the three MG17s is taken from two containers fitted between the pilot's legs [!] and one container on the aft starboard side of the cabin. Bullet-proof glass is fitted in front of the pilot's gunsight and the pilot's seat is armoured. For defence, one MG17 [7.92mm] hand-operated machine gun was found in the lower rear-gunner position and one MG15 [7.92mm] in the top rear-gunner position; both magazine-fed. Positions for three crew only.

Herrmann was an experienced and successful intruder pilot, having been credited with seven kills before his capture. He crash-landed the Junkers at Hay Green, Terrington St Clement, near King's Lynn, with some injuries to the occupants, one of whom, Böttner, suffered a fractured pelvis. RAF Air Intelligence inspectors considered the cause of the crash was due to the failure of a conrod, which fractured and burst through the crankcase of the starboard engine. Their report also stated that no bullet strikes were visible – although the captured radio operator, Uffz Böttner, expressed an opinion that the starboard engine may have been hit by flak. Fire took hold of the port engine on the ground and when local Home Guard soldiers arrived on the scene they found Herrmann gamely trying to get the flames to spread. He was disarmed and the fire extinguished by the soldiers. Although the aircraft was badly damaged in the landing it was described as being painted matt black overall, with the code slate grey, the C outlined in white and the fin swastikas painted out.

At least one account of this incident erroneously credits this Junkers to Flt Lt Bill Denison, a Hurricane pilot with 79 Squadron, who at that time was based at RAF Pembrey in South Wales. It seems slightly odd, even allowing for the considerable distances frequently covered during Fighter Night or freelance sorties, that one of their aircraft should be associated with a combat so far away over south Lincolnshire. The error is probably due to someone misreading the date of a combat claim submitted by Flt Lt Denison and then making an assumption in relation to the Herrmann incident. In 79 Squadron's records there is no mention of any combats or claims on March 10/11. In fact the only combat claim by 79 Squadron between January 2 and April 2 1941 was made on March 13 when Flt Lt Denison did indeed shoot down a Junkers Ju88 but that was over Pembroke Dock and confirmed as such.

Interestingly, from information contained in the same documentation one can also get a feel for the size of the forces being ranged against one another on occasions such as these. Data in Air Ministry ASO Summary 111 indicates the Luftwaffe despatched 160 bombers, 30 fighters and 90 mine-layer aircraft against the British Isles on the night of March 10/11, against which the RAF launched 109 single and twin-engine night fighter sorties.

Richard Stevens, back in action after a spell off flying with an ear infection, was sent off at 00.50 on March 13 on a freelance patrol off north Norfolk. Sector control directed him towards an outbound raider near Ipswich and he caught up with a bandit flying at 15,000 feet crossing the coast near Orfordness. In a cloudless, moonlit sky Stevens saw the bomber, a Junkers Ju88, as it passed across the moon's reflection in the sea some 3,000 feet below him. Diving on the bomber he closed to seventy-five yards, fired and saw hits on the fuselage and port engine. Trailing glycol and with its gunners firing back at him, the Junkers climbed steeply away but Stevens could not stay with it. He tried selecting fine pitch on the propeller but the pitch control had frozen up so he fell behind. Continuing the chase, he finally lost contact about twenty-five miles out to sea and returned to Wittering to claim one Ju88 damaged.

April 1941 saw the Luftwaffe making heavy raids on Midlands targets, in particular against Coventry and Birmingham on the nights of 8/9 and 9/10. In addition to those equipped with airborne radar these raids consisted of several RAF night fighter units on Fighter Night patrols, including 151 Squadron, from which the Defiants of Sgt Wagner and Flt Lt McMullen and the Hurricane of Plt Off Stevens were in the thick of the action. Wittering-based fighters had to operate well to the west of base in order to get among the bombers on this night and combats during this particular period serve to illustrate well the prevailing state of night air defence in general.

Sgt Alan Wagner – equally at home in either the Defiant or the Hurricane – and his air gunner Sgt Sidenberg, left Wittering at 00.48 on the 9th with orders to patrol Coventry. There was a big raid on and the night was bright from a quarter moon. In conjunction with a cloud layer below the patrol height, the moonlight made picking out other aircraft relatively easy – which of course worked both ways. While right over the city Wagner's Defiant was itself attacked and hit by gunfire from the equally alert crew of a Ju88 as it shot underneath the fighter, going so fast in the opposite direction that Sidenberg had no time to draw a bead on it. The damage seemed slight so the patrol continued with better results to come. Wagner spotted a Heinkel 111 a few miles north of the city flying south-west at 13,000 feet. He brought the Defiant to within forty yards where, from a position under the bomber's port wing, Sgt Sidenberg opened fire at point blank range. He reported seeing flames in the cockpit and forward fuselage, and return fire stopped at that point, but the Heinkel was already diving away and was last seen with smoke streaming out, disappearing into a cloud layer. Now south of Coventry, again Wagner resumed his patrol at 18,000 feet and found another Heinkel travelling south. Closing in to point blank range once more without being seen, Sgt Sidenberg poured in about a thousand rounds in three long bursts from under the port wing. Explosive rounds were seen hitting the fuselage but there was neither return fire from nor evasive action taken by the bomber. It simply flew straight on and was lost to sight, leaving Wagner and his gunner to surmise that all its crew may have been killed or had abandoned the aircraft. What was even more remarkable about this patrol was that after the hits registered by the Ju88 the Defiant's gun turret jammed, although later this was found out to be due to a burned-out fuse and not the enemy's gunfire. In the subsequent two engagements with Heinkels the four turret guns had to be fired from a fixed position, requiring a very special degree of cooperation and coordination by both the pilot and gunner to achieve the results they got. To round off their action-packed eighty-minute sortie Wagner and Sidenberg also reported they saw no less than three other enemy aircraft, which they identified as two Junkers Ju88s and one Heinkel He111, but were unable to engage them in combat.

Birmingham was the objective of a major Luftwaffe raid on April 9/10 and 151 launched several Hurricanes and Defiants on Fighter Night patrols over the city. Flt Lt Desmond McMullen with air gunner Sgt Fairweather were back in action and theirs was the first of the Defiants into the air at 23.15 on the 9th. Fires were much in evidence when they reached the city but the glow made it somewhat easier to spot the enemy. As the Defiant circled above the fires Sgt Fairweather saw a Heinkel He111 below and about 400 yards ahead. McMullen closed the range and came up on the bomber from below to give his gunner a twenty-yard point blank shot for a three-second burst into its belly. As the Defiant drew ahead the enemy pilot threw the Heinkel into a series of climbing and diving turns but McMullen kept the Defiant in close and Sgt Fairweather, now with one of his four guns jammed and useless, continued firing short bursts into his elusive target, until its port engine caught fire. With the fire spreading rapidly the enemy pilot appeared to try to ram the Defiant but as it turned towards the fighter, Fairweather caught it with a one-second burst into the cockpit area and the bomber crashed to earth west of RAF Bramcote. McMullen and Fairweather claimed to have destroyed a Heinkel He111 and despite at one point attacking from as close as twenty yards, it appears that the only enemy aircraft crash that fits this engagement was that of a Junkers Ju88, 3Z+AL from I/KG77 which came down near Bramcote.

One Defiant crew with cause to remember this night's action more than most was that of Sgts Bodien and Jonas and to say it was an eventful sortie would be quite an understatement.

A nearly full moon gave excellent visibility when Henry Bodien took off from Wittering at 01.10 on April 10, with air gunner Sgt D Jonas, for a Fighter Night patrol 13,000 feet over Birmingham. Twenty-five minutes later, while circling anti-clockwise round the city, they were in action. In the bright moonlight Sgt Bodien saw a Heinkel He111 flying north-east 500 yards ahead of him. Bringing the Defiant in from behind and below the target, Bodien presented an upward, no-deflection shot to Sgt Jonas who hit the bomber with a four-second burst of machine-gun fire from 200 yards. Still closing, Jonas fired again at thirty yards and as he did so, three of the crew baled out and the bomber dived hard to port. Bodien followed it down and when the Heinkel zoomed out of its dive at 8,000 feet, Jonas put another long burst into it from just 20 yards range. With one engine on fire the bomber half-rolled and dived vertically – followed again by the Defiant. Ominously close to the balloon barrage now and clearly doomed, the bomber continued its headlong dive towards the ground as Bodien hauled hard to bring his fighter out of its own dive and back to patrol altitude. It was then that he noticed the red and green intercom lights, linking him with his gunner, were both lit up and he assumed this indicated Jonas had passed out from the G-force effects of the last manoeuvre. Patrolling with a disabled gunner was no use so, with an emergency homing from Wittering, he landed back at 02.30 hours to find to his astonishment that the gunner's turret was empty. Sgt Jonas had baled out!

Many hours later the whole story emerged when Sgt Jonas returned to Wittering, clutching his parachute, having become another involuntary member of the Caterpillar Club. So steep was the angle of the Defiant's last headlong dive that Jonas reckoned his pilot must have either been killed or wounded so he made a very rapid exit from the turret, landing unhurt in the Birmingham suburb of King's Norton. The following report was submitted describing his experience.

> Sgt Jonas confirmed that two or three objects fell from the E/A which he presumed were members of the crew as he believes he saw parachutes open. The E/A was going down in a spiral with engines on fire and there was a large explosion on the ground just afterwards. After jumping from the Defiant he reported to a Balloon Barrage Unit and they informed him that an E/A had crashed just previously in Birmingham, killing about twelve civilians. The combat had taken place just east of Birmingham. Another E/A had also crashed in the Birmingham area.

Research by *The Blitz Then And Now* team identified the Heinkel as wk nr 1555, 1G+KM from II/KG27 which crashed onto houses in Hales Lane (later renamed St Mark's Rise) in the Smethwick area of Birmingham at 01.45 on the 10th. Although some accounts suggest this bomber should be credited to Flt Lt Deansley of 256 Squadron, that is now felt to be incorrect since all the facts clearly support Sgt Bodien's claim.

Lining up for take-off on the runway immediately behind Sgt Bodien was Sgt Lionel Staples (pilot) and Sgt K Parkin (air gunner) in Defiant N3479, also detailed for a Fighter Night over Birmingham. As he flew towards the patrol area Sgt Staples saw and attacked what he thought might be a Dornier east of the city. Staples brought the Defiant under the starboard wing of the bomber to within twenty-five yards and Parkin raked the fuselage with a very long burst. As usual the bomber crew seemed to have been caught totally unawares since there was no return fire. Staples had to climb rapidly to avoid collision, though, when the bomber turned towards the Defiant then dived, weaving from side to side as it went down. With only two of his four guns working now, Sgt Parkin hit it again with three more bursts as they followed the bomber down. Smoke started to pour out then something – probably one of the crew – was seen to fall away from the aircraft. When it seemed certain that the bomber would crash, Sgt Staples broke off, climbed away from the looming balloon barrage and headed back to Wittering to claim one Dornier destroyed. The subsequent combat report was altered to show the type as a Heinkel He111 or a Do17 and the claim amended to a probable. The question of recognition seems odd in view of the Defiant managing to get so close to the target and when no Dorniers seem to have been involved in this night's raid.

Flt Lt Donald Darling with his air gunner Plt Off J Davidson followed the other two Defiants bound for Birmingham, where they were detailed to patrol at 11,000 feet altitude. At 01.40 on the 10th when east-north-east of Birmingham they found a Junkers Ju88 heading south-west and Darling, unseen, brought the Defiant into a firing position just below its fuselage. Davidson fired a couple of two-second bursts into its belly from fifty yards as the Junkers turned away to port. Again there was no return fire and the bomber dived steeply with the Defiant clinging to its tail. At 3,000 feet they lost sight of the bomber in mist and smoke over the city and he returned to Wittering. Again amid the confusion of that very busy night there is some doubt about which aircraft Darling and Davidson attacked and what might have been its fate. They were officially credited with, "One Ju88 destroyed (shared with AA)", but their combat report is another that was later amended to include the following handwritten comment, "This E/A was identified as the Ju88 found in Windsor Great Park, damaged by AA fire. It is now claimed by 151 as a destroyed shared with AA."

However, in recent times it has been stated the enemy aircraft that crashed in Windsor Great Park was Heinkel He111, G1+LS of III/KG55, shared by Darling/Davidson and AA, but with the crash time/date given as 02.40 on April 9 rather than April 10. If Darling's identification of his Ju88 is correct then there is clearly an anomaly here. Furthermore, a Ju88, V4+JV of II/KG1, said to be attacking Coventry, is listed as brought down by an unidentified night fighter and AA to crash at Whitwell in Hertfordshire at 02.00 on April 10. Perhaps that might be the enemy aircraft claimed by Flt Lt Darling. Such are the joys of research!

The following night, April 10/11, the Luftwaffe returned to Birmingham and gave Flt Lt Richard Stevens another opportunity to notch up two kills in one night. His first sortie was a Fighter Night to the city, taking off at 22.45 on April 10. It would seem he had no intention of tying himself to the metropolitan area since one hour later he intercepted what he described as a Ju88, heading south at 16,000 feet ten miles north-east of Banbury. Attacking from astern, Stevens fired 1,600 m/g rounds in two long bursts into the target, causing pieces to fly off it and the Hurricane to be covered with oil. The bomber went down in a vertical dive, exploding into flames in a field below. There were no survivors. For this combat Richard Stevens is generally credited with bringing down Junkers Ju88, V4+FV of I/KG1 at Murcott, a village between Bicester and Oxford, and this final location certainly seems to fit the tracks of the combatants. For reasons not explained, Stevens' combat report was altered later to show the E/A type as a Heinkel He111, but the only He111 to crash anywhere near was believed to be 1H+FS, shot down about eight miles north-west of Banbury by another squadron.

Plt Off Stevens returned to Wittering at 00.25 hours to refuel and rearm and was off again at 02.15, this time on a freelance patrol within the sector. The moon was still up as he set off westwards from Wittering and within fifteen minutes his eagle eyes spotted a Heinkel above him heading in the opposite direction. Bringing his Hurricane round onto the tail of the bomber Stevens opened fire with a three-second burst from his eight guns at 150 yards range. He said, "The whole burst hit the bomber and I was temporarily blinded when something in the E/A blew up."

When the bomber's shadow filled his sight ring again he put another long burst into the fuselage. Its engines and fuselage on fire, the Heinkel slowly turned over, fell into a steep dive and Stevens saw it explode on the ground. He estimated his position was between Kettering and Thrapston when he saw the bomber and is credited with bringing down Heinkel He111, G1+AT from III/KG55, found at Rothwell Lodge near Kettering. Of the crew, three died and two baled out to become POWs.

Plt Off Stevens scored one more success that month when at 04.15 in the morning of April 20 he shot down Heinkel He111, 5J+JR from III/KG4, near Chatham, during a freelance patrol of the London area.

Enemy air activity was of such intensity now, that on some nights, Spitfires of day-fighter 266 Squadron at Wittering were even thrown into the sector's Fighter Night operations and it was not unknown for between 200 and 300 AI and non-AI equipped RAF fighters to be airborne on a single night in the skies over the British Isles. For example on May 4/5 when the Luftwaffe was piling on the pressure, 450 bombers were sent against Belfast, Liverpool, Barrow-in-Furness and Tyneside, against which the RAF launched 260 night fighter sorties.

Defiant crews were still notching up successes, too. KG30 sent bombers to Merseyside on May 2/3 and one of its Ju88s, an A-5, 4D+BH, was caught by Plt Off Guy Edmiston and Sgt Albert Beale (gunner) of 151 Sqn as it made its way home over The Wash. Sgt Beale managed to inflict enough damage for Major W Seeburg to need all his skill to pull off a good belly landing on the beach at Weybourne, north Norfolk. Seeburg and his crew, Fws Altmayer, Geiger and Laser got out safely and were all made POW.

Newly commissioned as a Pilot Officer, Henry Bodien continued to harass the enemy in battle and his sharp eyes brought him into combat again on the night of May 3/4. Half an hour before midnight, crewed with air gunner Sgt Wrampling, Bodien eased his Defiant into the air from RAF Wittering for a Fighter Night patrol. Turning north, he was led by search-lights towards potential enemy activity and soon he spotted a white light – possibly an aircraft tail navigation lamp – about five miles distant and just north of Wittering, moving across his track from west to east. Bodien went flat out after the target, but having caught up with it near Boston at 00.20 hours on the 4th, he thought at first it might be a friendly. Easing in to just fifty yards astern to check, he and his gunner agreed it was a Heinkel He111 whereupon Wrampling, without further ado, opened fire. This pro-voked a hot response from the Heinkel's upper and lower rear gun positions, then Wrampling was forced to stop firing when the solenoid (an electrical component that controlled the firing mechanism) of one of his four machine guns flew off after the first burst and two others suffered link-chute jams.

They were crossing the coast now, north of The Wash at about 7,000 feet altitude. Wrampling was able to keep one gun firing with two others working intermittently before he could clear the jams. The fourth gun, loaded with de Wilde ammunition, failed to fire at all. Despite this handicap the gunner kept up his attack as Bodien, still flying over sea but by now uncertain of his whereabouts, clung to his quarry like a dog after a fox. One good burst from Wrampling appeared to put the lower rear gunner out of action, then another burst stopped the port engine and a stream of white vapour began to pour from it. Now the Heinkel was losing height and all return fire had stopped. Still Bodien kept close in and slightly below so that Wrampling, even with his reduced firepower, could not fail to hit the target – which he continued to do with good effect.

The action had descended to 1,000 feet altitude where it became obvious to both sides that the bomber could not escape its fate. The enemy pilot turned on all his navigation lights and banked towards where the coast should be. Henry Bodien was not about to let the matter rest and now at 800 feet altitude, bored in for another pass. This was his last opportunity because, when they circled back, the Heinkel was next observed burning slightly, as the Defiant's crew described it "in the sea", almost certainly off the north Norfolk coast. In all Bodien estimated they had made no less than thirty to forty firing passes on the Heinkel and Sgt Wrampling had managed to fire 850 rounds, of which 600 were through his one fully serviceable gun. It had been a tough nut to crack with this handicap but as the combat intelligence report said, "The attack was carried out with great determination", and with this great team effort they had gone in close and made every round count. Out of Wittering R/T range by now, Bodien got a homing from Digby where he landed at 01.17 to refuel and give Wrampling an opportunity to examine his faulty weapons, before landing back at Wittering at 03.15.

That night a German pilot had belly-landed an aeroplane near Sharrington, a small village between Holt and Fakenham in north Norfolk, just four miles inland from the coast at Blakeney Point. It was subsequently established that this Heinkel was He111H-4, A1+LL of I/KG53, wk nr 3235, flown by Leutnant Alfred von Bachfelden who, having bombed Liverpool, was returning to his base in northern France. Could the flicker of flames mentioned by Bodien have been this crew setting fire to their aircraft, as it was was pretty well burned out by the time the German airmen were rounded up as prisoners-of-war? Of the other crewmen, Gefr B Reynat and Uffz W Richter were made POW, but Gefr B Kauhardt died in the engagement. Although A1+LL is generally credited to Plt Off Bodien and Wrampling, in a subsequent chapter it will be seen that all may not be quite what it seems about this night's work.

Mid May 1941 saw the culmination of the Luftwaffe Blitz and some of 151's Hurricanes continued to be detached to other sectors – this month for example to RAF Coltishall in Norfolk. Meanwhile the pace of night action was hotting up as – unbeknown of course at this point – the Luftwaffe Blitz moved towards its peak. On the night of May 7/8 bombers attacked Liverpool and Hull and Plt Off Richard Stevens, one of more than 300 RAF fighters sent up in the overnight period, notched up two more He111s out of the thirteen E/A claimed that night.

Airborne from Wittering at 01.12 on the 8th for a freelance patrol, he was at first drawn towards Grantham by AA fire. Searchlights lit up a

Heinkel but Stevens could not make up the altitude deficit before the bandit disappeared. Now flying at 10,000 feet he could see fires in the direction of Hull and radioed for permission to fly into that sector to investigate. Group gave the 'OK' and off he went. Over the city at just after 02.00, in the light of the half moon he saw a Heinkel about 2,000 feet below and swooped down on its rear quarter. He fired two bursts, the second of which hit the starboard engine, bringing a stream of oil and glycol back over the Hurricane. Stevens calmly cleaned the windscreen and went back into the attack. Making violent S-turns, the bomber tried to evade the Hurricane but Stevens fired another telling burst that caused the bomber to go into a slow rolling dive and be lost to his view in some low level cloud. Five minutes later, while climbing back up to resume his search, Richard Stevens saw another Heinkel flying eastwards, possibly one of those on its way home from Liverpool. He banged open the throttle and caught up with it but the crew was more alert than most and it dived towards the cloud cover. Firing from 250 yards – pretty far out for Stevens – as the range closed his first burst hit the port engine, which exploded in sparks and shed large parts of cowling. Following the bomber in its dive, Stevens put in a final burst and more pieces flew off before it, too, was enveloped by cloud. Climbing back up once more he continued looking for the enemy but could find none so, when the fuel in his main tanks was exhausted he returned to Wittering, landing at 03.35 with another job well done. It is believed Heinkel He111, 5J+ZB from Stab I/KG4 and G1+GH of I/KG55 are those brought down by Plt Off Stevens.

Under a full moon, London on the 10/11th became the cauldron for the Luftwaffe's last maximum-effort raid of the Blitz. With other squadrons from the sector and other crews from 151 Squadron, Sgt Percy Copeland and Flt Lt Des McMullen in Defiants and Plt Offs Richard Stevens and Irving Smith in Hurricanes were again in combat, this time over the Thames as part of the RAF's maximum-effort Fighter Night response. Moonlight gave good visibility to both sides and over 500 enemy bombers attacking the capital were met by swarms of single-engine fighters. Fighter Command records indicate over 300 fighters were deployed throughout the night and many aircraft – on both sides – flew more than one sortie.

Inevitably, among the latter was Plt Off Stevens, who claimed one bomber shot down (possibly He111, 1T+HH of KG28) and one probable, in the vicinity of the capital. Having had no luck on his first sortie of the night he had hung about the capital for so long that he had insufficient petrol to make it back to Wittering and just managed to find refuge at RAF Fowlmere, Duxford's satellite airfield. Re-fuelled, at 03.11 hours on the 11th he took his Hurricane back over the fires raging in the north-east of the city. Seeing AA fire to the west he set off towards it and found a Heinkel He111. In amongst the AA barrage, Stevens set about the Heinkel, his machine-gun fire causing an explosion in the fuselage, the engines streaming white smoke as it dived away into dense smoke from fires below. In an understatement Stevens thought "it inadvisable to follow" so he climbed over north London to resume his patrol. AA gunfire had a go at his Hurricane but diving out of danger he saw another Heinkel in front and above him at 7,000 feet. Its ventral gunner was awake and fired at the Hurricane as it approached. Plt Off Stevens gave the bomber a burst from 100 yards but as he broke left the dorsal gunner got in his own burst, peppering the underside of the Hurricane and damaging the engine, wings and a wheel. Bringing the Hurricane in faster this time, Stevens tried to get beneath the bomber but its wily pilot slowed down and the fighter almost overshot. Throttling back quickly, Stevens put a burst into the fuselage centre section but stalled and the Heinkel dived towards some cloud cover. As it passed him in the dive Stevens fired into the centre section again and the bomber seemed to go out of control. With his engine running roughly, he managed to make it back to Wittering intact to claim one destroyed and one probable. Strictly speaking these two particular Heinkels are unconfirmed, although several Heinkels are listed by the Luftwaffe as failing to return from ops or were severely damaged when they got back. Furthermore in the mêlée of aircraft over the capital that night it is quite possible that more than one fighter attacked the same bomber.

Sgt Copeland and his New Zealand air gunner Sgt R Sampson left Wittering at 01.50 on a Fighter Night over Gravesend. Bombers were attacking the docks and it was around 03.00, against the smoke and flames from this, when Copeland spotted a Heinkel flying east. Despite the target taking violent evasion Copeland kept the Defiant in the classic attacking position beneath the starboard wing, allowing Sampson to rake the whole of the fuselage with four bursts of gunfire. The Heinkel gunners fired back but the Defiant's position made it impossible for them to reach their target and after the second burst, return fire ceased. With one engine stopped the bomber slowly turned over and dived earthwards. Sgt Sampson hit it with two more bursts and riddled by 1,000 de Wilde and armour piercing rounds, the Heinkel exploded on the ground somewhere near Gravesend. Heinkel He111, A1+CL of I/KG53, was later found to have crashed not far away, near Gillingham.

Then, at 03.30, Desmond McMullen and air gunner Sgt Fairweather, on their second (freelance) sortie of the night, headed towards the fires that could be seen from Wittering itself. At 03.15 over the West End, Fairweather saw a Heinkel He111 heading south at a rapid rate of knots and McMullen, 'pulling the plug', overhauled it quickly. In another classic Defiant interception they came in under the port wing of the bomber, from where Sgt Fairweather put four long bursts into it at seventy-five yards range. Both engines and the fuselage caught fire and down went the Heinkel into a field about five miles from Tunbridge Wells. Their victim is believed to be Heinkel He111, G1+BT of KG55 that crashed at Withyham (East Sussex).

At 03.45 Plt Off Irving Smith, in one of the last Fighter Night combats of that frenetic night, claimed a Heinkel He111 as damaged in an engagement that was fought out all the way from the East End of London to Southend. Smith got in three bursts at the bomber while managing to avoid being hit by return fire. The Heinkel dived from 11,000 feet down to 1,500 feet at which point a Bofors light AA gun opened up on the Hurricane and Smith had to break off the combat. He landed at Wittering at 04.45 hours.

Following the fortunes of 151 Squadron's Hurricanes and Defiants on such a night illustrates graphically just how far and wide these fighters roamed. Many night squadrons and day squadrons were equally heavily engaged of course – 1 Squadron for example claiming no less than eight E/A destroyed that night. The battle raging was of a scale not seen since the daylight battles of the previous summer, with the defenders claiming twenty-four E/A destroyed – later found to be half that number in reality with fifteen damaged. Nevertheless, it was a 'hot' night and while all this was going on down south, RAF Wittering itself came in for some punishment when the Luftwaffe bombed it for the fourth night in a row. Plt Off Gayzler with air gunner Plt Off Pfleger, in N3372, one of the crews left minding the shop, intercepted what they thought was a Messerschmitt Bf110 over Peterborough around 23.59 on the 10th, but their Defiant was too slow to catch up with it and the E/A got away.

Gradually, from June onwards, it became clear that the Luftwaffe had substantially scaled down its activity over the UK, not only due to the short summer nights but also because of the start of the Russian campaign. On the night of 13/14 though, with one of the squadron's new four-cannon Hurricane IIs in his capable hands, Plt Off Richard Stevens continued to build up his score by shooting down a Heinkel He111 that crashed south of Royston. The hitting power of the four 20mm cannon in a pair of steady hands is amply demonstrated by Stevens' report: "A burst of one second from 250-300 yards dead astern caused a tremendous explosion in E/A, audible above the noise of the engine and the Hurricane was thrown violently upward and turned on its back." He had fired just forty rounds.

The arrival of the Turbinlite Havoc onto the night fighter scene – of which more later – marked another change of role for 151 when they sent a number of Hurricanes on detachment to RAF Hunsdon for Turbinlite cooperation training. Back at Wittering in August the whole of that month and the next were devoted to day and night training sorties with the Searchlight Havocs of 1453 Flight. The first pukka Turbinlite patrol by 151 Squadron was launched on October 22/23 1941 with Z2361, one of four Hurricane II cannon-armed aircraft now on charge and Defiant AA431. Both were in the hands of experienced night flyers with the Hurricane flown by Plt Off Richard Stevens and Plt Off Alex McRitchie at the controls of the Defiant. During the one-hour patrol, Stevens became separated from the formation but claimed to have destroyed an enemy aircraft he had spotted. The story of that interception is detailed in Chapter 5.

The squadron was still mounting Fighter Nights from Wittering and also by using a detachment at RAF Coltishall. September was a lean month, though, with the best opportunity coming the way of Defiant crew Plt Off John Haviland and his air gunner, Sgt R G Stolz-Page. John Haviland was actually American by birth but had spent most of his early life in England. While at Nottingham University he joined the RAFVR and was called up on the outbreak of war. His first posting, to 1 School of Army Cooperation was not to his liking so, at the height of the Battle of Britain, when pilots were being trawled from all sorts of units, he volunteered for Fighter Command. Trained at 6 OTU, RAF Sutton Bridge, on Hurricanes, he was posted to 151 Squadron in late September 1940.

This pair was scrambled from Wittering at 01.43 on September 12 to intercept an incoming raider. Langtoft GCI directed the pilot to the general vicinity of the bandit and searchlights beckoned him even closer until at 02.25 Haviland got a visual near Luffenham, to the west of Wittering. There in the half-moonlight was a Dornier Do215 heading south-west, cruising along at 4,000 feet altitude, silhouetted just above the cloud tops. Haviland, a couple of thousand feet higher, had no trouble picking out his quarry in the good visibility and immediately dived at the port side of the Dornier, giving his gunner the chance of a quick squirt as the Defiant zoomed underneath. Pulling up and round to his left, Haviland now came at the bomber from head on below, this time allowing Stolz-Page a four-second burst at a hundred yards range. Turning to port, the fleeing Dornier was quickly lost in cloud and although Stolz-Page was confident many of his 400 armour piercing (AP) and de Wilde rounds would have hit the enemy he did not actually see any strikes on the bomber. Plt Off Haviland scoured the area but no further contact was made. Later it was reported that the local Observer Corps heard a bomber circle once before flying off at high speed, estimated at 340mph, towards the east. Haviland landed back at Wittering at 03.00.

It might be appropriate at this point to provide some detail about the ammunition called 'de Wilde' that has been mentioned in this narrative from time to time. This was the name given to incendiary bullets used by the RAF and should not be confused with 'tracer' rounds. Tracer rounds tended to take a lower trajectory so did not mark the path of other rounds entirely accurately. Generally speaking, the guns of an RAF night fighter were not loaded with tracer so that, when they were fired, its position would not be compromised. On striking a target de Wilde incendiaries could cause any flammable material or liquid to ignite or explode. Additionally, the flash of light produced when the chemical compound in the tip of these rounds struck would show the gunner that he was hitting the target. This particular incendiary bullet was developed at Woolwich Arsenal and issued just in time for use in the Battle of Britain. It was named 'de Wilde' to deceive the Germans that it was derived from ammunition designed by a Swiss gentleman of that name. The British, however, had discovered that de Wilde's original design could only be produced by hand – an impractical proposition – whereas the British 'de Wilde' bullets were the invention of a soldier, Captain Aubrey Dixon, whose design, crucially, could be mass-produced.

One night in October Plt Off Alex McRitchie and his air gunner Plt Off Sampson in Defiant AA417 intercepted no less than four Junkers Ju88s twenty-five miles off Great Yarmouth, claiming one destroyed and one damaged. Trade was a bit thin by this time though and McRitchie had to wait nearly a month before he was again in action at dusk on November 15 in Defiant AA408 and could claim another Ju88.

Cooperation with the Turbinlite flight was back on 151's menu at Wittering in December and this even included experimenting with the Havocs, dropping parachute flares on possible targets from altitudes of 5,000 feet. However, that idea was soon scrapped as a complete waste of time.

By the end of 1941 there were nine squadrons of Beaufighters, six squadrons of Defiants – including 151 Squadron – and ten flights of Turbinlite Havocs, operating in the home defence night fighter role throughout the UK. Even better news though, was in the offing for the squadron when it was announced that 151 was to convert to the new Mosquito night fighter. Although this was an enormous boost for the squadron's morale, life went on as usual at Wittering because officialdom still persisted with the 'in-between' Turbinlite concept. The squadron's A Flight received its first Mosquito NF II on April 6 1942 but B Flight had to soldier on with its Defiants for a while. How they fared with the Mosquito while they remained at RAF Wittering will be dealt with later in this story.

CHAPTER 4

Patrolling the Blue Lines

Moving from RAF Debden to RAF Digby on June 27 1940 to replace 229 Squadron, 29 Squadron began its contribution to the defence of sectors around The Wash equipped with a complement of Bristol Blenheim Mk I fighters. A few weeks later, with the squadron now operating from Digby's satellite airfield at Wellingore, also known at this time as L1, the energetic Sqn Ldr Charles Widdows took command and Wellingore Hall, a large mansion in the village, was commandeered as the officers' mess. The Hall was only a mile from L1 dispersal and since non-commissioned aircrew were also found accommodation in the village, this arrangement enabled pilots and gunners to meet a thirty-minute availability commitment and get more sleep by avoiding the need to travel to and from Digby airfield itself.

Operational night patrols along various pre-determined compass bearings radiating from the airfield began immediately, interspersed with airborne practice flights to get used to the new AI equipment, usually referred to at this stage as RDF trials. The enemy was rarely found but on the night of June 30/July 1 the squadron received a rude awakening when Blenheim L1374 flown by nineteen-year-old Plt Off Peter Sisman with his air gunner, twenty-year-old Sgt Andrew Reed, crashed near Wellingore airfield while trying to engage an enemy bomber. Their patrol began at 22.50 and was uneventful until just after midnight when Plt Off Sisman reported his recognition lights had gone u/s and he was ordered to return to base. Approaching the airfield he told Digby Ops that he had spotted a bandit and was off to investigate. The term 'bandit', as used either by ground control or aircrew, meant that the target was almost certainly an enemy aircraft but positive identification was still essential.

He then reported that he could not keep the bandit in sight because his aircraft was coned by searchlights and these were dazzling him. So, with no recognition lights to use, ops recalled Sisman and gave him a course to steer for base. Shortly afterwards people on the airfield heard the sound of a crash and the explosion of bombs lit up the sky. L1374 had gone down, believed to be due to loss of control while held in searchlight beams and when the Blenheim caught fire, an enemy aircraft had laid a stick of bombs across the wreckage, blowing it and its crew to pieces with a direct hit.

Modifications to the Blenheims, to make them a little more war-like, kept filtering through and in July all squadron aircraft were fitted with self-sealing fuel tanks. A Fraser Nash gun mounting, consisting of two Browning .303 machine guns located in the hatch just forward of the gun turret, was fitted to one aircraft as a trial and two other aircraft were fitted with armour plating to protect the turret gunner. It was intended to modify all squadron aircraft in the near future.

Towards the end of July the squadron spread its wings on the operational patrol side by detaching two aircraft to RAF Ternhill every evening to add their weight to the air defence of the Merseyside area. Although sector boundaries would be redrawn from the beginning of 1941, at this time Digby's sector – in common with Wittering, Kirton in Lindsey and Church Fenton sectors – ran across the width of England with, in Digby's case, Ternhill more or less at its north-western corner. Patrols from Ternhill were actually controlled from Digby sector ops room and upon completion the Blenheims either landed back at Ternhill if they were on duty next night or made their way back to Wellingore if they were to be relieved. There was little success to record from these sorties but the most significant fact was that many of the Blenheim aircraft sent on these detachments were equipped with early production AI Mk III sets.

A so-called 'friendly-fire' incident involving the squadron occurred at the end of July, illustrating how fraught with danger night interceptions could be in those days. Plt Off Richard Rhodes and his air gunner Sgt Service were on a Red Line patrol just before midnight of July 31 when Rhodes saw an aircraft with its navigation light on. Reporting this to Digby control he was told to investigate and followed it as it climbed away. At 7,000 feet altitude the navigation lights went off and the Blenheim crew believed that the silhouette was that of an enemy aircraft. Digby control advised them there were no friendlies in the area and told Rhodes to open fire. The target went down in flames but was subsequently found to be an RAF Fairey Battle.

During August there were an increasing number of references to 'special equipment', for example on August 12/13 when Sqn Ldr Widdows, with air gunner Fg Off Charles Bell and AC2 Bill Wilson as AI operator, took Blenheim L1472 to Ternhill but, as the ORB mentions, "the special equipment in the aircraft did not pick up any contacts during the patrol."

Charles Widdows was always at the forefront of the action and when he was not flying a Blenheim he was, as often as not, out hunting the enemy alone in a Hurricane, often carrying out freelance patrols on consecutive nights and sometimes more than one sortie in a night. This enthusiasm and tenacity can be seen in one of his sorties on the night of August 29/30. He left Digby in a Hurricane at 04.50 on the 30th to intercept a raider that was travelling east from the Mersey area. Climbing to 10,000 feet over base, Digby control vectored him onto a bandit in the vicinity of Newark. Widdows never actually found the bandit, which was plotted going south-east until it reached Bedford, where it then turned north-east and crossed the coast at Cromer. Sqn Ldr Widdows chased the enemy aircraft on various vectors from control and at one time actually over-ran it. He crossed the coast behind the target and although out of touch by R/T, continued the blind chase for several miles out to sea before, with petrol running low, he finally gave up and returned to R/T range, whereupon control ordered him to refuel at RAF Coltishall and then return to Digby.

By the end of August 1940 the squadron had on charge nine Blenheims equipped with 'special equipment' (AI Mk III) sets and their crews were practising hard to achieve night operational status. These Blenheims were L1290, L1292, L1324, L1330, L1472, L6637, L7135, L7153 and L8661. Appearing amongst the crew names was that of a certain Pilot Officer John Randall Daniel Braham. On August 17, Plt Off Braham carried out his first 'RDF' trial, an uneventful 2½-hour patrol off the Lincolnshire coast to get experience with the new AI equipment. Better known in RAF circles as 'Bob', Braham had been with the squadron since December 1938 and was destined to become one of the RAF's top-scoring night fighter aces and one of its most highly decorated airmen.

Different coloured flares distinguished the individual blue, green, red, yellow or white patrol lines and in his memoirs Braham described these patrol lines thus:

> We had no airborne radar and there was then only the most primitive form of ground control. Our night patrols consisted chiefly of flying over groups of flares set out in various patterns on the ground. Flares were laid out in a particular pattern and repeated every few miles over a distance of twenty to thirty miles to form a visible patrol line. From these lines we could be directed to some point in space in an attempt to intercept the enemy. It was a hit and miss affair, dependent on there being little or no cloud so that the fighter crew could see the flares from 10,000 feet or more. At other times we worked with the searchlights.

But 29 Squadron's first confirmed 'kill' went to Pilot Officer Richard Rhodes and air gunner Sgt William Gregory in L6741, a non-AI Blenheim, while they were detached to Ternhill. Taking off at 01.32 on August 18 to patrol what was called the 'Mersey Blue Line', Rhodes was vectored on to a bandit and at 02.28, about fifteen miles south-west of Chester, he spotted what appeared to be a light on the rear part of the fuselage of an aircraft. Flying towards the target, he identified it as a Heinkel but it took him no less than two hours of chase before he could bring the Blenheim into range. By this time, having flown south at first, the enemy aircraft turned east and was making for the Lincolnshire coast, but Rhodes stuck doggedly to his quarry and finally came within firing range about twenty-five miles off Spurn Point. He was in no mind to let the enemy off the hook after such a long chase and opened fire at 400 yards range, expending all the ammunition in his five front guns. Now this would normally be regarded as a pretty optimistic range but his fire on this occasion was sufficient to slow down the enemy aircraft and it began to circle and lose height. Seizing the initiative, Rhodes brought the Blenheim up on its starboard side to allow his gunner to bring the turret Vickers K machine gun to bear and Sgt Gregory promptly emptied a whole drum of .303 rounds (97) into the bandit. The target continued to lose altitude until eventually Gregory saw it settle gently on the sea about ten miles west of Cromer Knoll. Sgt Bill 'Sticks' Gregory later retrained as a radio/observer (Rad/Obs or RO) and subsequently teamed up with Bob Braham to forge one of the most successful night fighter crews in the RAF.

Although ultimately successful, this combat is yet another classic illustration of the relatively poor performance of the Blenheim for the task it was assigned to. In addition, this incident gives an idea of the difficulties of research that can be encountered when trying to find that elusive thing called 'the truth'. For example, one version of post-war research suggests Rhodes' victim was a Junkers Ju88 intruder aircraft from II/NJG1, briefed to intrude over The Wash, and crewed by Ofw Fritz Zenkel (pilot), Fw Gustav Schramm (radio) and Gefr Hans Roth (flight engineer), all of whom were posted as missing. It was said to have been shot down off Spurn Head at 03.00, on August 17. However, this information is at odds with 29 Squadron's ORB in which the Rhodes incident is clearly timed and dated August 18. With take-off from Ternhill stated as 01.32 hours, the squadron ORB records the initial contact time as 02.28 to the south-west of Chester – a long way from The Wash – and the length of chase as nearly two hours, putting the time of combat at almost 04.30 when the enemy aircraft crashed off the north Norfolk coast. According to aviation historian John Foreman, intruder unit II/NJG1 did indeed operate Ju88s – and Fw Schramm was among its aircrew at that time – over England in July and August 1940, before it was reorganised to create NJG2 in September 1940. However, Foreman admits he cannot find confirmation of the date 17/8/40 in official Luftwaffe loss records. Another historian, Simon Parry, on the other hand bases his version of events on the PRO data, adding that NJG1 had just begun operations from Schipol/Amsterdam airfield at the time and that this particular Junkers Ju88C-2 was the unit's first operational loss. Another key point he raises is that NJG1's early sorties were not to the patrol areas in Yorkshire, Lincolnshire and Norfolk (known as Raum A, B and C) that were created later as NJG1/NJG2's operational expertise developed. This may account for the assumption that Schramm's objective that night would have been to one of those later-designated patrol areas. 'Overnight' times, too, can often lead to a misinterpretation of the relevant date and that may be so in this case.

Just to confuse matters even more, some books, magazines and internet sites have been found that credit Bob Braham with shooting down the first enemy aircraft for both 29 Squadron and himself, into the Humber on the night of August 24/25 1940. One source states the victim was a Heinkel He111 of III/KG55, while another has AC2 Jacobson as his AI operator that night. No Luftwaffe losses are recorded near the Humber and KG55 archives record only one loss that night, a Heinkel shot down off Hastings and credited to Flt Lt Sanders of 615 Squadron. Furthermore, for reasons explained below, the reference to AC2 Jacobson in this context cannot possibly be correct either.

In conclusion, then, these anomalies are highlighted here not as criticism but simply to demonstrate that the task of any researcher – all striving for that tantalising thing called 'accuracy' – faced with such a mass of information relating to this violent period, can be quite difficult.

August 19 saw Sgt Victor Skillen and Flt Sgt Wellesley Munn each taking up an aircraft for AI experience, while Bob Braham carried out that night's operational Blue Line patrol in a non-AI Blenheim. He reported considerable enemy activity with incendiaries dropping in the Grimsby area and even spotted two E/A as searchlights flicked over them, but they couldn't be intercepted as the searchlights were unable to track them due to cloud.

A similar chase to that of Plt Off Rhodes took place on August 20, when Flt Lt Jack Adams and air gunner Plt Off Lionel Watson were on a Digby Blue Line patrol. Airborne at 02.17 hours they were vectored to intercept a raid and at 03.10 hours Adams spotted a bandit flying south. Once again the enemy was careless because Flt Lt Adams could see a light in the rear gunner position and was able to follow its gleam. Even so it took him fifty minutes to gain on the bandit and then he was only able to do so because the target inexplicably circled when it reached the coast. So far had the Blenheim travelled that the 'coast' in this case was in fact near the Isle of Wight! No wonder that it was, by that time, out of R/T contact and right off Digby's plotting table. Adams fired a long burst at the target from the front guns but unfortunately it made a diving turn and was out of sight before it could be re-engaged.

Bob Braham opened his own score on the night of 24/25 August 1940. With Sgt Wilsden as air gunner the pair left Wellingore at 23.20 hours in non-AI L1463 to patrol the Digby Yellow Line. After a couple of hours Digby control vectored Braham towards the Humber and at 8,000 feet altitude in good visibility he saw what he thought was a Heinkel or Dornier caught in a searchlight beam. Despite the bomber twisting and turning to escape the glare, Braham came in behind it and fired four long bursts from the front guns at 500 down to 100 yards range while Wilsden got in two good bursts from his turret gun at close range. With smoke and sparks issuing from it, the enemy aircraft lost height. Braham and Wilsden didn't see the bomber crash but Humber searchlight units reported seeing an aircraft on fire, coming down in the sea immediately after the combat. While the squadron diarist confidently recorded that it: "…confirms that Plt Off Braham destroyed the enemy aircraft…", his combat report claim for a 'destroyed' was actually amended to a 'probable'. However, a Heinkel He111 of III/KG55 is believed to have crashed in the Humber that night and it may well have been the bomber claimed by Braham and Wilsden.

Reflecting the general feeling of frustration, Flt Lt Alex Campbell complained after another patrol on the 23/24th, that even with AI equipment, getting a contact was one thing (which was indeed being achieved) but holding it was very difficult owing to the Blenheim's lack of overtaking speed. As the squadron still retained a few Hurricane fighters on strength, Flt Lt Adams at least used the benefit of rank to organise the occasional freelance Hurricane sortie to relieve some of his frustration. On September 3, for example, he patrolled the Skegness area waiting for inbound raiders but although the Hun was out so was Adams' luck.

Tragedy struck the squadron on the evening of August 25. Pilot Officer Richard Rhodes, of whom we heard earlier, was ordered off on a dusk patrol along Digby's Blue Line that ran southwards to The Wash. Taking off at 21.00 hours in L1330, with Sgt Ronald Gouldstone as air gunner and AC2 Norman Jacobson as special equipment operator, Rhodes had reached The Wash and reported to his controller that he was investigating a "light in the sky". That was at 21.52 hours and was the last message received from the aircraft, which did not return to base. Later, reports from a searchlight unit suggested there might have been an air combat in the vicinity of Wainfleet. At dawn next day, Alex Campbell made a recce of The Wash out as far as the Inner Dowsing Light but could find no sign of the missing aircraft. Then the squadron's worst fears were confirmed when, on the 27th the skipper of HM Trawler *Alfredian* reported recovering the body of AC2 Jacobson from the sea near Inner Dowsing. Aircraftman Jacobson was buried at sea that same day and his wallet and papers were returned to the CO of 29 Squadron when the trawler docked. The body of Sgt Gouldstone was found on the beach at Gibraltar Point near Skegness on September 5, but of Pilot Officer Rhodes no trace was found. An assumption was made that the Blenheim had got the worst of an engagement with an enemy aircraft. Pilot and gunner were both nineteen, while Norman Jacobson at eighteen is believed to be the youngest airman to die in the Battle of Britain. He had only joined the squadron that morning.

In common with many of its contemporaries, for 29 Squadron September 1940 saw the beginning of a gradual change. The Luftwaffe night blitz on Britain began in earnest while, in equipment terms at least, RAF night fighter squadrons saw signs of an improvement. There were still regular detachments of aircraft to Ternhill and others to Wittering and still a frustrating lack of effective combats in the Blenheims but, on September 2, the first sign of what the future held arrived in the pugnacious shape of Bristol Beaufighter R2072, sent to the squadron for evaluation.

Designed to meet a perceived need for a long-range heavy fighter, the Beaufighter first flew in July 1939, but it was as a night fighter that it found the first of its many roles in RAF service. Early in 1940, before he took over control of Fighter Command, Air Vice-Marshal Sholto Douglas chaired what was known as the Night Interception Committee and had this to say about it.

Dowding made it clearly understood that he preferred the idea of a
powerful radar-equipped, twin-engine night fighter with a pilot and
navigator: the former concentrating on flying the aircraft and the
latter on controlling the interception through the use of his radar set
and he [Dowding] had pinned his faith on the new Beaufighter. The
idea of this special night fighter and crew had appealed to me from
the beginning.

September proved to be a busy month and Sqn Ldr Widdows drove himself
as hard as anyone. At 22.10 hours on September 17 he took off on a
freelance patrol in a Hurricane and immediately spotted incendiary bombs
dropping south of Cranwell. Looking around for signs of a bandit without
success he headed further south to investigate some searchlight
concentrations, but was warned to keep a sharp lookout for friendly aircraft.
Turning north again, suddenly he passed beneath an aircraft that had eluded
the searchlights. Quickly confirming with ground control that no friendlies
were in the vicinity he made a tight turn to attack but misjudging his
position, he again flew underneath his target, which confirmed its
credentials by firing at him as he passed. When he hauled the Hurricane
round for a third try the enemy had made good his escape and despite
further searching, Sqn Ldr Widdows could not re-establish contact, so he
returned to Digby.

Later that same night he went out on patrol again, this time in the
Beaufighter, but his luck was still out and no enemy aircraft were sighted.
Although several patrols were flown over The Wash area that night by 29
Squadron Blenheims detached to Wittering, they too had no success. For
example, Plt Off Roy Davies and air gunner Sgt Edwin Jones chased a
bandit for over half an hour by following vectors from control and
searchlight beams, but frustratingly, even though bomb explosions were
spotted from time to time, no E/A was sighted. The same thing happened
again to this pair on September 23, when there was much AA gunfire,
searchlight activity and bomb dropping but still no contact with the enemy.

There was still some daylight left when Charles Widdows and his air
gunner Plt Off Lionel Watson took Beaufighter R2072 up in the evening of
the 18th as one of the Ternhill detachment. They were ordered off at 20.50
to patrol Hoylake at 17,000 feet but despite seeing anti-aircraft fire in the
distance, no bomb bursts were observed. As darkness fell this situation
changed and although the Beaufighter crew could now see bombs dropping
on Liverpool, they were ordered to leave the area clear for AA guns. This
did not please Sqn Ldr Widdows at all and he remarked later that as there
was a little light left he felt sure he could have "done something if I was
allowed to go in."

The two Beaufighters evaluated by 29 Squadron appear to have been
popular aircraft with those who flew them. Although no formal speed test
was made, the Beaufighter appears easily able to hold on to a Hurricane and
it was considered not much more difficult to fly at night than a Blenheim –

in fact it was thought generally more pleasant to fly at night due to its superior manoeuvrability. Pilots commented that the short nose made approach and landing seem rather strange but the view, although better than a Blenheim, was still somewhat restricted by the thickness of the windscreen supports. Neither of the two Beaufighters initially issued to 29 Squadron were fitted with AI apparatus so the crews had no opportunity to test the performance of the latest AI Mk IV that was to be installed for squadron service.

Sqn Ldr Widdows got in one more night patrol with R2072 on the 19th before it was flown to St Athan next day to be fitted with AI Mk IV equipment. Imagine the disappointment (and no doubt the strong comments) when news reached 29 Squadron that not only would 'their' R2072 not be returned after the mod but it was being issued to rival 600 Squadron at Redhill.

Throughout those September nights there was plenty of 'trade', but with their appetite whetted for the new Beaufighter, 29's crews had no choice but to soldier on with Blenheims, whose AI Mk III sets were like the curate's egg – only good in parts. Flt Sgt Wellesley Munn and his operator Sgt Jack Ashworth patrolled Skegness on the night of September 10/11 in good visibility conditions, but though Digby control vectored them onto the track of three 'bogeys' (term for target unconfirmed as enemy aircraft and could be friendly), nothing was picked up on the AI set.

Four Blenheims were again detached to RAF Wittering on September 12 and it seemed as if Wittering returned the favour next day by releasing Beaufighter Mk I, R2077, to Digby. It had been under evaluation by 23 Squadron at Wittering but the squadron was in the process of relocating to RAF Ford in Sussex. After just three days with 29 Squadron it is recorded as being flown out to RAF Ford, presumably back to 23. That squadron however, having changed from a night fighter to an intruder role, did not re-equip with Beaufighters but instead, retained its Blenheim Mk 1F until March 1941 then re-equipped with the Douglas Havoc.

No wonder the squadron diarist wrote wistfully, "It is to be hoped the Beaufighters will be received in the near future."

Detached to Wittering, Plt Off Donald Anderson with air gunner Plt Off Percy Byng-Hall almost pulled off an interception at 02.15 on September 20, while they were on a VHF air test. They set off in hot pursuit only to be recalled when it turned out to be a friendly. One of the Ternhill detachment crews, Plt Off Jack Buchanan with gunner Sgt Victor Wingfield and AI operator AC2 Arthur Jackson were ordered to patrol Hoylake at 10,000 feet in 9/10ths cloud cover. Take-off was at 19.15 but they, too, had no joy and when the R/T failed an hour later they beetled off back to Ternhill. Other Ternhill patrols had a similar outcome.

Next night Plt Off Anderson with Plt Off Byng-Hall and Sgt Donald Isherwood were airborne again from Wittering at 00.40 hours on the 21st. Bomb explosions were seen but after only thirty minutes in the air the R/T transmitter packed up and the Blenheim was recalled.

In the evening of the same day Sgt Skillen with air gunner Sgt Isherwood, on detachment to Ternhill, were ordered off at 19.05 hours to patrol Merseyside in a non-AI Blenheim. Although they, too, saw many incendiaries dropping on the city they reported that the patrol "was uneventful". This was something of an understatement since, at the end of the allotted patrol time, not only was their Blenheim fired on by friendly AA guns but when landing back at Ternhill the aeroplane struck a floodlight and was rendered unserviceable with a damaged wing. Next night one of the Wittering aircraft, flown by Sgt Sydney Stokoe with Sgt Albert Wilsden, was ordered to patrol Skegness at 15,000 feet altitude to await possible 'trade'. They were directed towards a 'hostile' raid and although searchlights had been ordered to light up the raid they were unable to illuminate the bandit.

Probably the closest anyone got to a real interception occurred when an AI Blenheim, flown by Sgt Fraser with air gunner Sgt Thomas Menage and AI operator AC2 Harold Gilyeat, was ordered up to investigate a raid at 00.40 hours on September 23. Searchlights surpassed themselves and two enemy aircraft were seen. Sadly both bandits were flying in the opposite direction to and above the Blenheim, and by the time Sgt Fraser had turned to intercept both E/A were out of sight and never seen again. On top of this the AI set had become u/s, so they were recalled, landing back at Wittering at 03.00.

Patrol reports all told the same miserable tale. Blenheims without AI couldn't spot the enemy and those interceptions with AI – assuming the set actually worked – often turned out to be friendlies. Furthermore there were R/T failures; they were fired on by so-called friendly AA guns; had crash-landings; poor searchlight cooperation or – even when it was good – the Blenheims were simply not agile enough to catch up with their targets.

Searchlight (non-?) cooperation and aircraft recognition issues can best be illustrated by two patrols flown by Flt Sgt Wellesley Munn and Sgt Victor Skillen on September 25. First up was the experienced, pre-war trained Flt Sgt Munn, with air gunner Sgt Geoffrey Everitt. They took off at 19.20 and when west of Digby were given a vector and told to follow any searchlight activity. Munn observed bombs exploding and incendiaries dropping in a line parallel to his track and a couple of miles to the north. Although searchlights were active to the south of the bombs he decided to head for the bombing area itself, but as he did so his Blenheim was coned by yet more searchlights. Flt Sgt Munn frantically switched on the downward recognition light and fired a Very cartridge for the colour of the day and much to his relief, that batch of searchlights released him. He was not out of the woods yet, though. In spite of leaving on the downward light, Munn's Blenheim was coned again and he had to fire another recognition cartridge and take evasive action. By now his altitude was down to just 1,100 feet when he was lit up for a third time and because he thought he had run out of Very cartridges, he beat a hasty retreat from the searchlight's glare. When he found he had one more cartridge left, commendably but perhaps rather unwisely, he returned to search for the enemy and was yet again picked up by searchlights so, firing his final cartridge, he called it a day and returned to base.

At 20.10 that same night Sgt Skillen and his AI operator Sgt Donald Isherwood were ordered off from Wellingore to patrol RAF Bircham Newton. Twice their Blenheim was illuminated by searchlights and twice released when Skillen fired the colours of the day. Then they saw bombs dropping to the south and west of The Wash and Isherwood even picked up two contacts on his AI set, both of which were chased without success due entirely to the slowness of the Blenheim. They returned to base, landing at 22.20 after a fruitless patrol.

Detachments were still the order of the day, but these were put on a more formal basis at the end of September when the whole of A Flight – about one hundred men all told – was packed off to Wittering. It was to remain there for one month, at which time it would return to Wellingore and be replaced by B Flight. While checking the squadron ORB for operations during September, Bob Braham's name was noticeably absent and this seemed curious until the following entry dated September 27 provided the reason: "Plt Off Steele and Plt Off Braham discharged from RAF Hospital Rauceby (Sleaford) where they had been since September 6, as a result of injuries sustained in a car accident. They went on sick leave."

It must have been quite a 'prang' to keep them hospitalised for three weeks and it is to be wondered how close it came to curtailing a very promising career.

Blenheims were still being detached to support air cover around both Birmingham and Liverpool and patrols were flown over the Point Of Aire on most nights during October. One Blenheim crew, returning to Wittering from an evening patrol over Birmingham on October 11, was advised of a bandit in their vicinity. Although the weather was cloudy it was bright moonlight above the cloud but despite a search, no contact was made.

While it was usual for a crew to be ordered off on a specific patrol line, subsequent events might dictate a change of plan and a crew could find itself wandering far and wide. At 20.50 on October 12 one of 29 Squadron's Blenheims was sent off to patrol 10,000 feet over Spalding but on reaching his line the pilot was ordered to fly south-west to intercept hostile raids in the Midlands. He saw considerable AA gunfire and the explosion of many bombs and incendiaries in the Coventry area, but the complete absence of searchlights made interceptions impossible. At one time control informed this pilot that he was surrounded by no less than twelve enemy aircraft – and yet still he saw nothing.

On a more positive note, 19.05 the next night saw Sgts Arthur Roberts and Ronald Mallett on a searchlight cooperation sortie when they observed bombs dropping in the Grantham area. Roberts spotted an enemy aircraft at 13,000 feet altitude and followed it down to 3,000 feet where he opened fire with his front guns at 500 yards range. The enemy returned fire but it was wide of the mark and Roberts continued to shoot at the bandit's starboard engine using nearly all 2,400 rounds in the ventral gun-pack. That engine seemed to stop just as the enemy aircraft disappeared into a cloud layer so Sgt Roberts could only claim a damaged.

Although there was plenty of trade and quite a large number of RAF fighters in the air looking for it, in the dark and in all kinds of weather there was always the possibility of mistaken identity. This was mainly due to too many aircraft milling around in a relatively small area under limited ground control and with few navigational aids. Earlier on the 13th the two Blenheims detached to Ternhill took off to patrol the Point Of Aire when they fell victim to another case of mistaken identity. Plt Off Jack Humphries flew L7135 with air gunner Sgt Douglas Parr and AI operator AC1 Joseph Fizel. L6637 was crewed by Sgt Robert Stevens, Sgt Oliver Sly and AC2 Arthur Jackson. At 18.20, when ten miles north-west of Liverpool, L7135 was attacked from above by a Hurricane of 312 Squadron. Humphries' aircraft was hit but not seriously, none of his crew was injured and he managed to make it back to Ternhill. He fired off two Very lights and shouted a warning on the radio to Sgt Stevens but it was too late. The Hurricane had shot L6637 into the sea with the loss of all on board. Arthur Jackson's body was recovered later but the other two were not found.

November 13 would be remembered for a couple of other events of significance too. It was the day, for example, that Flt Lt Guy Penrose Gibson (later of Dambusters fame) arrived at Digby to take up a flight commander post with 29 Squadron. That same day Beaufighter R2140 was delivered to the station from RAF Shawbury, followed next day by R2141 from RAF St Athan. Things were looking up indeed! By the end of November Sqn Ldr Widdows had reorganised the squadron into A Flight with Beaufighters, four pilots and the squadron leader himself, and B Flight with Blenheims and nine pilots. At the same time six other pilots were undergoing conversion training for the Beaufighter.

Sadly this reorganisation did not come soon enough for the squadron to have any beneficial impact on the biggest air raid on Coventry on the night of November 14/15. To a large extent the ineffectiveness of the RAF that night is a graphic endorsement of tactics adopted by the Luftwaffe bomber force, together with the inherent difficulty experienced by defenders looking for the proverbial needle in a haystack. Air historian Alfred Price points out that, guided by pathfinder target-marking aircraft using the new X-Geraet precision radio beam navigation system, the Luftwaffe bomber force "would cross the British coast singly, moving on parallel tracks confined to a narrow belt some fifteen miles in breadth." He describes these tactics as:

> ... 'crocodiles' that were quite different from the 'stream' tactics employed by the RAF later in the war. German crews made no attempt to concentrate in time and space. Instead they flew in at

intervals of about four minutes, with an average spacing between the bombers of twelve miles. This made it very difficult for the 'cat's-eye' fighters to intercept, for there was only one raider per 180 square miles. Taking into account the altitude dispersion of the bombers between 10,000 feet and 20,000 feet, there was an average of one aircraft per 345 cubic miles of airspace!

It was evident that moonlight could be a two-edged sword also. As duty officer that night in the main Air Ministry Y-Service listening station, Aileen Clayton recalled:

There was a brilliant moon and the evening had been crisp and clear with excellent visibility. Over 500 aircraft took part in the raid but only one bomber was destroyed over England that night. So clear was the sky that single searchlight beams were ineffective; the raiders had no difficulty in spotting any approaching night fighter and were easily able to take evasive action.

Of three 'crocodiles' despatched against Coventry, one came in over The Wash, and Digby and Wittering sectors were desperate to get to grips with the enemy. Numerous patrols were flown by 29 Squadron all through the night of the 14th and morning of the 15th, with the last aircraft landing back at Digby at 06.10 hours. Most crews observed bombs bursting in and around Coventry and fires breaking out, but they had precious little to show for their efforts.

Flt Lt Alex Campbell sighted one aircraft near Warwick but could not determine what it was before it disappeared. Only Fg Off Lionel Kells and air gunner Sgt Robert Lilley, who were detailed to patrol Leicester in a Blenheim, engaged the enemy just before midnight.

With take-off at 22.33, after an hour Kells spotted a light in front of him in the vicinity of Grantham and taking this to be from an aircraft cockpit, he gave chase. It took him until he reached Swaffham in Norfolk to get close enough to his target to open fire. At 500 yards range he gave it a three-second burst from the front guns. Another three-second burst caused the enemy aircraft to swerve downwards and to the left. His third burst of fire missed the target entirely, the light he had been following disappeared or was turned off and Kells lost sight of the enemy. Both airmen were sure the enemy aircraft had been hit by the first two bursts, but as there was no subsequent report of any crashed enemy aircraft to support the claim, a 'damaged' was the best they could hope for.

Later the same day, Flt Lt Charles Winn and Fg Off Braham went to St Athan to collect Beaufighter R2144 and this was followed next day by R2150. Beaufighter R2095 was also a recent delivery and very nearly 'did for' Sqn Ldr Widdows on October 17.

On a late evening searchlight cooperation sortie the squadron commander took off with Plt Off Len Wilson in the back seat but shortly before midnight the Digby controller diverted him onto a bandit. Of the enemy nothing was seen but Widdows soon had his hands full when the port engine of the Beaufighter failed and the aircraft fell into a steep dive. When the starboard engine also lost power he realised that the Beaufighter was out of control and ordered Wilson to bale out. Widdows was about to jump himself when he saw Wilson trapped inside the stricken aircraft – later found to be because he could not open his escape hatch. With the aircraft in a spin – or at best, in a spiral dive – and with complete disregard for his own life, Sqn Ldr Widdows climbed back into the cockpit. With extreme skill he managed to get the fighter out of its dive and pull off a belly-landing at Walks Farm near Sleaford. It was fortunate the aircraft did not catch fire and except for superficial cuts, Widdows emerged unhurt to release Wilson, who was in some pain from a broken ankle. Extricating Wilson, he carried him to a safe distance until help arrived to take him to Rauceby hospital. The Beaufighter was severely damaged and in coming to earth had ripped up fencing and killed five sheep but undoubtedly the magnificent action of Sqn Ldr Widdows had saved Wilson from certain death.

Widdows was not alone in having a prang. On the 16th Sgt Thomas French landed Blenheim L1508 downwind at Wellingore and ended up in a hedge, damaging the aircraft, but he and his gunner emerged unscathed. A couple of days after that, Sgt Sydney Stokoe and his gunner Sgt Willins, too, were lucky to escape without injury when Blenheim L1507 caught fire on landing.

The cannon armament in the new Beaufighters was not without teething problems either and the perils of dealing with these are described as follows. Both crew members entered the aircraft via a ladder attached to a hatch that opened downwards from the belly and led up to a compartment in the fuselage centre section. Here a pair of armoured doors separated the pilot's cockpit from the rest and the AI operator occupied a swivel seat under a bubble canopy about halfway down the fuselage. He faced rearwards to work the AI apparatus, enabling him to turn his seat and move forwards to attend the guns when required. In the centre section a catwalk allowed the crew to move into position and accessible in a well below this floor were the breech mechanisms of the four 20mm cannon; two on either side. A sixty-round drum of ammunition was loaded into position on each gun before take-off. Replacement drums – each weighing an unwieldy 60lbs – were secured on racks in the compartment and it was the AI operator's job to change the drums during a combat or attempt to clear jams. Quite a challenge!

Patrols were launched whenever a raid threatened but for the remainder of that year there was little to show for the effort. Bob Braham chased a couple of enemy aircraft – one south of Grantham and the other south-east of Leicester – in one of the new Beaufighters on the night of 20 November but was unable to catch either, while during the evening of December 10 Guy Gibson chased a 'blip' that Sgt Ken Taylor picked up on his AI set, until it turned out to be a friendly. Gibson and Taylor went up again at dawn next day in R2150 after departing raiders. They chased one Ju88 that was going like a bat out of hell over the Lincolnshire coast near Mablethorpe and eventually managed to get within 800 yards range about sixty miles out over the North Sea. Gibson fired two short bursts at the fleeing Junkers but without any visible effect before it was lost to view in cloud. Although he sent in an intelligence report of the incident, the Squadron ORB recorded that, as he did not claim to have inflicted any damage on the enemy, Gibson did not submit a combat report. Guy Gibson made several more sorties during the remainder of December but without bringing the enemy to battle.

The weather turned sour during January 1941 and although it started to improve towards the end of the month there was little enemy activity on 29 Squadron's patch. On January 3 three of its Beaufighters, with Sqn Ldr Widdows leading from the front as usual, with Bob Braham and Flt Sgt Munn, were detached to RAF Middle Wallop to reinforce that sector.

At the end of January the squadron started to operate from Digby airfield itself rather than Wellingore as the latter was quite wet and although still flyable, it was pretty small to operate Beaufighters in those conditions. It was around this date, too, that Fighter Command changed the command structure of night fighter squadrons and 12 Group – into which 29 Squadron fell – promulgated new ranks. As a result of this Charles Widdows was promoted wing commander and one flight commander would step up to squadron leader in due course.

February was equally non-productive for Gibson and the other pilots. They put in plenty of sorties but it was rare to come even within sniffing distance of a bandit. On February 4 he and his RO Sgt Richard James followed up an AI contact near Mablethorpe and found an enemy aircraft dropping flares, but though Gibson fired a burst at a dimly lit target, when the flares died he lost sight of it and James lost the AI contact. A second chase also ended inconclusively after Gibson had fired another burst at his target. He would no doubt have had some strong words for the armourers on his return as it was found that only one of his four cannon functioned properly during the sortie. One of the other guns fired at only half the normal rate while the remaining two wouldn't fire because their cocking levers were left down. It seems there were a spate of these problems for next day Plt Off Victor Lovell could only use one cannon on a dawn patrol over a convoy off Skegness. He engaged a Dornier Do17 out after the convoy but it got away. Three of the four cannon stopped firing after a couple of rounds, each with a damaged round in the feed mechanism. It was Flt Lt E Parker's turn to suffer next when he returned from an inconclusive engagement with a Ju88 on February 12 to find both inner cannon had been left on 'safe'.

Sunshine returned in March but inevitably brought with it mists in the early mornings and evenings which made take-offs and landings tricky. Fg Off Braham and his RO Sgt Ross were also having no success, losing two contacts, for example, off Grimsby on March 1. Of three patrols launched on March 3, only Sgt Robert Lilley, Plt Off Lovell's RO, managed to get a contact. Lilley held it for six minutes before the bandit out-manoeuvred the Beaufighter and he lost the contact. After all that, because conditions had deteriorated at Digby, Lovell had to divert to RAF Kirton in Lindsey.

Then there came signs that things were beginning to liven up.

First, at midday on March 7 the Luftwaffe laid a stick of four 250kg bombs across Digby's green sward, fortunately without causing casualties. Then, in mid-afternoon, Flt Lt Parker, patrolling from Skegness to Mablethorpe, got a squirt at a Ju88 about four miles off Donna Nook. He was still firing as both aircraft went into cloud and could not see if his gunfire was having any effect. Emerging from the cloud base, Parker saw what he thought was the result of bombs having burst on the surface of the sea but the bandit seemed to have got away – probably after dumping his bombs. Changeable weather – including everything from sun through low grey cloud and rain to snow showers – slowed down activity on both sides. One posting of note at this time involved the highly experienced Wellesley Munn. Newly commissioned as Pilot Officer Munn he was transferred away to 54 OTU, a night fighter operational training unit, having served with 29 Squadron with distinction for no less than six years.

Patience was needed on the night of March 12/13 as success eluded the squadron again. It was a clear night for a change and the Luftwaffe came in strength, with over 300 bombers going for Liverpool. 29 Squadron put up eleven patrols in the Lincolnshire area that night and among these, Charles Widdows' RO held two AI 'blips' for about two minutes each but the WingCo could get no visual on the targets. Fg Off Jack Humphries had a similar outcome on his patrol, while Guy Gibson and Dick James chased a contact near RAF Sutton Bridge also without success, possibly due to a faulty AI set. Last crew up in the early hours of the 13th, Sgts Alan Roberts and air gunner Victor Wingfield, had R/T failure and had to land at RAF Leeming. To cap it all Orby GCI station had been 'non-op' that night so although conditions were ideal for GCI procedure, the vital initial component for an effective interception was sadly missing.

But success finally came next night, March 13/14, when the bombers returned to Liverpool and this time, Hull. Orby GCI was back on line and in top form and 29 Squadron got a slice of the action with two enemy aircraft shot down from nine patrols.

With Sgt Ross at the radar set of R2148, a new cannon-only Beaufighter, Bob Braham was first to claim a Dornier Do17Z, one of the raiders bound for Hull. Two hours into their patrol at 12,000 feet over Skegness and The Wash, Orby GCI put Braham onto the course of a bandit and Sgt Ross very soon picked up a blip. With Ross quietly issuing small course corrections then telling his pilot when to throttle back, Braham peered ahead and saw a Dornier 500 yards in front and slightly to starboard, heading north. Closing smoothly to 250 yards range Braham opened fire. As he did so there was a short burst of answering fire from the Dornier's ventral gunner, but this stopped under the onslaught of a hail of cannon shells lasting eight or nine seconds. There was the flash of a small explosion on the fuselage side but the bomber steadied and turned south. Keeping his quarry in sight and having expended all 240 rounds in the four magazine drums, Braham told Sgt Ross to leave his AI set – which had been switched off anyway when visual contact was made – and reload the cannon. Braham fired again at 200 yards range with just one gun in action but with no discernable effect. Ross reseated the drums again. Braham pressed the firing button – nothing! Ross tried again. Braham pressed again – still nothing! For the third time Ross sweated in the confined space above the guns trying to clear the weapons and this time Braham, from just sixty yards out, fired a three-second burst. No doubt about the result this time. The Dornier exploded in front of him, sending large chunks of metal flying in all directions and the blazing aircraft fell into the sea. U5+DA, of Stab/KG2 crashed about six miles off Wells-next-the-sea at 22.00 hours with its crew, Oblt H von Keiser, Lt B Meyer, and Fws Genahr and Rucker all killed.

It took just 32 cannon rounds for Charles Widdows to despatch R4+GM, a Junkers Ju88C-4 that crashed at 03.30 hours on March 14 at Smith's Farm, Tathwell, near Louth. This was actually a Ju88, wk nr 0604, from NJG2 modified as an intruder – no doubt looking for enemy targets just as Widdows was. But it was Widdows and his RO Sgt Derek Ryall who gained the upper hand, due in the main to the advantage that the GCI/AI combination gave the defending fighter. Wg Cdr Widdows began his patrol by providing protective cover over RAF Waddington but after working his way south chasing and losing several AI contacts he finally got on the tail of this Ju88. Firing from one hundred yards range he thought his first burst must have killed the pilot outright for it to crash so rapidly. The rear fuselage of the all-black intruder displayed substantial evidence of the effectiveness of a one-second burst from the Beaufighter's 20mm cannon punch and its three crewmen, Gefrs Hans Körner and Karl-Heinz Spangenberg and Uffz Willi Gesshardt, were found dead in the wreckage.

Next evening it was Guy Gibson's turn, and it was not without its own share of drama. The Luftwaffe targeted Glasgow and Sheffield and flying Beaufighter IF, R2250, he caught up with an incoming bandit tracking north off the mouth of The Wash. Leutnant G Stugg of I/KG1 was in Heinkel He111H-3, V4+HK, wk nr 5683, heading for Glasgow. Orby GCI put Gibson onto the course of the Heinkel, Sgt Richard James got the AI contact and his precise instructions brought the target into Gibson's vision at 400 yards range and slightly above. Closing gently to one hundred yards range, Gibson opened fire but his burst was cut short by an ammunition jam. In his book *Enemy Coast Ahead*, Gibson describes the incident thus:

When the centre spot of the ring sight was right in the middle of the Heinkel I pressed the button… instead of a blinding flash there was nothing. The Heinkel flew on and I throttled back to avoid over-shooting; in doing so flames and sparks spat from my exhausts and I swore, anxiously hoping that he wouldn't dive away. The next time I got into position, I pressed the button again. This time only one cannon fired and again nothing happened. There was no return fire, so I reckoned my first burst must have killed the rear gunner. The third time we got into position, no cannons fired. I began imploring Sgt James to get one going so that I could finish him off. But it was ten minutes before he was able to do so. The Hun, meanwhile, had turned out to sea and began diving for home. At last Sgt James got one cannon going and we aimed at the port engine. As shell after shell banged home there was a yellow flash. Sparks flew out and the engine stopped. Then we aimed at the port engine and this stopped within a few seconds. Someone baled out and we followed it right down and watched it land in the sea off Skegness pier. When I first saw him I screamed over the R/T full of excitement. When he was gliding down completely helpless I felt almost sorry for him.

The crew of the Heinkel, Uffzs L Auer, H Pauer and H Seidel, all died.

The question of the drum-fed cannon had plagued many of the foregoing interceptions but the problems were found to be human as well as mechanically induced, as a memo from SHQ Digby to HQ Fighter Command makes clear. It reports the findings of an investigation into the cannon stoppages recently experienced by Guy Gibson.

The reason for the stoppages of the guns is due to the following contributory causes:
(1) A foreign body jammed between the trigger release mechanism and the lever of the port outer gun. This foreign body was a brass union from the oxygen apparatus probably carried in the breast pocket of the overalls of a mechanic, which had probably fallen out unobserved and been vibrated into the lowest position of the gun nacelle.
(2) Both starboard guns (particularly the starboard outer) excessively lubricated with unsuitable lubricant.
(3) Firing button giving intermittent contact.

The morning of March 15 dawned sunny and warm and after the whole squadron had been 'available' and had flown operations on three consecutive what he called 'blitz nights', Wg Cdr Widdows considered his crews needed rest and sleep so he directed that "all pilots should sleep as long as possible." Fortunately the weather became foggy during the next three nights and ops were scrubbed anyway. This inactivity and fog appears not to have been much to Guy Gibson's liking, though. When fog descended for the fourth evening Gibson, having decided the weather was quite good enough for him to fly a night patrol, had to be ordered not to take off by the station commander himself. In fact the weather remained poor with little operational activity in the sector during the rest of the month.

But NJG2 showed it was still operating and could hit hard, too.

On the night of March 17/18 Lt Pfeiffer of NJG2 caught Wellington R1474 of 149 Squadron on its final approach returning to base at RAF Mildenhall at the end of a sortie to Bremen, and shot it down. The RAF bomber crashed near Beck Row with the loss of all on board.

Fw Hans Hahn is believed to have been responsible for shooting down Wellington Ic, R1470 of 115 Squadron at Terrington St Clements, near King's Lynn at 00.30 hours on April 4. This Marham-based aircraft was part of a large force of bombers despatched to attack the *Scharnhorst* and *Gneisenau* warships in Brest harbour. Of the six crew, five died: Sgt C M Thompson, pilot; Sgt H Y Chard, co-pilot; Plt Off S S Barnett, nav; Sgt J S C Sherman wireless op; Sgt E Keetley, front gunner. Although badly injured, rear gunner Sgt Russell survived the crash. Next night Fw Hahn was also thought to have shot down a Hampden, P2092 from 14 OTU at Cottesmore, to crash on the main railway line at Little Bytham near Bourne, Lincs. Sgt Holborrow's crew had just finished a practice bombing exercise on Grimsthorpe Park range when the Hampden was hit by gunfire. It caught fire over the village of Holywell before crash-landing on the railway line. Home Guard soldiers succeeded in stopping trains and dousing the fire but Sgt Holborrow and two of his crew died.

Returning from a raid on Mannheim on the night of April 29/30, Wellington T2721 of 99 Squadron, based at RAF Waterbeach, was shot down into The Wash with the loss of all six crew. At about 03.00 hours Sgt F Hewitson, pilot, radioed that he was under attack by a night fighter. The Wellington was not seen or heard from again after that 'mayday' call and is believed to have fallen victim to NJG2's Ofw Sommer. Others in the crew were Sgt N O Bennett, co-pilot; Sgt W P James, wireless op; Sgt E C Stevens, nav; Sgts S J Holt and R R Thomas, air gunners. Quite by chance research among some wartime Lincolnshire Police records turned up a curious item that could be linked to this last incident.

On the evening of June 22 1941 a pilot of the inland waterways reported he had discovered the wreck of an aircraft in The Wash at the mouth of the Welland river at map ref F8657. Believed to be a Wellington, the wreck is deeply embedded in sand and is submerged except for twenty minutes at low tide. Two metal component plates were removed from the wreck:
1. Wellington serial FL/VACH/1515 model numbers P50 P161 P168 P226 P27- P298 P32-.
2. Folland A/c Ltd Hamble serial FL/VACH/1515. Date 20/1/40. Drg No 40816/Sht 5 issue F. Insp FL18 AIDG 09.

This wartime map reference places the wreckage on Black Buoy Sand about two miles out from the sea bank at Holbeach St Mark's, and with the wreckage embedded in the sand it suggests it may have been there for some time.

Flt Lt Gibson's own flying career was almost brought to an equally abrupt end. He was on finals to land at Digby after a patrol in the Manchester area during the evening of April 8 when a German intruder got on his tail. At fifty feet over the boundary hedge, navigation lights on, flaps and wheels down, he was a sitting duck. The intruder pilot fired, but luckily the majority of his rounds missed the target. Most damage was done to Gibson's RO, Sgt Bell, who was shot in one leg. Gibson got the Beaufighter down on the ground but it careered across the airfield, probably because the brakes had been hit, too, and crashed into trees. Both airmen escaped without further injury. It is believed crews from NJG2 made several claims for damaging RAF aircraft around that time but it is unclear which Luftwaffe pilot very nearly cut short the career of one of the RAF's most charismatic pilots.

Intruders were at large again on April 16/17 when Gibson got a whiff of the action in the small hours of the 17th. He chased a target south of Digby for about fifteen minutes but could not catch it. His final flourish in this region came on April 23/24 during a large raid.

Having gained and lost something like ten 'blips', at about 01.00 Sgt Dick James was finally able to bring Gibson into visual range of a Dornier 215 near Boston. Closing to 150 yards Gibson fired but was greeted with accurate return fire. He broke away then lined up for another attack and this time his burst of fire hit the enemy aircraft fuselage. But the rear gunner was still on the ball and his fire was too close for comfort so Gibson broke away again. This time he could not regain contact and returned to Digby at the end of his last sortie from that station. Guy Gibson was destined to stay with the squadron for several more months before returning to bomber operations.

The change from Blenheims to Beaufighters marked a key point in the fortunes of 29 Squadron during its time in the Digby sector. At the end of April 1941, the squadron moved south to RAF West Malling in Kent where it continued to operate in the night fighter role, reinforcing air defences on the southern approach to London, and as we shall see later, it fell to 25 Squadron to enter this arena to help carry on the fight.

CHAPTER 5

Airborne Searchlights

In earlier chapters reference has been made to the Turbinlite Havoc in its night fighter role, and operations involving this aeroplane began in early 1941 and continued until the end of 1942. Because it is an intriguing subject and as there is also a particular human-interest story relating to the region under discussion, it is proposed to deal with this topic in more depth in this chapter.

In October 1940, eighteen-year-old Jack Cheney began the transition from sixth-form schoolboy at Spalding Grammar to night fighter pilot in the RAF and in 1941 his first operational posting brought him to RAF Wittering. He spent a substantial part of his operational career in the night sky above The Wash region and had first-hand experience of the Turbinlite era. Flying Officer Cheney kept a diary that survived after his untimely death in air combat in June 1943 and this chapter describes his experiences while training to become a night fighter pilot, and then his involvement with one of the more unusual aircraft to be created in the quest for supremacy of the wartime night sky. This is his story.

After three glorious weeks of leave at home in Spalding, looking up old friends, putting my feet up and sampling home cooking with my mother and three sisters, I was summoned to 54 Operational Training Unit at RAF Church Fenton in Yorkshire. This was to be the last part of my training as a night fighter pilot and I arrived at the station on August 3 1941.

I was not immediately impressed by what I saw of the base but later that day, I met up with 'Tosh' Bramley, Jimmy Smith, Arthur Howard and 'Hammy' Hamilton, all of whom had been with me on 22 Course at 7 Service Flying Training School, Kidlington (Oxford airport). Life, it seemed, would not be quite so bad after all.

Church Fenton was considered to be the crack night fighter OTU in the country but we soon discovered it had also earned a reputation as a killer station.

Now designated as 11 Course, we were obliged to do some day flying in Airspeed Oxfords just to get our hand in again. However, before being permitted to fly at Church Fenton at night we first had to go to RAF Catterick and do a few hours at night in Tiger Moths. We were at Catterick for only a week and flew from a satellite landing ground called Forest Farm. What a week that was! It was really great fun being back in the old Tiger again. All too soon though it was back to the serious business at Church Fenton, where night flying dual was carried out in the Oxford, augmented by day solo flights in the ropey old Bristol Blenheim.

September saw the arrival of our observers. For this seemingly important event, the actual teaming up process was, in fact, pretty informal. We were all assembled in a large room and told to get on with it. A fair-haired fellow, calling himself Sgt Mycock, made the first approach to me. He was about my own age and we seemed to hit it off from the word go and from that day he became and still is, my observer. His name is James Kenneth Mycock but from that first day I met him I called him Mike and so it remained.

A tragic blow came on September 2, when my pal Arthur Howard and his observer were killed in an Oxford. They were out on an R/T homing and map reading exercise one morning when their aeroplane, V3150, went out of control in cloud. The story went the rounds that the recovery from a spin may have been a bit too violent and the machine dived in when the ailerons and elevators broke away.

Blokes were killing themselves right, left and centre in those ropey Blenheims, which we had now begun to fly at night. As far as the prospect of night flying is concerned, there is really nothing to say, except that ground control was good but the Blenheims were bad and the accidents frequent.

At the end of September 1941, the aircrew sergeants of my course moved out of the Church Fenton mess, to be rehoused in an old country house known as Barkston Towers about three miles from the aerodrome. It was a marvellous old place, with ornate gardens and a splendid interior. George, our cook, had been in the submarine service in the last war and vowed he would never go near an aeroplane. He was good to us though and served up colossal meals and we lived like kings to the end of the course.

Together now with our observers, we put in a tremendous amount of both day and night flying in an effort to become an efficient team and yet again the end of the course was rushed. It was not the hard work I minded, it was more of a desire to get away from the OTU in general and the CFI, Sqn Ldr Aikens in particular. The CO at that time was Group Captain Richard Atcherley, who with his twin brother David, also a flyer, had earned quite a reputation as an airman and was an all-round good type. The chief ground instructor was Sqn Ldr R de W K Winlaw who, with a variety of colleagues, went over the now familiar range of subjects slanted this time towards our operational requirements.

One week before the course was due to finish, on October 17, another blow fell on my small circle of friends, Sgt T C 'Tosh' Bramley was killed during an altitude test at night in Blenheim IV, V5622. His observer, Wood, had been off flying for a few days so, luckily for him, he was not on board when the aeroplane crashed a mile south of Everingham village in Yorkshire. 'Tosh' was the fourteenth casualty in three months.

The course duly finished and on the day I left I found out I was due to fly a Beaufighter for the first time. However, we were rushed out of the OTU in such a hurry that I did not get the chance but from what I heard about their handling qualities, I can't say I was particularly sorry to miss the opportunity.

Those of us left in my group of pals said our farewells again and on October 28 1941, almost one year to the day after I joined up, parted company to go to our respective operational stations. Church Fenton at least had lived up to its grim reputation while I was there. Now I was off to Wittering, not far from my home town of Spalding, for my first operational posting to 1453 Air Target Illumination Flight.

We will digress at this point to take a closer look at the Turbinlite concept. The emergence of the Turbinlite aeroplane has its roots in the air situation following the Battle of Britain. Due to the not unreasonable previous concentration on single-seat high-performance day fighters, when the Luftwaffe turned to its night offensive there was no suitable specialist RAF night fighter or control system to take them on. As we have seen earlier, those few AI-equipped Blenheims that did exist had little success but like all such ideas, that was more a reflection of the very newness of this particular man/machine system, together with inadequate aircraft, rather than an indication of the true potential of the AI-night fighter concept itself. Lack of results seems to have diverted attention away from acceptance that the subject had simply been neglected and that it needed a focused and swift injection of resources. Critics of the system – and there is always competition for resources or competing ideas – were the catalyst for some of these alternative ideas gaining a lot more prominence than their true practicality really warranted. Among the latter was the idea to mount a searchlight in the nose of an aeroplane. The RAF had acquired some Douglas Boston aircraft originally destined for the French and this was the most suitable aircraft to hand.

Now, to the modern eye at least, any basic description of the Turbinlite Havoc concept cannot fail but engender some incredulity about its practicality. It was based around the American-designed Douglas Boston twin-engine light bomber, designated by the RAF as Havoc I, with its nose compartment sawn off and replaced by an enormously powerful searchlight.

The idea was the brainchild of Wing Commander W Helmore and the light, named Turbinlite, was built by the General Electric Company (GEC) in England and powered by forty-eight 12-volt batteries that weighed a total of about 2,000lb. These were stowed away on reinforced flooring in the bomb-bay, the batteries themselves being laid out in four banks of twelve with two banks placed in each of the two halves of the bomb-bay. They were charged up from an external ground-based source with special attention given to providing forced ventilation inside the aeroplane to avoid the build up of hydrogen fumes during the charging process. A description of the Turbinlite by another former pilot, Michael Allen DFC**, will convey the sheer power of this airborne searchlight:

> Its batteries were capable of producing a current of 1,400 amps and discharging totally in two minutes. The lamp – reputed to be the most powerful in the world at that time – produced a beam from mechanically adjusted carbon rods located in front of a para-elliptical mirror reflector with a small frontal area approximating to the size of that cross-section of the forward fuselage. The light thus produced had an illumination intensity of over 800,000 watts [try to imagine 8,000 x 100 watt domestic light bulbs] and blazed out as a horizontal, sausage-shaped, beam of light that illuminated an area 950 yards wide at one mile range. It was not, however, simply a case of detecting a target then throwing a light-switch! The carbon rods took some seconds to bring the arc-light to full power during which time, in order to avoid a situation where the beam was not at full strength but nevertheless provided an enemy with a juicy light to fire at, the light source and reflector were hidden behind shutter doors on the inner surface of the lamp glass. Only when maximum luminosity was achieved (code name: Boiling!) did the pilot open the shutters, expose the beam and (hopefully) pinpoint the target like a blinded moth.

Equipped with an AI Mk IV set, with arrowhead transmitter antennae protruding either side of the lamp glass, the aeroplane carried a crew of two. The pilot sat in a single seat front cockpit and a radar operator occupied the glazed rear compartment originally intended for a gunner. But, in this AI configuration the Boston carried no armament, because with the weight of the batteries, light and radar there was no spare capacity for guns and ammunition. Despite this peculiar arrangement and – as will be seen – the lack of combat success, it nevertheless provided night fighter crews with many months of valuable – if boring – night flying and radar interception practice. This was to stand them in good stead when the Luftwaffe stepped up its activity over Britain and also when RAF night fighters carried the fight to continental and other skies.

One of an eventual ten such units in Fighter Command's 11 and 12 Groups, 1453 Air Target Illumination Flight, to give it its full title, was formed at RAF Wittering in July 1941 from elements of 1451 Flight which itself was based at RAF Hunsdon. CO of the new flight was Sqn Ldr Kenneth Blair DFC – already mentioned in Chapter 3 – who had seen active service both in France with 85 Squadron and in the Battle of Britain and was transferred from 151 Squadron based at Wittering at the time.

These Havocs cooperated with one or more single-engine fighters, usually Hurricanes, but on occasion Defiants or even Spitfires are recorded as taking on the role of satellite fighter. Take-off would be carried out in close company, with the Hurricane keeping formation to the rear of the Havoc by reference to a few tiny, variable-intensity lights playing over broad white paint stripes on the upper and lower rear surface of the wings.

Of course, to formate in this manner at night would have been no mean feat in itself but how was this unwieldy group going to bring the enemy into combat? Well, the scenario goes like this. Ground control would vector the Havoc onto a bandit to a point where the AI operator could take over and use airborne radar to try to pick up the target. If a target was found the AI operator guided his pilot towards visual range. The pilot might of course be fortunate to get a visual contact first but the whole idea was to bring the Havoc within searchlight range – without needing to rely on a visual sighting – and that was when the Turbinlite would be switched on. The pilot of the formating satellite fighter was supposed to spot the enemy in the beam, move in on it and shoot it down. There were many imponderables that could affect the success of this sequence of events – not least that it was highly unlikely that an enemy aircraft so illuminated would stay mesmerised in the beam sufficiently long enough for the satellite fighter to catch it! Or, that either of the two RAF pilots would not have their night vision ruined by the sudden intense light. So far, successful interceptions had been a quite rare event.

It was in July 1941 that 151 Squadron began cooperating with the Turbinlite Havoc unit at Wittering. As a first step several of its aircraft and pilots were sent to RAF Hunsdon to learn the ropes from one of the first Havoc units formed. When they returned to Wittering almost all flying in August, September and much of October was then devoted to training with 1453 Flight.

As the flight was more or less up to personnel strength, training started in earnest with the Hurricane and Defiant boys from 151 Squadron. It was recorded in 151 Squadron's Operational Record Book that "on October 22, Pilot Officers Stevens in Hurricane Z3261 and McRitchie in Defiant AA431 carried out a pukka Turbinlite patrol for the first time."

It also records, "Plt Off Stevens broke away and independently destroyed an enemy aircraft." On deeper investigation this latter statement turns out to be an over-simplification of an event which provides yet another example of the hunting spirit of the legendary Plt Off Richard Stevens. The wording also implies the incident took place in the vicinity of RAF Wittering and of the other aircraft on the exercise but that, too, is not the case. This is what actually happened.

Flying a cannon-armed Hurricane IIc, one of four of that model now on strength, Richard Stevens indeed took off from Wittering, at 20.30 hours, on a Turbinlite exercise but early into the flight he claimed to have lost contact with the formation during a tight turn.

There was no moon but it was a clear, starry, night, so rather than land back at base he looked about him and saw a lot of AA fire to the north-west. He was at that time to the west of Wittering so he headed off in the direction of the AA fire in the hope of finding a target. At about 21.30, lo and behold his eagle eyes spotted an aircraft 250 yards away, flying slightly above him at 10,000 feet. He was not certain but thought it to be a Heinkel He111. Closing in to 150 yards he was left in no doubt when gunfire came towards him from the dorsal and ventral positions, so he opened fire with several bursts, scoring hits on the fuselage as he followed the bomber down until it dived into the ground and exploded. Stevens had actually begun his interception twenty miles south-west of Wrexham – almost a hundred miles from Wittering.

His fuel state was now critical and he was forced to land at RAF Wrexham at 22.35 hours where it was found the Hurricane had just ten gallons of fuel left in its tanks. He refuelled and landed back at Wittering at 01.30. It was later confirmed that a Junkers Ju88, 7T+CH of I/Kustenfliegergruppe 606, part of a raid on Liverpool, had been shot down at Adderley near Market Drayton but despite all his efforts, Stevens was obliged to share the kill with a 256 Squadron Defiant crew – on whose patch this was – who made a claim for the same time and place. But it was a better outcome than being tied to a Havoc! This was Richard Stevens' last known kill.

His meteoric rise as a 'cat's eye' night fighter pilot began on January 15/16 1941 and ended with his death, just eleven months later on December 15/16 when, having been posted to 253 Squadron, he was shot down over Holland on his first intruder sortie.

Jack Cheney continues:

The weather deteriorated into December but practice interceptions continued whenever there was a break. In spite of the cold, our dispersal was very comfortable during the bad spells and we sat around line-shooting whenever there was little else to do.

However, the calm was quickly shattered when, on December 18, Sgt James Sudders, who had been with us at Church Fenton and posted in during October, spun in and crashed his Havoc at Stowgate railway crossing, between Crowland and Market Deeping (Lincs). At this time radio observers outnumbered pilots so it was quite usual for a pilot to have two observers attached to him. On this occasion, Sudders had both Sgt Eric Welch, his regular RO, and Sgt William Fradley, a spare RO, in the back of BD120 and they were all killed in the accident.

Later on in December there were a few sorties in company with Hurricanes of 151 Squadron to try out a new wheeze. The Havocs were to fly around at 5,000 feet dropping flares on possible targets as an alternative method of illuminating the enemy. Bit of a shambles all round! Since the flares were loaded in the bomb bay, the Havocs used for these sorties were the battery-less non-Turbinlite aircraft that the squadron had on charge for crew training purposes.

As we had not yet been declared fully operational, the whole flight was allowed Christmas leave, which suited me down to the ground being so near to home. While I was away some members of the flight, being less fortunate, wangled a trip to the GEC factory in Coventry.

There was precious little flying for us in January 1942 and we were still 'non-op'. The bad weather made our other activities scarce but we did have several ice hockey matches on the frozen Whitewater lake at the edge of the airfield. There was also bags of snow-clearing to be done and it was both back-breaking and heart-breaking as, every time an area was cleared, it snowed up very soon after.

The CO was dead keen on playing soldiers so, when flying was scrubbed, we used up many Very cartridges and thunderflashes on these ground exercises. I ruined a perfectly good pair of flying gauntlets putting up his damn barbed wire fences.

In February the snow abated a little and although it was still cold enough to keep skating, we were able to get some flying in too. My pride took a bit of a blow when I taxied a Havoc into one of the dispersal bay walls. The brakes failed and the starboard engine cowling was a trifle bent but there was no serious damage and I got away with it.

The station dance, held on February 17 in Stamford Grammar School, was a good opportunity to give Flt Lt George Turner, one of 1453's original pilots, a good send-off. He was being posted to RAF West Malling and a replacement crew arrived from 51 OTU Cranfield even before he had left.

A milestone was also reached before the end of that month when the flight was, at long last, declared operational. Night readiness routine was started, with bags of panic, Mae Wests and things. Despite all this readiness routine though there was not much trade and the only excitement occurred during the night-flying tests (NFT), when one could indulge in a spot of low-level work over the wide-open space of the Fens. I was warned off doing this after word got back to the CO about my regular aerial visits to my home in Spalding, which also happened to be just across the road from my old school. My mother – and of course the boys of the school – got an enormous kick from the sight of my big black Havoc thundering down the school road just above rooftop height. But it had obviously upset someone else!

On March 18, Plt Off Ole Bechgaard, a Swedish pilot, pranged Havoc BJ467, which happened to be Sgt Joe Gunnill's usual mount. Any Bechgaard landing was a sight to behold at the best of times and all the ground crews usually turned out to watch when he came in. This particular landing was a beauty. He came in too fast after an NFT and was forced to brake very hard. This put such a strain on the nose wheel gear that it collapsed and the aeroplane slid merrily along the runway with its tail cocked up in the air. I pitied poor old Andy Cunningham, his observer, in the back seat!

Shortly before the end of March the flight was re-equipped with Douglas Boston III aircraft to replace the lower powered Havoc Is. These new mounts were handled gingerly at first, in view of the extra power, but when we got used to them they were found to be aces up on the old Havocs.

Two new crews arrived from Cranfield on April 7 but sadly only one week later one of these was lost in an accident. Plt Off Jacques Henri Horrell (English father, French mother) and Sgt Samuel Capewell were on an NFT with Plt Off Frank Darycott BSc, the flight's special signals (radar) expert, also on board. An enquiry into the crash suggested that Horrell became aware that two unidentified Spitfires were diving on him from astern. It was surmised that he took violent evasive action and fell into a spin from which he could not recover, the aeroplane crashing at Aldwincle St Peter in Northamptonshire.

Now that the weather was getting better, our thoughts turned to outdoor pursuits to relieve the waiting. Someone had the bright idea that we should take up sailing on the lake near dispersal, so a sailing dinghy was purchased from the aircrew fund. The first trips were made, a bit too daringly, and in the strong April winds quite a few duckings followed, including Mike who tried to go solo too soon.

Flying livened up a bit in May when mine was one of three crews detached for readiness duty at RAF Swanton Morley, Norfolk. Each day the detachment took off at dusk for Swanton and returned to Wittering at dawn the next morning. 151 Squadron had by now exchanged its Hurricanes for Mosquitoes so the flight was now cooperating with 486 (New Zealand) Squadron instead. Another change of scene occurred in the middle of this month, too, when I underwent a blind approach course with 1529 BAT Flight at Collyweston, Wittering's second satellite. It was a pleasant change to fly a single-engine aeroplane again, this time the Miles Master II.

Upon my return to the fold I continued to do readiness at Swanton but there was precious little doing. Plt Off Gallagher got a scramble one night and chased an unidentified target until it was discovered to be a friendly aircraft. That was the only chase during the month but it did at least relieve the monotony of the continual waiting.

Late in the month my pride and joy, Boston Z2184, went u/s with a radio fault. It had only flown once with the flight and was practically brand new. It was, however, repaired by the 30th, just in time to take Sgt Dave Glen to RAF Church Fenton to start his leave. I found that the station had changed considerably since my time there. The OTU had disappeared and night fighter operations had taken its place with the return of 25 Squadron from RAF Ballyhalbert in Northern Ireland.

Detached aircrews continued to go regularly to Swanton Morley well into June but there were no more scrambles. There was plenty of activity, though, on the night of the thousand bomber raid on Germany at the end of May. Both Swanton and Wittering were littered with bombers coming back in one piece or in several pieces.

On the subject of pieces, our illustrious CO came a real cropper on June 3 when he was taking off at dusk to cooperate with me. He had borrowed a 616 Squadron Spitfire Vb, AE246, and the starboard tyre burst during the take-off run. With 100mph on the clock he just managed to get airborne as he touched the perimeter of the main runway. He decided to hold the machine down on the other part of Wittering's two-mile strip so he cut the throttle and prayed. First the starboard leg was torn off, followed in turn by the port leg, the starboard wing, then the port wing. The propeller and half the engine was next to part company and the whole of the tail structure broke away completely. What remained of the fuselage, including the cockpit, finally came to rest intact on its side.

The wonder of it was that Sqn Ldr Blair was able to step out and walk away from the wreckage practically unscathed. He was conveyed to the sick bay by no less a person than Group Captain Basil Embry [the station commander] and after recovering he was despatched for a week's sick leave.

I had an opportunity to revisit another old haunt when I was detailed to fly over to Kidlington to put the Boston through its paces for the residents. The old FTS had gone, its place taken by some glider schools. I was the envy of those glider tug pilots in my nippy Boston.

At the end of the month our flying from Swanton Morley was washed out. July got off to a good start, though, as the flight was one year old and it was decided to have a party to celebrate. All the aircrews and many of the technical NCOs were invited to Pilsgate, the CO's house near Stamford, where copious quantities of strawberries and cream were consumed and the beer flowed freely. When the CO persuaded us to leave, the party departed in two cars (eighteen in the Humber!) to continue the merry-making at the White Hart in nearby Ufford, before finally retiring somewhat worse for wear for a nightcap in the mess.

Standing patrols began at Wittering during this month but although these were flown regularly, no trade came our way. 486

Squadron converted to Typhoons but still kept a few Hurricanes to cooperate with us.

On July 26 1942 the flight upped sticks to go on detachment to RAF Hibaldstow, eight miles south of Scunthorpe, to reinforce 1459 Flight and maintain standing patrols cooperating with the Hurricanes of 253 (Hyderabad) Squadron. This was all very well but still no trade came our way.

Aircrew were billeted at RAF Kirton in Lindsey and we had the bind of travelling daily to and from Hibaldstow to do our flying. The dispersal at Hibaldstow was definitely ropey compared to the comfort of Wittering and the food was lousy, too. But, you can get used to anything eventually and after a few days this was no exception.

Kirton in Lindsey mess was full of Polish Spitfire pilots from 303 Squadron led by Sqn Ldr Jan Zumbach. They were a grand bunch of chaps, full of beans and they would listen to our woeful tales of fruitless chases then shoot us a line about their recent slice of real action near the airfield and we'd all have a good laugh. I was very envious of their cannon-armed Spits, though.

The incident to which Jack refers concerns the shooting down of two Junkers Ju88s by the Poles between Horncastle and Spilsby at 20.30 hours on July 2 – an incident that is believed to have contributed to 1453 Flight's rapid detachment to Hibaldstow. Research in the National Archives turned up what is undoubtedly a gripping story about this particular incident but all the signs are that it was more of a one-off, 'gung-ho' enterprise than a portent of renewed bomber activity in the sector. The following edited account of the raid is based on a contemporary RAF AI 1(k) report containing information distilled from interviews of Luftwaffe prisoners of war. The report, like others of its ilk, contains a proviso that: "the statements have not as yet been verified", but its version of this raid and its outcome nevertheless makes fascinating reading.

The two Ju88s shot down in Lincolnshire were bombers from the 2nd Staffel of Kustenfliegergruppe 106 (2/106) based at Dinard/Pleurtuit airfield in Brittany, France and they were the only aircraft involved in a daring low-level raid aimed at the de Havilland aircraft factory near Horwich in Lancashire. The operation itself was alleged to have been the outcome of conversations in the Luftwaffe officers' mess during the previous week, about the feasibility of bombing targets in England, at low level, by day – and getting away with it. Hans Bergemann, the staffelkapitän of 2/106 was adamant that such attacks were possible. New Luftwaffe intelligence information just in, detailing the importance of the Horwich factory, provided an ideal opportunity to put his theory to the test and he managed to convince his gruppenkommandeur that his bold plan for an attack on the de Havilland factory should go ahead. The staffel's two most experienced crews were selected for the operation – naturally Bergemann's was one – and the whole of the next week was spent practicing low-level attacks. Bombing height would be sixty feet and the flight was to be executed at wave- and tree-top height all the way in and out. An essential part of Bergemann's plan required the nature of the operation to be kept absolutely secret, so it was not until the morning of the actual raid that the target was disclosed to the crews. Both aircraft were to carry four 250kg HE bombs, with eight-second delay fuses, on the wing racks, with a mixed load of 50kg HE and 1kg incendiaries in the fuselage bomb bay. This heavy weight meant both aircraft would first fly unloaded to an airfield at Lanveoc-Poulmic, near Brest, where they would be fuelled and bombed up, after which each Ju88 would get airborne for the sortie using rocket-assisted take-off.

Weather on the day was predicted as low cloud cover all the way to the target and the gruppenkommandeur watched as the two bombers left Dinard at 13.30. Any misgivings he might have harboured about the wisdom of the whole operation must have got the better of him though because soon after the aircraft had landed at Lanveoc, he telephoned Bergemann and expressly ordered him to abort the flight. The staffelkapitän, however, was raring to go – it was even alleged that he savoured the prospect of the medal that would be certain to come his way if the raid was a success. So, at 16.00 hours the two Ju88s took off on the mission.

Their route to the target was in four legs: Lanveoc to Land's End then to St David's Head (Wales), on to a point south of the Isle of Man and finally the run in to Horwich, but it is the exit phase that seems the hairiest part of the plan. Carrying the large weight of bombs loaded – vital to make such an attack worthwhile – even with full tanks, the Ju88's fuel would not allow the aircraft to return to Brittany via the Irish Sea route. The exit route chosen from Horwich therefore was to fly straight to The Wash then out over the North Sea to land at Amsterdam/Schipol in Holland and this was the very reason they came to be flying over Lincolnshire. Further doubts existed about the fuel lasting all the way to Holland so the contingency plan was, if necessary, to conserve fuel by flying the exit leg on one engine.

Maintaining radio silence and skimming the wave tops to avoid radar, the flight up the Irish Sea went according to plan. The dot-zone of a radial beam from the German navigational radio beacon called 'Elektra 2' was intercepted just south of the Isle of Man. First the dots and then the continuous-tone zone was crossed, with the pilots making a right turn onto the final leg as soon as they heard the dash-zone signals. Landfall should have been the Ribble estuary. Six minutes at zero feet to Rivington reservoir then turn south along the reservoir to the factory. But this is where things started to go wrong.

Cloud cover was even lower than expected and the bombers' landfall was too far south of their intended track. In the lead aircraft, unable to spot the reservoir and with only a few minutes fuel reserve for a search, an argument seems to have taken place that only added to the confusion. Bombs were eventually released from both aircraft over what was thought to be a railway station and a gas works and a train was strafed, but British sources claimed the bombs caused little damage.

Both bombers managed to stay in close formation and – so far – no opposition had been encountered but now, identified as raid 301, the Royal Observer Corps monitored the Junkers' progress over land and passed a series of accurate plots to 12 Group. Sector control was advised that two Ju88s were flying at zero feet, forty miles west of Lincoln heading in an easterly direction. Sector controller, Sqn Ldr Mawdesley, immediately scrambled 303 Squadron (Spitfire Vb) from Kirton in Lindsey and handed over control of the Polish fighters to Flt Lt Ostaszewski. No misunderstandings were going to mar this interception!

Yellow section (Flt Sgt Wunsche, Yellow 1 and Flt Sgt Popek, Yellow 2) was airborne at 20.05, orbiting base until joined by White section (Plt Off Kolecki, White 1 and Sgt Rokitnicki, White 2) a few minutes later. The four pilots were instructed to maintain just sufficient height to keep in R/T contact and fly a course of 190°. The Spitfires were down at 500 feet when Flt Sgt Wunsche spotted the two bandits half a mile away, two miles east of Lincoln, flying close, fast and low. Calling out the contact he identified them as Ju88s and dived into the attack, opening fire with his two cannon and four machine guns from astern at 250 yards range, first at the leader, then the other aircraft. When he broke away, Flt Sgt Popek, ignoring return fire from the top gun position, closed to fifty yards range and fired at the second Ju88 – this was M2+BK, Fw Majer's aircraft, until with both engines on fire it hit a tree and crashed into some farm buildings. Wunsche and Popek now turned their attention to the leading bomber and fired their remaining ammunition at it. As they broke away, White section continued the attack with both pilots making firing passes from 300 yards down to fifty yards either side of astern until flames poured from the starboard engine. Desperately, Hptmn Bergemann tried to keep the bomber airborne on one engine but it was so low and so damaged that evasive action was impossible. When White section attacked again the fuselage was riddled, the electrical system shot to pieces and the other engine hit. There was no escape for M2+KK but Hptmn Bergemann managed to crash-land the badly damaged bomber in a field. Circling the crash, the Poles watched as four airmen clambered out of the aircraft and ran off just as a brilliant flash lit the sky and the bomber turned into a blazing wreck.

Cheney takes up the story again:

> Turbinlite standing patrols from Hibaldstow continued into August and things began to hot up a bit as most crews began to get their share of scrambles. Nobby Clarke got two head-on interceptions one night over Hull but was unable to turn quickly enough to follow them up. Jerry Clymer had the most atrocious bad luck. Almost invariably,

when he got the order to scramble his engines would refuse to start, or he would be recalled before he could get off the deck. Mike and I chased an unidentified aircraft and almost came within range, only to be told it was a friendly.

On August 24 Mike and I were sent off on yet another detachment, this time to RAF Coltishall with Havoc BJ467 and a ground crew of six. We stayed three days doing some ground control exercises for Fighter Command under the watchful eye of Flt Lt Derek Jackson, a university don and electronics boffin. There were endless snags between Coltishall and Wittering control and I was heartily fed up with the job by the time we left for home. No sooner had we arrived back at Kirton in Lindsey than I was told to report back to Coltishall on the 31st. Another binding few days!

The pace of life took another upward turn on September 3 1942, when 1453 Flight was re-formed as 532 Squadron. A number of Hurricanes were sent to us and pilots for them were drawn from 486 Squadron and from various OTUs. The idea now was for the squadron to become self-contained, in that it comprised A Flight with Havocs (Boston III) and B Flight with the Hurricanes. The other good news was that we were to return to Wittering on the 6th.

Back at Wittering, the first two days were spent rearranging and clearing up our old Whitewater dispersal. Training under the new structure started immediately but after only two days, would you believe it, it was all change again and off we went back to Hibaldstow. In order to become operational there, it was necessary to borrow three Hurricane pilots from 486 Squadron at Wittering, which was now fully fledged on Typhoons. Does anyone really know what they are doing in this war?

Once the move to Hibaldstow was complete we settled down to get the new Hurricane pilots operational, so that the 486 chaps could return to their squadron. Just before they left we had the only scramble of the month. At 21.30 on the 19th, Sgt Preston, one of the 486 boys and I took off to intercept a bogey. We were airborne for only forty minutes though before the hated recall came through. The Hun had gone further north and some of the squadrons in that direction took over the hunt. That was the nearest any of us got to the Hun in September. For the rest of the month we got stuck into our training programme in order to become fully operational, spending much of the time on instrument tests, since the artificial horizons in the Havocs were playing up at this time.

A change of command brought the month to a close. We bid a boozy farewell to John Willie Blair, posted out to 51 OTU Cranfield and an equally rousing celebration was held for his deputy Flt Lt C L W Stewart on his appointment as the new CO. Henceforth 'Stew' must be known as Squadron Leader Stewart or even Sir, which took a bit of getting used to. Needless to say this historic occasion was dealt with in style and lunch that day finished at 16.00 hours. At 17.00 that same afternoon I flew Sgt Joe Gunnill down to Wittering to attend the Beam Approach training school and I don't think I have flown a steadier course in my life!

With the coming of the moon period in mid October the weather turned duff and night flying was reduced to practically zero and it was not until the 24th that the weather decided to clear. Although the squadron was on readiness and could only put up one Boston at a time, Mike and I managed to jam in six and a half hours of night flying, the first for a fortnight. I crawled into bed at 08.00 next morning well satisfied after such a splendid session.

The weather clamped down yet again so odd jobs were the order of the day. The latest wheeze is for us to scrape off the matt black dope from the Havocs in order to get the new grey and green camouflage on in the specified time. Well, at least it's warm and useful work, though some of the aircraft began to resemble patchwork quilts.

In general terms, up to November 1940 aeroplanes used for night operations were usually painted in the standard RAF day paint scheme. When night fighter operations became common it was felt that black or a similar dark colour might be the most suitable for camouflage at night. As a result a black paint with an almost 'fuzzy' finish to it called 'Special Night' or 'RDM2' was applied first to under surfaces from September 1940 then overall by about mid November 1940. However, by the time the Blitz ended, Special Night was considered not to be the best colour for night fighters. This conclusion had already been reached in WW1! Flying experiments discovered it tended to turn a fighter into a dark silhouette and rather than it merging with the darkness it could, under certain conditions and at reducing ranges, actually make it more visible. Unfortunately no one seemed to have an alternative and it took many more experiments and almost another eighteen months before a replacement colour scheme was settled upon. It seemed that, contrary to expectations, disruptive patterns of grey seemed to render aeroplanes less visible under most conditions including the night sky. Thus in October 1942 it was promulgated that night fighters would be painted medium sea grey overall with a disruptive pattern of dark green on upper surfaces, hence the hard work referred to by Jack Cheney.

On my day off Joe Gunnill flew my beloved Z2184 on an NFT and over Goole the port fuel pump packed-up. By a clever bit of juggling with the interfeeds he managed to keep the port engine running and brought it back all in one piece.

Wonder of wonders, on October 31 the weather cleared up and patrols were on again. Three of the others were detailed for these while I was briefed to carry out a bomber affiliation sortie with a

Left: In the control gondola of German Naval Zeppelin L14; Hptmn Kuno Manger, second left. *(Aeronauticum, Deutches Museum fur Luftschiffahrt und Marinefliegerei, Nordholz)*

Middle left: The effects of aerial attack were brought home forcibly to the civilian population of King's Lynn when they saw the extent of the bomb damage on January 20 1915.

Middle centre: Kptlt Alois Böcker, commander of L14 on the air raids of September 8 1915 and January 31 1916. While commander of L33, he and his crew were captured when their Zeppelin was hit by AA gunfire over London and crash-landed at West Mersea, Essex on September 24 1916.

Middle right: Another German aerial Baron. Front: Horst Freiherr Treusch von Buttlar-Brandenfels, wearing the 'Pour le Merite' decoration at his neck, commander of L14 on the air raids of September 8 1915 and January 31 1916. Seen here with his first officer Hans von Schiller, both airmen had a long and distinguished airship career both during and after WW1. *(Philippe Saintes)*

Bottom: Kptlt Joachim Breithaupt, seated second left with officers and ratings of German Naval Zeppelin L15, which took part in the large raid of January 31/February 1 1916. *(Author's collection)*

Top left: Oblt-z-S Kurt Frankenberg, commander of Imperial German Naval Zeppelin L21. He died when L21 was shot down by Flt Lt E Cadbury and Flt Sub-Lt E Pulling on October 1/2 1916. *(Aeronauticum, Nordholz)*

Top right: Imperial German Naval Zeppelin L31, in which Kptlt Heinrich Mathy and his crew died on October 13/14 1916.

Middle left: Kptlt Heinrich Mathy, commander of German Naval Zeppelin L13 on the raid of September 8 1915. Mathy died in L31 when it was shot down by 2/Lt Tempest at Potters Bar on October 13/14 1916. *(Aeronauticum, Nordholz)*

Middle right: Kptlt Kurt Friemel at the window of the black-painted main control gondola of German Naval Zeppelin L52. *(Aeronauticum, Nordholz)*

Right: Flt Sub-Lt Edward Pulling (left) and Flt Lt Egbert Cadbury from RNAS Gt Yarmouth, who jointly destroyed L21 off the Norfolk coast on November 27/28 1916. *(via Putnam)*

Top: Kptlt Hans-Kurt Flemming, standing ninth from right, with the crew of German Naval Zeppelin L55. Note the two outside gunners wearing different headgear, sixth and tenth from right. L55 took part in the Silent Raid of October 19/20 1917. *(Aeronauticum, Nordholz)*

Middle left: Fregattenkapitän Peter Strasser, Director of the Imperial German Naval Airship Service. He died in L70 when it was shot down during the last airship raid on England on August 5/6 1918. *(Aeronauticum, Nordholz)*

Middle centre: Kptlt Franz Stabbert, commander of German Naval Zeppelin L44, which took part in the last airship raid on England on August 5/6 1918.

Middle right: Thick, warm clothing for machine gunners was absolutely essential when manning the extremely exposed gun positions on top of German airships.

Left: The exposed nature of defensive machine-gun positions on the top forward part of the outside of a Zeppelin. Access to the gun position is by ladder through the interior, emerging from the small hatch seen in the foreground.

Top left: Zeppelin chaser. A BE2c, B3707 from 3 Gunnery School at Frieston, Lincs, a satellite of RNAS Cranwell.
(J M Bruce/G S Leslie collection)

Top right: BE12, A6303, a single-seat conversion of BE2 used by the RFC for anti-Zeppelin night patrols.
(Author's collection)

Right: Planning the raid. Oblt Joachim von Arnim, second left; Oblt Ulrich Jordan, right; going over final details before the raid by KG4 on 18/19 June 1940. *(Goss/Rauchbach archive)*

Below left: Oblt Joachim von Arnim (third left) and his crew, Fw Karl Hauck (left), Fw Wilhelm Maier (second left) and Uffz Paul Gersch, in front of Heinkel He111, 5J+AM, before the sortie on 18/19 June 1940. *(After The Battle)*

Below right: Raymond Myles Duke-Woolley, who shot down He111 5J+DM on June 18/19 1940, as a Wg Cdr just back from his fourth sortie on the day of the Dieppe raid. *(Robin Duke-Woolley)*

Top left: Riddled by gunfire in the air battle of June 18/19 1940, Heinkel He111, 5J+DM, the bomber flown by Oblt Jordan with KG4 Gruppenkommandeur Maj von Massenbach on board, wallows like a stranded whale in The Hood shallows off Blakeney Creek. *(Peter Brooks collection)*

Top right: Flying a Hurricane, New Zealander Plt Off Irving Smith of 151 Squadron intercepted a Heinkel He111 over The Wash on October 2 1940. While commanding 151 he also shot down a Heinkel off the north Norfolk coast, in a Mosquito NFII on 24/25 June 1942. *(NZFPM)*

Middle: 23 Squadron, RAF Wittering, July 1940. Seated, from left: Ensor, Baker, Harding, Duke-Woolley, Sqn Ldr Bicknell, Sqn Ldr O'Brien, Knight, Anderson, Cooper-Key, Gawith. Standing, from left: Swan, Young, Sgt Bicknell, Willans, Atkinson, Grogan, Duff, Hoole, Orgias, Pushman, Gillespie, Burton, Penford, Dann, Rose. *(23 Squadron Association)*

Above left: An early production Bristol Beaufighter, believed to be R2059, a Mk IF of 25 Squadron. Delivered in September 1940 with AI equipment yet to be installed. *(Ernie Sutton)*

Left: Hurricane I, V7434, DZ-R of 151 Squadron, in which Plt Off Irving Smith shot down a Heinkel He111 at Chapel St Leonards on October 2 1940. His NZ Maori emblem can be seen painted above the fuselage roundel. *(P H T Green collection)*

Top left: A pre-war studio portrait of Richard Playne Stevens in the uniform of an airline pilot. *(Simon Parry)*

Top right: Dornier Do17, 5K+EA, from the unit KG3, one of whose aircraft was shot down by Plt Off R P Stevens of 151 Squadron on the night of January 15/16 1941. *(Luftwaffepics.com)*

Middle left: Ogefr Wilhelm Beetz, pilot of Ju88C-2, R4+BM of NJG2, who died when his intruder aircraft was shot down at French Drove, Gedney Hill on April 17 1941. *(Simon Parry)*

Middle right: Excited schoolboys! This is usually how the public got to see RAF successes. A Junkers 88C bomber, 4D+DR, of KG30 on display in Peterborough for War Weapons Week in December 1940. The 151 Squadron Defiant night fighter team of Edmiston and Beale shot down a bomber from KG30 on May 2/3 1941. *(Author's collection)*

Bottom: Given that 151 Squadron Defiant gunner Sgt Beale only fired thirty-two rounds at it accounts for this Ju88A-5, 4D+BH of KG30 showing little sign of battle damage after its forced landing off Weybourne beach on May 2/3 1941. *(Peter Brooks collection)*

Top left: Junkers Ju88A-5 of KG77 from which 3Z+CL crash-landed in Welney Wash on the night of May 4/5 1941. *(Heinz Nowarra)*

Top right: Originally mustered as an air gunner, Plt Off Dennis Britain re-trained as an AI operator and served with distinction in 25 Squadron. Flying with Plt Off David Thompson, Britain helped to bring down Dornier Do17Z-10 near Boston on May 7/8 1941. *(Dave Stubley)*

Middle left: Uffz Herbert Thomas, one of the crew of NJG2 Dornier Do17Z-10, R4+GK, shot down on May 7/8 1941 at Carrington, Lincs. *(Herbert Thomas via D Stubley)*

Middle right: Merlin-engine Beaufighter IIF, R2375, the type flown by Michael Herrick in his combat of June 22 1941. Clearly visible on the nose is the arrowhead transmitter aerial for its AI Mk IV radar. Azimuth receiver aerials are on the leading edge of both wings and those for elevation protrude above and below the starboard roundel. *(Cheney collection)*

Left: New Zealand night fighter pilot Flt Lt Michael Herrick DFC of 25 Squadron, who shot down Junkers Ju88, R4+JH at Deeping St James on June 22 1941. *(Simon Parry)*

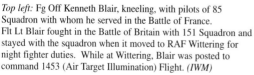

Top left: Fg Off Kenneth Blair, kneeling, with pilots of 85 Squadron with whom he served in the Battle of France. Flt Lt Blair fought in the Battle of Britain with 151 Squadron and stayed with the squadron when it moved to RAF Wittering for night fighter duties. While at Wittering, Blair was posted to command 1453 (Air Target Illumination) Flight. *(IWM)*

Top right: Oberfeldwebel Otto Wiese, pilot, of the night fighter unit NJG2, who died in combat with Michael Herrick on the night of June 21/22 1941. *(Wiese family via Robert Bates)*

Middle: 151 Squadron at the height of its success as a night fighter unit in mid-1941 at RAF Wittering. Front, from left to right: Staples, Nicholls, Atkinson, McRitchie, Stevens, Edmiston,

C L W Stewart, Turnbull, McMullen, Sqn Ldr Adams, Darling, Turner, I S Smith, Ellacombe, Bodien, Wagner, Davidson, Lynes, Copeland. Back, from left to right: Parkin, Maguire, Sidenberg, Elvin, Beale, Fairweather, George, Hart, Wain, Cartwright, Fielding, Wrampling, Broit, J G Stewart, Jonas, Lammin, Gudgeon. *(Ron Durant)*

Bottom left: Defiant N1791, DZ-K, of 151 Squadron, in 1941. *(Ron Durant)*

Bottom right: Junkers Ju88C-2 of NJG2 at Gilze-Rijen, seen here with a cannon and three machine guns fixed in the 'solid' night fighter nose section. *(Simon Parry)*

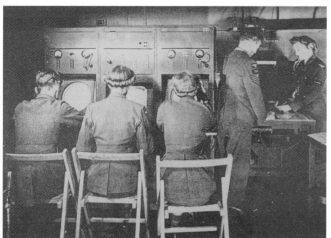

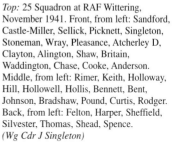

Top: 25 Squadron at RAF Wittering, November 1941. Front, from left: Sandford, Castle-Miller, Sellick, Picknett, Singleton, Stoneman, Wray, Pleasance, Atcherley D, Clayton, Alington, Shaw, Britain, Waddington, Chase, Cooke, Anderson. Middle, from left: Rimer, Keith, Holloway, Hill, Hollowell, Hollis, Bennett, Bent, Johnson, Bradshaw, Pound, Curtis, Rodger. Back, from left: Felton, Harper, Sheffield, Silvester, Thomas, Shead, Spence. *(Wg Cdr J Singleton)*

Middle left: A primitive mobile GCI interception room similar to that used at Langtoft in 1941. *(J Baxter)*

Middle right: Ready for battle. Sgt Jack Cheney shortly after he joined 1453 (Air Target Illumination) Flight at RAF Wittering in December 1941. *(Cheney collection)*

Above left: A Defiant with attitude! Shark's mouth Boulton Paul Defiant I, N3328, DZ-Z, of 151 Squadron based at RAF Wittering in 1941/42. *(P H T Green collection)*

Left: Despite being shrouded in covers protecting it from the harsh winter snow of 1941/42 the characteristic arrowhead AI Mk IV aerial can be seen on the starboard wing of this 151 Squadron Boulton Paul Defiant IA. The receiver aerial protrudes from the engine cowling cover.
(P H T Green collection)

Above: Air gunner Sgt Fred Barker (right) and his mascot, in the turret of a Defiant night fighter. Sgt Barker is wearing the special 'parasuit' parachute smock whose D-ring release cable can be seen passing under his left arm. Pilot Sgt Ronald Thorn (left) and his gunner are credited with thirteen day and night air victories with 264 Squadron. *(Alec Brew)*

Above right: 'Round the bend NCOs, Wittering April 1942'. NCO aircrew from 1453 (Air Target Illumination) Flight. Back: Harrison, Alfie West. Middle: Godfrey, Mycock, Cheney, Smith. Front: Gunnill, Compton, Thomas 'Jock' Grieve.

Right: Turbinlite Havoc Is of 1453 Flight flying in formation from Wittering to RAF Heston to be exchanged for the more powerful Boston IIIs. Spring 1942. *(Cheney collection)*

Bottom left: Bob Braham (right) and Bill 'Sticks' Gregory in front of a Mosquito. This distinguished and highly successful night fighter crew learned their trade patrolling The Wash area with 29 Squadron based at RAF Digby, Lincs. *(Wg Cdr Gregory via Key Publishing)*

Bottom right: A 'Kolynos' toothpaste smile from observer (radio) Sgt James Mycock, 1453 Flight, RAF Wittering, spring 1942. *(Cheney collection)*

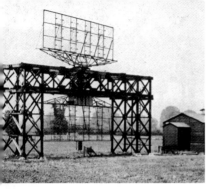

Top left: Initiating many successful interceptions around The Wash, one of the first operational GCI sites is this AMES type 8 intermediate transportable ground controlled interception (GCI) installation at Orby near Skegness. *(After The Battle)*

Top right: Flying searchlights. Douglas Boston III 'Turbinlite', Z2184 of 1453 Flight (later 532 Squadron), the personal mount of Fg Off Jack Cheney. *(Cheney collection)*

Middle left: The parabolic mirror and light ignition apparatus of a Helmore Turbinlite, mounted in the nose of a Douglas Boston III. *(Simon Parry)*

Middle right: Taking Satan for a ride. A Heinkel He111 with a large calibre bomb attached to the external portside rack. This may have been the object Wg Cdr Irving Smith reported as a torpedo during his interceptions on June 24/25 1942.

Bottom: Spitfire Vb RF-H of 303 (Polish) Squadron at Kirton in Lindsey airfield, Lincolnshire, involved in the destruction of two Junkers Ju88s near Spilsby on July 2/3 1942. *(Cheney collection)*

Top left: Flt Sgt Popek, 303 Squadron, one of the four Polish pilots who shot down two Ju88s near Spilsby on July 3 1942. *(Wilhelm Ratuszynski)*

Top right: Pilots of 303 (Polish) Squadron at RAF Kirton in Lindsey. Sgt Rockitnicki is second from left and Fg Off Kolecki is leaning on the elevator. Both were involved in the combat of July 3 1942. Sqn Ldr Zumbach is fourth from right. *(Wilhelm Ratuszynski)*

Middle left: Dornier Do217E-4, F8+CN, wk nr 4279 of II/KG40, clearly showing a 'two-tone' black night camouflage. This aeroplane was shot down at Fleet Fen, near Spalding, on July 23/24 1942. *(Bundesarchiv)*

Middle right: Flt Lt E L 'Peter' McMillan (right) with Wg Cdr Paul Davoud of 409 Squadron, admiring a prop blade from the Dornier McMillan intercepted over Fleet Fen on July 23/24 1942. *(Gp Capt E L McMillan via Bill Norman)*

Bottom: Beaufighter Mk VI with 'arrowhead' AI Mk IV radar antennae on nose and wing leading edges, as flown by Flt Lt McMillan of 409 Squadron on the night of July 23/24 1942. *(IWM)*

Top: All that remained of a Dornier Do217 after it was caught by a night fighter and crashed at Salthouse Heath on the north Norfolk coast on July 30/31 1942. *(Peter Brooks collection)*

Middle left: New Zealander Flt Lt Harvey Sweetman, 486 Squadron, left: Group Captain Basil Embry, RAF Wittering station commander, centre: Sqn Ldr Bob Roberts, OC 486, right, in front of a Hurricane II at RAF Wittering, July 1942. *(Paul Sortehaug)*

Middle right: Aircrew of A Flight 532 (Turbinlite) Squadron, on being re-numbered in September 1942. OC Sqn Ldr Stewart is seated fifth from right. Fg Off Jack Cheney is seated second left, with his radar operator, Flt Sgt James Mycock second left on back row. *(Cheney collection)*

Bottom left: Group Captain Basil Embry, station commander RAF Wittering 1942. *(Cheney collection)*

Bottom right: Sqn Ldr Stewart takes command of 532 Squadron while on detachment to RAF Hibaldstow in September 1942. *(Cheney collection)*

Top left: Heinkel He111 H5, werke nummer 3769, showing the effects of battle damage from .303 machine guns. *(Don Hannah)*

Top right: Dornier Do217E-4, U5+ZN of KG2, with crew relaxing in the summer sun at Gilze-Rijen airfield in 1942. *(Bundesarchiv)*

Middle left: 151 Squadron's South African night fighter ace Flt Lt Henry Bodien DFC in 1943. *(Mick Kelsey)*

Middle right: Mosquito NFII, DD750, clearly showing off all its AI antennae and factory-fresh in its early night fighter all-black paint scheme. DD750 flew operationally with 25 Squadron but was destroyed in a flying accident near Keighley, Yorks, on March 22 1943. *(Roy Bonser collection)*

Bottom: 25 Squadron with Mosquito NFII, RAF Church Fenton, June 16 1943.
Front, from left: Davies, Snell, Wg Cdr Maude (OC), Gp Capt Stannard (Stn Cdr), Flt Lt Joe Singleton, Cooke.
Middle, from left: WO Ben Bent, Gibbs, Cummings, Hogarth, Haigh, Cairns, Norris, Grey, Gallagher, Guthrie, ?, ?.
Back, from left: Franklin, Cooke, Underdown, Sewell, ?, ?, Skinner, ?, Wilson, Charman. *(Joe Singleton)*

Top left: Mosquito bite! The devastating power of the four .303 machine guns and four 30mm cannon of a Mosquito night fighter is being demonstrated in the butts.

Top right: The revolving aerial of a 'final' AMES Mk 7 GCI radar installation. The partly subterranean 'Happidrome' operations bunker in the background is believed to be that of RAF Langtoft. *(J Baxter)*

Above left: 'Helga' prepares for a raid. Heinkel He177A-3 of I/KG100 based at Châteaudun at the time of Operation Steinbock. This Luftwaffe four-engine heavy bomber, specifically designed for the long-range role, used coupled pairs of engines. It was the type shot down by a Mosquito of 307 Squadron off Skegness on March 19/20 1944. *(Luftwaffepics.com)*

Left: Flt Lt Joseph Singleton DFC, (centre) and his Nav/RO Fg Off Geoff Haslam, both with heads bandaged, in Coltishall officers' mess after a night patrol in which they destroyed three Junkers Ju88s in fifteen minutes on March 20 1944, fifty miles out from The Wash. *(via Wg Cdr J Singleton)*

Below: Dornier Do217E-4 with dappled camouflage pattern on upper surfaces and black on lower surfaces. Individual aircraft and staffel letters 'HN' are visible on the fin leading edge but unit codes have been painted out. *(Bundesarchiv)*

Top left: A Mosquito 'office'. Interior view of an NFII cockpit with pilot's control column on the left and the AI Mk VIII radar display unit in front of the navigator's seat on the right. *(via Wg Cdr J Singleton)*

Top right: Sqn Ldr A I (Alex) McRitchie (left) learned his trade as a night fighter pilot with 151 Squadron. Posted to 464 Squadron, he is seen here with navigator Flt Lt R W Sampson before taking part in the famous Mosquito raid on Amiens prison. *(Hawker Siddeley Aviation/BAe)*

Middle left: A V-1 flying bomb attached to the port wing root of a Heinkel He111 for air-launching trials.

Middle right: Heinkel He111H-22, 5K+GA of Stab/KG3 with a V1 attached for air launching. In operational service, V-1 flying bombs were carried on a release shackle attached to the reinforced main spar at the starboard wing root. *(via Heinz Nowarra)*

Bottom: The ill-conceived Turbinlite Mosquito, W4087, test flown at RAF Wittering on February 5 1943. *(Simon Parry)*

Lancaster from 44 Squadron at Waddington. Everything had been previously arranged with the Lancaster crew who were word perfect, so I cracked-off at 19.05 to rendezvous with them. By that time there was quite a haze over the aerodrome and the lights were very dim, even in the circuit.

To start with, the Lanc took off before it should have done but luckily I caught a glimpse of its lights as it left the ground. There then followed the most gruelling time I have had for many a long time as far as night flying goes. The Lanc proceeded to do turns, with about 40° of bank on, around the aerodrome at low speed. I must say the Boston stood up to it very well even though I must have been very close to stalling many times. Unfortunately I was unable to get to the exact range to carry out my orders and after an hour of trying I gave up in disgust and went home. I found out later that, although I was burning all my lights, not one of the bomber crew ever saw me even though I was in visual range all the time. That seems to auger well for our night fighters – but not so good for the bomber boys!

Fighter Command declared all our aircraft unserviceable at the beginning of November, pending a new modification – whatever that means. What with the weather being u/s as well as the aircraft we are doing an awful lot of Link trainer time these days. On the 4th visibility rose to all of two yards so how appropriate it was that we were assembled for a lecture on new blind flying techniques. By midday visibility had risen to about ten yards but it is so cold here now that Jimmy Green had to put his feet into my hot bath to get them warm!

Life at the dispersal gets very boring with no aeroplanes to fly, even if the weather is so duff. Fortunately I managed to wangle some leave again and while I was away things livened up again with a few incidents. One afternoon the whole of A Flight – with the sole exception of Sgt Gunnill – and most of B Flight took off on NFTs. While they were airborne, the weather clamped in and our aircraft were scattered to the four corners of 12 Group. Some got down at Church Fenton, some at Coleby Grange and a few at Wittering and they just had to stay put overnight. Poor old Joe Gunnill was left holding the fort at Hibaldstow with just one aircraft and the AOC was tearing his hair out.

On the 7th Sgt Carter wrote off Hurricane BE581 when he crash-landed on a Q-site a mile west of Mablethorpe. It burst into flames and he was damned lucky to get out alive and only with cuts and bruises. The very next day one of our sister 538 Squadron Havocs taxied very prettily into Church Fenton's telephone exchange. I have never seen a taxying accident look so much like the result of spiralling in from 20,000 feet in my life. Both mainplanes had at least 50° of dihedral and the rest of the machine is a complete write-off. Sgt Lowndes, the unfortunate pilot, was injured in the prang, which was attributed to the windscreen completely misting up and poor lighting on the peri-track.

I managed to get airborne for the first time this month for an NFT on the 13th but it was only for ten minutes before the inevitable bad weather closed in. Hibaldstow is a helluva place for lousy weather! It was another week before I put in more night hours and even then I had to turn back early with a spot of engine trouble. I managed to squeeze in another sortie at 04.00 and it was wizard to have that peace and quiet of the last patrol of the night.

Except for the odd NFT, flying was washed out for the rest of the month and the monotony was only relieved by the bind of the group captain's inspection of dispersals and being invited to attend a colossal binge at Wittering's annual dance. On December 1 the squadron's official photographs were taken and the rain just managed to hold off until they were completed. The weather is marginally better now, allowing all NFTs to be got in and a session of night flying until about midnight but it is exceedingly cold up there now and there is not much sign of the Hun.

As December wore on it was back to foul weather again and I had to wait until the 10th before getting airborne again. At long last the Hun decided to liven things up a bit and twelve enemy aircraft came over on a minelaying sortie. Just our luck that they were too far north for us to cooperate successfully against them. We heard later that the Czech boys of 68 Squadron at Coltishall caught one Dornier Do217 on its way home, so that relieved the tedium, as these were the first Huns to venture our way for ages. It was the 20th before the enemy sent another foray but 532 was not on readiness that night so 538 scrambled a couple of aircraft with bags of flap all round but no result.

For once no one moaned when the weather went delightfully non-op for four whole days from Christmas Eve. From teatime on the 24th until the early hours of the 28th everyone, almost without exception, was gloriously tight. There were dances in the various messes and the WAAFs were on top line all the time. What a smashing party and it lasted four whole days! There were many sore heads and lively stomachs when flying resumed on the 29th, although the first snow of the winter soon put paid to that. It was my 21st birthday on the 31st and I went home on a week's pass.

January 1943 and back at Hibaldstow we passed the time snow clearing mostly but I did manage to put in some night flying on the 9th. Between then and the 18th little flying of any sort took place and the only event of note was that my promotion to flying officer came through.

Well, it looks like the writing is on the wall for the squadron because 12 Group declared us non-operational on January 18 and big changes are rumoured. A hint of what was in the wind came when the CO went over to Wittering to test the new Mosquito night fighter.

One of my last flying duties on the squadron was a little test-flying job. Fg Off Johnny Limbert and I were detailed to go by train to Loughborough to test fly two Boston Havocs that had been assembled by the General Airwork Trading company. We duly reported to a Mr Davies, an AID inspector who briefed us for the tests. The runway on which we had to take off and land was situated behind the repair shops and was, to our amazement, just 700 yards long! Now, in our experience, we normally operated the Boston Havoc with 1,200 yards for its take-off run and not only was the runway on offer very short but also the landing approach was between an electricity pylon and a darned great chimney as well.

Johnny tested his aircraft during the afternoon and for want of something to do, I went up with him in the back seat. The undercart took a lot of persuading to come down and we lost a flame trap but otherwise Johnny managed to get it up and down without mishap. Next day, January 25, it was blowing half a gale across the runway but we were both anxious to get back to Hibaldstow to hear the fate of the squadron, so it was decided to take a chance and complete the wretched testing. Johnny went up this time with Mr Davies in the back and I took up Mr Woodward, another AID official. What with that crosswind, the rain, the electricity pylon and positively the shortest runway I have ever landed on, we did jolly well to get down at all. Both of us burst a port tyre in the process because of the heavy braking necessary but were congratulated for our efforts. All the blokes at the factory were very nice to us but the aircraft, in my opinion, were somewhat ropey.

Back at Hibaldstow, the news was out that 532 and all the other Turbinlite units are disbanded with effect from January 25th and all personnel are to be posted. Most of us in A Flight will go to 25 Squadron to fly Mosquitoes at RAF Church Fenton. B Flight is being split up among various single-engine fighter squadrons, with a few of the boys choosing to go to OTU to convert to twins.

The Turbinlite scheme is finished and I can't say I'm very sorry about it but the pity is that the squadron has to break up as a result.

It was lunchtime of January 29 1943, when I set out by train for RAF Church Fenton to embark on this next phase of my career. I was delighted to find a familiar face upon my arrival, for none other than my former CO, John Willie Blair, is now the senior controller at the station. Fg Off Jimmy Wooton, who was with me at 54 OTU was another welcome sight together with several old pals who should make the squadron quite lively.

After converting to the DH Mosquito NF II, Fg Off Jack Cheney and his RO, Plt Off Mike Mycock, went on to night fighter operations with 25

Squadron during which, in addition to home defence night fighter patrols, they carried out several 'Night Ranger' intruder sorties deep into Germany and 'Instep' long-distance offensive patrols over the Bay of Biscay. It was during one of the latter sorties that Cheney and Mycock were shot down and killed in combat with FW190s off the Brest peninsular on June 13 1943.

CHAPTER 6

Night Hawks

From November 1940 onwards, the RAF felt the benefit of a series of changes that turned its night fighting force into a potent, cohesive organisation. Principal among these was, first, the arrival of the Bristol Beaufighter IF with AI Mk IV and second, the employment of Ground Controlled Interception techniques.

GCI stations providing radar cover over the approaches to the Midlands (and of course beyond) were located in an arc round The Wash at Orby, in Digby sector near Skegness, Langtoft, in Wittering sector south of Spalding, and Neatishead in Coltishall sector near Norwich. From spring 1941 almost all night fighter actions over this region were controlled by one or other of these three GCI stations, acting as the long range eyes of the fighters and guiding them to within the shorter three or four mile range of their airborne sets. Although the date on which it opened is unclear, Orby was one of only six mobile GCI units operational in the UK at the beginning of 1941 and as seen in the last chapter, it was certainly handling interceptions in early March. In its initial form it was composed of mobile antennae units mounted on trailers and lorries parked in a grass field, connected by a veritable knitting-pattern of cables to control room trailers that owed their origin more to caravans and tents than anything else. The height finding capability of those early mobile-aerial units was limited due to the same antenna being used both to transmit and receive signals and even with a programme of continual modifications, it was accurate only to within about 1,000-foot units of altitude until the advent of more accurate centimetric equipment. However, this was still good enough to bring night fighters to within striking distance of their targets. With a range of detection initially in the order of fifty miles up to 25,000 feet altitude, this range decreased as the altitude of a target got lower. As technology improved, detection ranges increased in excess of one hundred miles.

Langtoft soon joined Orby on stream and as will be seen below, was in full operation by May 1941. Research by *The Blitz Then and Now* team established that:

On April 7 1941 the first of a limited batch of twelve 'intermediate transportable' stations with rotating aerials was opened at Langtoft. The whole station could be transported using six lorries and six trailers. However, once at site the gantry and aerial had to be erected on ground foundations... which employed ten men for three days. These, like the mobile GCIs were termed Air Ministry Experimental Stations (AMES) Type 8.

During 1942 Langtoft GCI was re-equipped with what was called AMES Type 7 permanent equipment and brick buildings which, with a series of more modern radars and underground bunkers, continued to perform that role until 1958.

Langtoft GCI's visible component, the above-ground aerial array known as a 'revolving mattress', stood thirty-five feet high and was split into two segments, an upper and lower, revolving six to eight times a minute. With this split-aerial arrangement, height was now deduced from the time difference between a signal sent out from the upper segment being received by the lower segment and this substantially improved its accuracy in that respect. Signals indicating aircraft positions were relayed to an adjacent control huts (later, concrete bunkers) and traces projected onto a circular plan position indicator cathode screen, while indications of target height were displayed as synchronised traces on a separate cathode display tube. Initially only one interception at a time could be controlled but as the system developed, more than one fighter could be handled by a number of controllers at the same station. Each would interpret a display, allocate targets to fighters and because they could distinguish friend from foe by emissions from the former's 'identification friend or foe' (IFF) signal, pass interception instructions to their fighter to bring it into AI range of about two to four miles. After that it was up to the RO's (later re-designated navigator) with their airborne interception sets to guide a pilot to within a few hundred yards, at which point it was then all up to the pilot and his 'eyeball Mark 1' to finish the job. By the way, while an IFF signal meant 'friendly', the absence of an IFF signal did not automatically mean 'enemy' since the transmitter could have been switched off or faulty – so targets still had to be positively identified by an attacking fighter before firing.

It is clear that human teamwork, too, was a vital component throughout the whole of the chain. According to former 25 Squadron night fighter pilot, Wing Commander Joseph Singleton DSO DFC AFC, the process of relaying the target altitudes through the control chain was somewhat fraught with error. It was therefore not at all uncommon he said, "for one or more component in the chain, including the pilot, to add a thousand feet or two to the reported height, just to be on the safe side in an effort to get above a bandit."

Additionally, in the New Year of 1941, this ground organisation was supported by night fighter operational training units, for example 54 OTU at RAF Church Fenton, turning out a steady flow of new crews. There were also gradual improvements to the quality and reliability of AI equipment itself, coupled with increasing experience of its use and finally, considerable improvements were made to VHF radio-telephony that directly linked GCI stations to the fighters. Without such fast and reliable communication, GCI would not have been as effective.

In his book *Radar Days* E G Bowen wrote:

In the first two months of 1941 the weather was unusually bad over Europe and this restricted enemy activity. In March the enemy resumed heavy night raids on Britain and during that single month the night fighters scored twenty-two kills. In April the number destroyed was fifty-two with a further eighty-eight probables. In May 1941 a total of 102 confirmed kills were made by night fighters over British soil... and 172 damaged. These were losses the German Air Force could not sustain.

Night fighter units active over this particular region in that period were 25 Squadron, with Beaufighters; 151 Squadron (Hurricanes and Defiants), both based at Wittering and its Collyweston satellite and 29 Squadron, having completed its re-equipment with the Beaufighter, based at RAF Digby located between Sleaford and Lincoln. Coleby Grange began its association with night fighters as Digby's second satellite airfield with the Canadians of 409 Squadron operating Defiant and Beaufighter aircraft there from mid-1941.

The first Beaufighter to be delivered to 25 Squadron at RAF North Weald on September 2 1940 was R2056, a cannon-only version, followed by three more during the month and the four were declared operational in October when the squadron moved to RAF Debden. It will be seen later that 25 Squadron used some Beaufighter IFs armed with four 20mm cannon only and some armed with four 20mm cannon and six .303 machine guns. This was because the first fifty Mk IFs rolled out from Bristol's Filton factory were built with cannon only and some of these were among the first issued to the squadron.

Another move in late November 1940 brought the squadron to RAF Wittering but it was not until during January 1941 that its re-equipment with the new fighter was complete. Thus, at the beginning of 1941, 25 Squadron had the tools with which to make its presence felt by the enemy. However, just as with 29 Squadron in Chapter 4, some months would elapse before the training, necessary with both a new aeroplane and a new version of AI, would pay off in operational success.

Flt Lt J 'Inky' Inkster and Sgt Charles Johnson were the first to cross swords with an enemy bomber in an unsuccessful engagement on January 16 and this was followed by another inconclusive engagement on January 27 off the north Norfolk coast. Initially controlled by Orby GCI, the Beaufighter went out of its range and had to revert to Wittering sector, relaying CHL information. Sector put them onto a bandit but although Johnson found an AI contact and Inkster managed to get in close enough to loose off a short burst of cannon and m/g fire, they lost visual and AI sight of the target.

Spells of bad weather throughout February and March brought Wittering squadrons little trade but from the beginning of April things began to look up, although sadly it was an accident that cast a shadow first. Sgt Harold Maxwell and his RO Flt Sgt D Roberts died when X7541 stalled on approach and crashed in Burghley Park just short of the airfield.

First enemy blood went to the team of Sgt S Bennett (pilot) and Sgt Frank Curtis (RO) in Beaufighter R2122 on the night of April 9/10. Intruder unit NJG2 was active that night in support of major attacks on Birmingham and Tyneside and at 20.00 hours on the 9th a Junkers Ju88 C-2 flown by Gefr Franz Brotz took off from Gilze-Rijen airfield in Holland, heading for airfields around The Wash. Patrolling a line east of Wittering, Bennett saw a shower of incendiary bombs being dropped in the distance. As he was still under the control of RAF Wittering he asked for and received permission to go and investigate. Almost immediately Curtis picked up a contact on the AI set and his instructions allowed Bennett to come in behind the bandit and spot it, silhouetted against some cloud, crossing in front and slightly below, but in his enthusiasm he overshot the first pass and lost sight of the bomber. Frank Curtis, though, held it on his set and brought Bennett back behind the target. This time he made no mistake. At 200 yards range two bursts of cannon fire devastated the cockpit, killing Brotz and badly wounding flight engineer Uffz Erich Gorlt. Radio operator Uffz Willi Lindner was slightly wounded but he and Gorlt managed to bale out to become POWs. The Junkers, R4+CM wk nr 0776, went down in flames, crashing with its pilot near Langham in Rutland about ten miles west of RAF Wittering.

Opinion differs as to who actually delivered the coup de grâce to Obergefreiter Wilhelm Beetz, Gefreiter Johann Mittag and Gefreiter Rudolf Cronika, the crew of another NJG2 Junkers Ju88. This C-2 intruder variant, wk nr 0345, coded R4+BM, was shot down on April 17 1941, to crash and bury itself on Hurn's Farm, French Drove, Gedney Hill, about eight miles south of Spalding. According to a local newspaper report, the enemy aircraft was heard circling the area for some time before the crash. It was a moonlit night and a number of people had what was said to be a clear view of a dogfight between a fighter and an enemy aircraft which crashed in flames and burned out. Set ablaze in the attack, the Ju88 was later found to have dived vertically at great speed into the ground, where it was almost entirely buried in the soft fen clay. Some seat armour and one MG15 was recovered, together with what remained of the bodies of the crew. The site of the crash was quickly turned into a quagmire of watery clay but the crater was eventually filled in and returned to farmland.

It has even been suggested that this Junkers may have been shot down by one of its own kind and no RAF combat report has yet come to light to refute that idea. Local people, however, recounted a story about a "black Hurricane" seen swooping very low over the crater next day, only narrowly avoiding collision with a nearby farm shed. Was this the victor taking a look at his vanquished perhaps, or maybe just a curious 151 Squadron pilot out on an air test?

There lay the Junkers for thirty-seven years – and this writer had occasionally found scraps of Perspex and aluminium where the ploughed field met the roadside grass verge – until October 1978 when Wealden Aviation Archaeology Group excavated the site. In a corner of that lonely field a crater some twenty feet across and twenty feet deep was opened up by an excavator. From this hole was recovered a large quantity of mangled wreckage together with both engines, propellers, undercarriage, ammunition, maps and numerous components which once gave life to an aeroplane. One of the most interesting finds was the survival dinghy, preserved in excellent condition and complete even to an intact bottle of medicinal brandy. These artefacts can now be seen in a refurbished and preserved condition at a museum on the former Tangmere airfield near Chichester.

There were clear signs now that the Luftwaffe was stepping up its operations across the whole of the country and – little did they know it – the night fighter squadrons would be severely tested during the next two weeks. 25 Squadron had been fully operational with the Beaufighter for only three months and the new GCI stations had been operational for just two of those months. However, the Luftwaffe had been relatively inactive during that period, so although the crews practiced hard, there had been few opportunities to carry out interceptions against an elusive, aggressive enemy. May 1941 was going to be the month in which 25 Squadron would feel great pressure and frustration in equal measure.

Orby GCI directed Sgts Arnold Hill (pilot) and Ernest Hollis (RO) onto an unidentified 'single-fin' enemy aeroplane which they intercepted south-east of Derby at about half-past midnight on the night of May 3/4, but at first sight there is little evidence to support conclusively their claim to have destroyed it. Certainly Sgt Hill fired over 200 cannon and 700 machine-gun rounds at his target, claiming: "I opened fire at 200 yards from dead astern with four cannon and six machine guns. I saw tracer disappear into the E/A and other rounds bounce off into the air. Quite a lot of sparks and what appeared to be red-hot particles shot off the E/A."

After last seeing it diving through 10,000 feet so fast, Hill decided not to try to keep up with it, and they didn't actually observe it crash and neither was a wreck reported near Derby. On a night when nearly 300 RAF fighters across the whole country were seeking an equally large Luftwaffe force it is not surprising that a duplicate claim might be made or, as seems possible in this instance, an enemy bomber loss as yet not attributed to any RAF pilot may be one of those Luftwaffe aeroplanes whose fate was unknown and simply listed as 'failed to return'.

As mentioned in a previous chapter, Plt Off Henry Bodien of 151 Squadron put in a claim that same night and he is generally credited with the Heinkel brought down on land at Sharrington near Holt in Norfolk. However, when one reads the details of both engagements, what appear to be two interceptions that began more than a hundred miles apart, may actually have ended quite close together and that could have caused the confusion. From details in Sgt Hill's combat report it is clear that the action was close to Derby and he adds, "I claim one unidentified E/A as destroyed and learn since that it crashed at Hold [*sic*] in Norfolk." In Plt Off Bodien's running fight he said, "the coast was crossed north of The Wash." It appears to have carried on out to sea until "the E/A turned towards the coast." Further firing passes were made until "the E/A was seen by pilot and gunner burning slightly on the sea." When, in the same report, Plt Off Bodien also says the visibility was good enough to allow him to see the enemy aeroplane exhausts at two miles range, it tends to support his being able to distinguish sea from land – and that his claim was actually a different victim to that usually attributed to him. It seems possible Bodien may have shot down a Ju88 from I/KG806. This scenario thus lends more weight to Sgt Hill's claim being the Sharrington Heinkel, which may indeed have been hit hard near Derby but managed to stagger nearly to the Norfolk coast before coming down.

25 Squadron's next Beaufighter success over The Wash corridor fell to the guns of its CO Wing Commander David Atcherley, in a Mark I, on May 4 1941. Together with his AI operator, Flight Lieutenant John Hunter-Tod, they took off from Wittering at 22.00 hours in R2251, under the control of Langtoft GCI. At 22.30 they were given some 'trade' and put onto a series of courses by the controller until Hunter-Tod picked out a target with his airborne set, about two miles ahead. Shortly after, Atcherley gained a visual sighting and began to close in. At an altitude of 12,000 feet and one hundred yards range it was identified as a Ju88 and immediately Wg Cdr Atcherley opened up with two short bursts from the full weight of his four 20mm cannon and six .303 machine guns. The effect was devastating; the cabin of the Junkers exploded in a brilliant flash and the interior of the fuselage caught fire. The enemy aircraft fell into a dive, shedding pieces as it fell. Wg Cdr Atcherley poured in one more burst before breaking away, leaving the stricken aircraft to plunge vertically to the ground. He had fired 189 x 20mm cannon shells and 535 x .303 inch machine-gun rounds in the course of the engagement.

Such is the tragedy of war that this Junkers, a Ju88A-5, wk nr 3358, coded V4+BS of III Gruppe, Kampfgeschwader 1 (III/KG1), part of a raid heading for Belfast, crashed directly onto the Butcher's Arms public house in Eastgate, Bourne, Lincolnshire. From the crew, Uffz Adam Becker (pilot) died in the wreckage; Gefr Reinhold Kitzelmann (radio) and Gefr Karl Focke (observer) also died. These latter appear, however, to have baled out as their bodies were found some little distance from the crash, but were probably too low for their parachutes to deploy. The gunner, Gefr Rudolf Dachschel, was slightly injured but escaped by parachute and was made a prisoner of war.

The wreckage of this Junkers was almost entirely buried in the ruins of the pub and the war was brought suddenly and tragically to this rural community when licensee Charles Lappage, his wife Fanny, together with two relatives staying in the house, Violet Jackson and Minnie Cooper, were killed instantly. In addition, an army officer and two soldiers of the Loyal (North Lancashire) Regiment, billeted in the public house, also died in the explosion. A fourth soldier was lucky to escape even though seriously injured, and five more soldiers in a house opposite were also injured by the blast. Fire prevented rescue parties from working on the building for some time, as when an attempt was made to move debris, flames broke out afresh because the whole site was drenched with petrol.

There was also a sequel to this combat many years later. Damaged beyond repair, the pub was subsequently pulled down and the site cleared. The area remained empty until 1964 when Lovell's garage and filling station was built on the vacant plot. The wartime incident came to life again when the new owner brought in an excavator to dig out foundations for a petrol storage tank. Down at a depth of eight feet the digger encountered a heavy object. Climbing out to clear the trouble, the driver got quite a shock when he saw what was clearly the nose of a bomb in the hole. The police were called in and they in turn sent for an RAF bomb disposal team, this time from RAF Newton. The bomb was a 500kg type but fortunately the fuse was not energised – suggesting the aircraft was en route to its destination. In addition to the bomb that was successfully removed, pieces of wiring, fuselage and some machine-gun ammunition were also found.

David Atcherley achieved prominence in both the pre-war and post-war RAF. Hunter-Tod was also to make his mark in the post-war air force rising, by the time of his retirement in 1973, to the rank of Air Marshal.

That same night, 25 Squadron was active elsewhere in the region when another Beaufighter, controlled by Orby GCI and piloted by Sgt Kenneth Hollowell with Sgt Richard Crossman as AI operator, engaged two unidentified enemy aircraft north of The Wash. They believed both were damaged by their attack and submitted claims for such. In the early hours of the 5th Sqn Ldr Harold Pleasance with his RO Sgt Bennie Bent, also with the assistance of Orby GCI, claimed a 'damaged' in T4629 near Aldeburgh, Suffolk.

At dawn next morning Norfolk police reported a Junkers Ju88 crash in Welney Wash, south of King's Lynn, but in view of the relative positions of these incidents it seems unlikely that they are linked. Aircraft of I/KG77 raided Liverpool that night and Leutnant Joachim Wreschnick in Ju88A-5, wk nr 4269, coded 3Z+CL, was on his way home when things started to go wrong. RAF crash inspectors looking over the Welney aircraft found the port engine had failed and burned, but apparently not due to combat action, and the starboard engine also showed signs of damage. The original factory code of DE+ES was visible beneath the standard camouflage paint. The letters CL were marked on the fin tip and painted on the nose beneath the cockpit was a crest bearing a condor in yellow. Subsequent interrogation found that Wreschnick had ordered his crew to abandon the aircraft whereupon Uffz Friedrich Podlesch, Uffz Rudolf Siegmann and Gefr Helmut Pix baled out and were captured unhurt. The pilot decided to stay with his stricken machine and pulled off a successful belly-landing on flat land near the Great Ouse river. On scrambling out of the Junkers he tried, unsuccessfully, to set fire to it by firing his pistol at the fuel tanks, before he too was captured.

The three who baled out caused a stir for a short time as local researcher Ivan Bevis discovered.

One of the three crew was discovered by a farm worker near March who looked after him until collected by an army escort. The other two enjoyed a little more freedom but they, too, were eventually picked up.

Driving along a lonely road out of March, a motorist saw someone walking in the road ahead of him. This was unusual in the middle of the night and aroused his suspicion. As he drew nearer, the person turned towards the car and the motorist was shocked to see what was clearly an airman in flying overalls, bearing all the hallmarks of the Luftwaffe. The motorist took one look, turned the car around and headed back to March police station as fast as he could go. A police patrol went out to the spot and apprehended what was indeed a German airman. The final member of the Junkers crew actually strolled along unchallenged and into the town of March itself. Mr D Gipson, a teenage railway messenger in those days, recalled how he came upon an airman in flying clothing in Station Road. The German was acting nervously and stood looking in Fell's shop window. He spoke to the young lad and having explained to the equally nervous boy who he was he made it clear he wanted to be taken to the police and not a civilian authority. Then calmly the pair went off to the police station where all three airmen were kept in custody until the army arrived.

Standing patrols continued to be the routine tactic, with the number of aircraft despatched varying according to the expected level of Luftwaffe activity in the sector. In seven nights between May 5/6 and 11/12, the squadron carried out seventy night patrols between the hours of 22.00 and 06.00, each patrol lasting about three hours and overlapping to keep at least two fighters airborne at any one time. During that period twelve interceptions were made, resulting in claims for three E/A destroyed and nine damaged. Four interceptions were controlled by each GCI station at Orby and Langtoft while the remaining four were controlled by the Digby sector operations room and the crews made these interceptions in an area stretching from Aldeburgh on the Suffolk coast to Hull and inland to Grantham.

As the Luftwaffe crossed the region in force again in the bright moonlight of May 7/8 1941, 25 Squadron was ready for them. Among the attackers was a Dornier Do17Z-10 intruder. Dubbed 'Kauz II' (Screech Owl II), this Z-10, wk nr 2843, coded R4+GK of I/NJG2, was a Do17 modified to carry a battery of two MG FF 20mm cannon and four MG17 (7.92mm) machine-gun armament, all fixed in a 'solid' nose to fire forward. This night fighter conversion job on the last nine aircraft off the Do17Z-3 production line originally married a Do17 fuselage to a Ju88C-2 cockpit, but it was not a success. Dornier therefore designed a completely new nose with the above-mentioned armament. In an effort to aid night interceptions this new nose was subjected to further modification by the installation of an infra-red sensor, codenamed Spanner-anlage (roughly translated as 'Peeping Tom equipment') but it had a poor range and so many practical limitations that only fifteen sets were actually installed operationally. It has been suggested in some quarters that Kauz IIs carried Spanner-anlage on intruder operations in 1941 but the device, built by AEG-Mayer was not developed and tested until 1942.

For the pilot, Fw Wilhelm Lettenmeier, it was a testing time because it was his first operational night fighter sortie. He was somewhat encouraged though by the presence in the aircraft of Uffz Herbert Thomas, an 'old hand' with forty missions to his credit already. Thomas was charged with the task of passing on his experience to new night fighter crews at Gilze-Rijen airfield, in Holland.

Plt Off David 'Tommy' Thompson, from 25 Squadron's A Flight, with his AI operator Plt Off Dennis Britain, took off from Wittering in R2181 just before midnight to patrol off the Lincolnshire coast under Digby sector control. After an hour they were directed south towards The Wash. While still north of The Wash, however, Britain picked up a contact independently on his own radar set which they chased for a few minutes until Plt Off Thompson was able to spot their target. There, off to port, clearly silhouetted by moonlight against a cloud layer below, was what they both agreed was a Dornier Do215. Easing the Beaufighter down to the enemy's altitude of 13,000 feet, at one point Thompson realised he was approaching the aircraft too fast and had to close the throttles quickly. This action caused flames to belch from the exhausts and gave away his position to the equally wide-awake enemy crew.

Eager not to let the chance slip away, Thompson loosed off a short burst at the Dornier's starboard profile. In that same instant Lettenmeier instinctively reacted to a warning shouted over the intercom and hauled the Dornier over in a steep turn to port, away from his attacker. Thompson followed his quarry in the diving turn, still keeping it at about one hundred yards range. Lettenmeier straightened out, thinking he had shaken off the Beaufighter but it was not so and Thompson, who now had the Dornier firmly in his sight, let fly with two more short bursts of cannon fire in quick succession. First of these hit the nearest, starboard, engine and as the Dornier rolled away to port the second hammered into the underside of the port engine. That engine immediately burst into flames and the enemy aircraft continued to roll over into a downward spiral.

Inside the Dornier at first pandemonium reigned as exploding cannon shells slammed through the fuselage, filling the interior with lethal flying metal splinters. Each member of the crew was hit but not seriously and quickly discipline and training took control. When the engine caught fire Lettenmeier carried out the well-rehearsed procedure: ignition off, petrol cock off, full throttle to clear out any petrol in the feed pipes and pray! Now the Dornier was in its ever-tightening spiral – pull back on the control column – can't budge it! Thomas saw Lettenmeier's frantic actions and lent his strength to try to haul the stricken machine from its headlong plunge, but to no avail. It was Herbert Thomas who saw they had no chance and gave the order to bale out. He saw the third crewman, radio operator Uffz Georg Herden jettison the canopy cover and start to climb out.

Interviewed many years later, Herbert Thomas said he had little recollection of what happened during the next few seconds but remembered feeling a terrific blow that stunned him and becoming aware of heat from all sides. Above all he felt a lot of pain.

At first all went quiet, as if he had been drugged, but then the pain came back. He had no sensation of falling through the air and when he regained his senses he found himself lying on the ground beneath his parachute canopy, through which he could discern the ghostly shape of the moon. He joked many years later that the "sight made me think I'd gone to heaven!" He believed that when Herden jettisoned the big top canopy he was dragged out by a suction effect and the blow he took was probably caused when he struck the tailplane.

Without realising it he must have tugged the ripcord or it caught on something that deployed the parachute and carried him away from the falling aircraft. Herbert Thomas could not remember just how long he lay on the ground in his semi-conscious state, but he heard voices, getting louder as they approached, and soon he was surrounded by a small group of people. The parachute was removed and someone pushed a cigarette between his lips. He drew on this with much relief. He was helped to his feet and hobbled to a waiting car, where he was delighted to find his companion, Georg Herden, thankfully alive. The pair were consigned to the care of local constable, PC Cutts, who broke the news that Willi Lettenmeier was dead. He had baled out too late and his parachute could not save him.

Thomas had suffered serious injuries in the crash and was taken off to hospital. He remembered waking up on an operating table, feeling quite embarrassed to find a young nurse cutting off his flying overall and uniform. Still dazed, he next awoke from an anaesthetic to find himself encased in plaster and with an armed soldier sitting beside him. That soldier became friendly during the course of Thomas's stay in hospital and the more so because he shared his Woodbine cigarette ration with the German. "I received good treatment from the hospital staff," he said, "and since I was in no fit condition to attempt an escape, the guard was removed."

Usually he was hidden from prying eyes by a screen around his bed but later this was removed and during visiting hours he became something of a novelty and the main topic of conversation in the ward. One day he was quite moved when a small boy came over to his bed and placed a toffee on the covers without saying a word. After two or three months he was considered fit enough to be transferred to a military hospital in Knutsford, Cheshire. Eventually, though, Herbert Thomas was repatriated to Germany as his injuries were considered too severe for him to take any further part in the war.

Forty-three years later the Lincolnshire Aircraft Recovery Group (LARG), located the final resting place of this rare Dornier Do17. Having obtained the necessary MOD and landowner permission LARG began their preliminary detector scan of the site, on the bank of Medlam drain at Carrington, north of Boston. At first sight little was found until it was explained by locals that the raised riverbank, into which the aircraft had crashed, had been levelled off some years previously, thus removing much of the wreckage that would have been close to the surface.

On a warm August morning in 1984, the LARG enthusiasts arrived at the site, complete with a Hymac digger to begin the real work. At a depth of fifteen feet, the first telltale signs of the presence of a buried aircraft were found when glycol coolant and oil began to seep into the hole. Shortly after, the first identifiable components emerged. Among these items was the still intact tail wheel, complete with tyre and tube. The inner tube was taken to a local garage and reinflated and remained thus for over a year. Vast quantities of crushed metal skin from the fuselage and wings were removed, together with many smaller artefacts. At a depth of thirty-five feet below the surface of the field, part of the reduction gear of one engine was pulled from the clay. At this depth the hole was becoming very difficult to work and with the risk of flooding from and possible damage to, the adjacent drain, it was decided to cease further excavation. The final tally of items recovered included machine guns (turned over to the police), a badly torn dinghy and a survival kit which contained a corroded flare pistol and spent flare cartridges. Among the more personal items was Georg Herden's flight briefcase, found to contain the navigation maps, signal code books, his kappi (forage cap) and a handkerchief with his initials embroidered on it.

Those pieces found capable of being preserved were painstakingly cleaned and placed on display, alongside the results of similar digs, in the Lincolnshire Aviation Heritage Centre on the former wartime airfield at East Kirkby. The final episode of this tale unfolded when LARG members had the opportunity to meet Herbert Thomas at the museum in 1987. There they presented him with some pieces of his rare Dornier, including one of the ignition keys, as a tangible reminder of his brush with death one moonlit night in 1941. Also present at the meeting was Herbert's old adversary Dennis Britain. Dennis is the former chairman of the UK's oldest toy manufacturing company that bears his family name. He actually became chairman in 1936 and when he joined the RAF in WW2, was officially too old for operations. However, he managed to bend the regulations and between March 1941 and September 1942 he flew more than eighty night patrols as a radar operator with 25 Squadron, for which he was awarded the DFC. Dennis died in 1996 at the age of ninety-three. David Thompson, on the other hand, despite his flying and combat experience, survived only a couple more months after the above combat.

Since February 1941 over 120 attacks had been made on bomber and fighter airfields across the country. Over a longer period, RAF Sutton Bridge, near The Wash, was hit five times and its decoy Q-site at Terrington St Clement was attacked eight times during the war. RAF Wittering, 25 Squadron's base, was bombed several times, too, including four consecutive nights in a row up to May 9/10. One of those attacks destroyed 25 Squadron's office and the loss of squadron documents accounts for the scarcity of archive information for the early part of the war.

On the civilian side, Spalding, a small market town in south Lincolnshire, received the attention of a single raider in the early hours of Friday, May 10. Four HE bombs damaged houses in King's Road, Pinchbeck Road and West Elloe Avenue, alongside the railway line to the north of the station. At first sight Spalding seems an unlikely target but a closer look at the combination of railway lines, junctions, embankments and road and river bridges carrying the railway through the town, shows it to play a strategic role in the east coast railway network. Fortunately there were no casualties on this occasion nor was the railway itself damaged.

An aeroplane linked to an intriguing mystery may well have been responsible for this attack. Night fighter pilot Plt Off Alan Picknett of 25 Squadron submitted the following combat report of an engagement with what he claimed was a Focke-Wulf FW200 Condor, also in the early hours of May 10 1941, very close to the time of the Spalding raid.

At 02.10 I took off with Plt Off G F Sellick as AI operator from Wittering in a Beaufighter and landed at 04.00, controlled by Langtoft GCI. After patrolling for about an hour I was vectored NE and after a series of vectors I obtained a visual at 250-300 yards of a large four-engine aircraft flying east at 13,500 feet altitude. I closed and identified the aircraft as an FW200 Condor. I immediately opened fire from astern and to starboard at 100-150 yards range with four cannon guns. The E/A almost instantaneously went into a steep dive to port. I followed it down to 8,000 feet, getting in another very short burst, causing green sparks to be emitted from the E/A's fuselage. As the E/A pulled out of its dive I managed to get in another very short burst before I passed over its top. Although I continued to search I could get no further contact, either visual or on AI. I have since been informed that Lincoln Observer Corps have reported that, at 03.30, the precise time of the combat, cannon fire was heard about three miles south of Fosdyke and that this was followed by the sound of an aircraft crashing, which was confirmed by the Fosdyke police and searchlight post WT045. At low tide in the afternoon of 10 May 1941 Plt Off Herrick and Plt Off Sellick made a reconnaissance of The Wash in a Magister and a patch of oil was observed in the vicinity of the combat, one inch to one mile map ref sheet 56: F970670; the area of Gat Sand.

The weather and visibility was excellent with nearly full moon and both I and Plt Off Sellick clearly identified the E/A as an FW200 Condor, which I claim as destroyed. No return fire was experienced.

It is clear the crew had fired at something, as Plt Off Picknett used a total of thirty-five cannon shells in three very short bursts. What seems unclear is whether they did in fact shoot down an aircraft. An oil slick is not conclusive evidence as it could have come from a ship. The Wash is shallow in the vicinity of Gat Sand and it seems odd that no wreckage was found nor any more detailed surface search initiated, particularly in view of the comment: "the sound of an aircraft crashing". Or was that sound really the noise of aero-engines slammed to full throttle, such as might happen when an aeroplane is diving hard – as it would do to evade its attacker? According to German archive sources, MOD (Air Historical Branch), and several reputable air historians both in the UK and Germany – such as the late Heinz Nowarra – no FW200 loss record exists to support the claim, or at least not one that matches the Spalding raid date. Enquiries about RAF four-engine aircraft (notably Stirlings that had just entered service) and aircrew losses on that date also drew a blank, thus allaying the fearful alternative possibility. Furthermore, despite the discovery in 25 Squadron archives of a photograph purporting to be of the mystery Condor, no evidence can be gleaned from that picture to make it in any way connected with this incident. Only four bombs were dropped in Spalding on this occasion and the local newspaper described them as "of small calibre" so that is not particularly helpful either. However, on the vexed question of aircraft identification in the darkness, it is also interesting to note that an RAF intruder crew from 23 Squadron claimed an FW200 over France on the night of April 21/22 1941, but it was subsequently found that they were mistaken and the aircraft they actually attacked and shot down was in fact a Junkers Ju88.

The mystery, therefore, still remains, but perhaps the simple explanation that this was a sortie by one bandit – 'wounded' or not – that got away under cover of darkness, may be closest to the truth. Who knows?

The night of May 10/11 1941 saw the Luftwaffe launch its last major attack of the Blitz, when London and many other towns were severely raided. Among the many single-seater Fighter Night sorties drawn to the London area were several by Hurricane fighters from 151 Squadron at RAF Wittering, as outlined earlier. Just twenty-four hours later the biggest attack on a civilian target in The Wash locality during this period occurred when twenty-four HE bombs were dropped in and around the market town of Spalding again. This time the centre of town itself was devastated by what was described at the time as hundreds of incendiaries, dropped by one of an estimated three enemy raiders in the early hours of Sunday, May 12 1941. This seems to have been part of a concerted series of attacks on communications and airfield targets across eastern England that night. What follows is a description of the devastation that could be caused by a small number of enemy bombers on an undefended civilian target.

Air raid sirens wailed at 23.57 on the 11th and soon the noise and vibration of exploding bombs was heard and felt with trepidation. This was the result of one aircraft unloading a stick of twelve bombs along Cuckoo Road, close to the railway line from Spalding to Bourne, on the western outskirts of the town. At 01.00 on the 12th another single bomber caused the greatest havoc by dropping shoals of incendiary bombs across business premises and homes in and around the old market place. An eyewitness said it sounded like "pebbles clattering as the bombs hit the roof tiles." Many were extinguished by fire watchers, Civil Defence and police but large numbers penetrated top floors of high buildings, locked and vacated for the weekend, where they soon caused major fires. Subsequent official reports made it clear that the devastation in the town centre was the result of incendiary bombs and not high explosives. These are thought to have been released by the same aircraft that dropped two HE bombs recorded as falling just to the north of the town centre; one exploding between the Lincoln and Boston railway lines where they converge, and the other just missing these lines as they approached the station itself – about a quarter of a mile from where the carpet of incendiaries began to fall.

Spalding Urban District Fire Brigade and Auxiliary Fire Service units were soon at work but fires were so extensive that these services were in danger of becoming overwhelmed. A call went out to neighbouring towns for assistance and fire brigades from Peterborough, Boston and Bourne promptly answered the plea, together with fire-fighting parties from soldiers of the 18th Battalion of the Welch Regiment stationed locally. The latter also provided parties to control spectators, remove furniture from burning buildings and act as runners. Then, at 02.45, while fires raged and the sky was lit up for miles around, another hammer blow fell as an enemy bomber swept in from the south-east, laying a stick of twelve bombs across residential areas. These fell in a mile-long swathe from Matmore Gate to St Thomas's Road, missing many properties but killing people in houses that took direct or near-hits.

This writer's father was one of many AFS firemen fighting the conflagration in the town centre that night. George Goodrum recalled how they were pumping water from the Welland river onto the Woolworths store and adjacent properties when that last bomber was heard. He said: "We all dropped to the ground in shop doorways as the explosions came nearer, thinking they would be aiming their bombs to stoke up the fires we were tackling." But this bomber was after another section of the railway and left the fires to wreak their own havoc while it went for the railway bridges.

The town post office had to be evacuated at 02.30 owing to the danger of it being engulfed by fire and the only telephones working were a private police line and the council's private system. It reopened at 04.00 when the danger passed. All off-duty policemen, special constables, civilian clerks and the staff of the United Services canteen were soon back on duty as the town got to grips with the disaster. It was a most serious blow to it though, as it suffered five people killed, twenty-five injured and all told, more than 300 properties damaged. Certain roads in the town were closed to all vehicles except essential services but by 06.00 an extended system of control was in operation, with the assistance of two sergeants and twenty-four men of the 80th Traffic Control Company.

In the cold light of a smoke-filled dawn the town counted the cost but by then the fires were out and temporary repairs and rehousing of businesses under mutual assistance arrangements were well in hand. Although business premises in the centre of the town had been hit hard, miraculously two-thirds of the HE bombs fell in open spaces such as bulb fields, allotments and playing fields so, despite 250 houses being slightly damaged, only one had to be demolished and eight were badly damaged. The relatively few people who were rendered homeless were billeted with friends so the council decided it was not necessary to open up official rest centres.

Speculation continues to this day over why this small market town was singled out by the Luftwaffe. Popular local theory is that a navigational error caused it to be mistaken for either Boston, fifteen miles to the north, where the docks might have been the target or Peterborough, an engineering and railway centre some fifteen miles further south. A glance at these three places on a map of the region is enough to show how such an error might well have been made from the air at night. Although smaller, Spalding, like both Boston and Peterborough, sits astride a river and that river flows into The Wash.

Another much more plausible theory however is because no less than six railway routes converged at Spalding station, these lines and not the town centre may have been intentional targets. This major junction straddled important north-south routes (Peterborough and Ely to Lincoln, Boston and Grimsby) and the west-east route linking Leicester to King's Lynn, Norwich and Great Yarmouth. If, for example, the east coast main line and other important lines in the region became congested or closed due to bombing then the railway lines converging on Spalding would become vital diversionary routes. It would certainly have caused disruption by disabling the lines or more importantly, the bridges and complex junction system through the town, and strong support for this idea comes from an analysis of the bombing patterns. The validity of this theory becomes much more apparent by consulting older, pre-Beeching, maps, showing lines and junctions that are no longer evident today. Bombs from both the Friday morning and Sunday morning attacks only just missed the station and the north and north-west railway junction. One of the Sunday attackers narrowly missed the line to the south and the west/east line junction. while another laid his stick close to and parallel with the east/west railway just missing a rail/river bridge, a rail/rail bridge and a junction. This pattern therefore seems quite deliberately directed at the railway targets. Whatever the reason though, the raid became a clear indication to the ordinary citizen of what 'total war' really meant.

There was much enemy air activity over the length and breadth of the region that same night, with Ju88 and He111 bombers attacking RAF Sutton Bridge and other airfields all round the periphery of the Fens. Between 01.00 and 02.00 – around the time Spalding was hit – separate attacks by three enemy aeroplanes were made on the airfield. Sixteen bombs fell among the parked Hurricanes, setting two on fire, seriously damaging seven others and peppering many more with shrapnel. A new intake of pilot trainees at 56 OTU arriving at Sutton Bridge during the morning after the raid were greeted with the sobering sight of smouldering craters and burned out Hurricanes.

25 Squadron at Wittering put up several Beaufighter aircraft to counter these raids and the Luftwaffe did not get off entirely scot-free. Two crews had some success when Sqn Ldr Harold Pleasance (pilot) with Sgt Bennie Bent (RO) damaged a Heinkel He111 near Wells-next-the-sea while Plt Off David Thompson (pilot), with Plt Off Dennis Britain (RO) claimed another Heinkel He111 damaged west of Skegness.

Both Beaufighters thundered down the runway within minutes of each other at 01.00 on the 12th with Pleasance in T4634 taking a patrol line to the south of The Wash under Orby GCI, and Thompson in R2181 to the north under Digby sector control. Bandits came in about an hour later and the two crews joined combat almost simultaneously. Dennis Britain picked out his own contact just inland from Skegness and brought Thompson into visual range of a Heinkel He111 at 6,000 feet altitude. It was down-moon of the Beaufighter, putting the fighter in an exposed position so, cool as a cucumber, Thompson slid the Beau underneath the E/A, came up the other side and opened fire at 300 yards range. But he was spotted and the E/A crew returned fire as the bomber dropped into a series of diving turns. Whenever he could get the elusive Heinkel in his gunsight Thompson fired a burst – five times in all. He saw hits but the fight had dropped to sea level and the bomber managed to wriggle free and escaped out to sea.

About the same time, Orby GCI put Bennie Bent onto the track of a bandit and he brought Sqn Ldr Pleasance into visual range of another He111, flying about ten miles off Wells-next-the-sea. Once again the Beaufighter was seen and the bomber crew fired first as it closed in. Pleasance, too, scored hits on the fuselage as the Heinkel went down in diving twists and turns but it was lost to view at 5,000 feet, eight miles east of RAF West Raynham. Harold Pleasance complained bitterly that it was "aimless searchlights" that deprived him of his kill.

On balance, the Luftwaffe seems to have had by far the best of the encounters, particularly when one takes into consideration the damage done to Spalding and RAF Sutton Bridge that night. 'Big week' was over but after a short lull the bombers came back.

Sgts Ken Hollowell (pilot) and Dick Crossman (RO) had flown together regularly in 25 Squadron since November 1940 and had become an effective team with several successful interceptions to their credit. Airborne on May 16/17 they were patrolling The Wash in Beaufighter R2156 when Sgt Crossman picked out a contact on his AI set and directed Ken Hollowell onto a course to intercept. As they closed on the target both agreed it was a Heinkel 111 and Ken Hollowell moved in for the kill. He put his gunsight ring onto the dark shape – it was a 'sitter'. The four 20mm cannon thumped out but after just a few rounds they stopped, jammed. Immediately Dick Crossman wriggled from his radar position into the centre section where he could get at the ammunition drums and breechblocks and feverishly set about clearing the blockage. With Crossman away from his radar it was vital that Hollowell kept in visual contact with the bandit. By now though that wasn't too difficult since, having spotted the Beaufighter, enemy gunners were blazing away at it from every position. Now Crossman yelled to his pilot that the guns were clear and Hollowell fired again – and again the guns fell silent after a few rounds. With Hollowell desperately hanging on to his target, in all Dick Crossman had to clear the cannon three times before the Heinkel could be hit hard enough to force it down near Cromer. But by keeping so close to the bomber the enemy gunners were themselves able to score good hits on the Beaufighter. With one engine stopped and some controls damaged Hollowell could not maintain height so he gave the order to bale out. Down to 1,000 feet altitude Crossman just made it out safely over Langham but Hollowell decided he was too low so he took a chance, stayed with the aircraft and pulled off a masterful crash-landing on marshland near Stiffkey, north Norfolk. Ken Hollowell was no stranger to forced landings as he had experienced his first back in January when he was unscathed after engine failure brought down R2129 near Wisbech.

After nearly three weeks with little by way of action for the squadron, Birmingham came under attack on June 4/5 1941, from Heinkels of III/KG4, based at Leeuwarden in Holland and at 02.00 hours on the 5th an He111 H-5 fell to the guns of 25 Squadron Beaufighter R2157 flown by Sgt Horace Gigney, with radar operator Sgt Gerard Charnock. They were instructed to orbit the northern side of The Wash at 12,000 feet altitude under the control of Orby GCI station. Shortly after being vectored onto an inbound bandit Charnock picked up a contact flying west, brought Gigney neatly in from astern and he got visual contact at 200 yards range. Throttling back so as not to overshoot, Gigney had time to fire one brief burst of forty-four cannon shells just as the target seemed to take evasive action. There was no return gunfire from the Heinkel and it transpired that Gigney's short burst was sufficient to bring down He111, wk wr 3793, coded 5J+FS.

The pilot of 3793, Oblt Hans Paas, struggled with the controls to keep the Heinkel airborne, when first one engine was shot out then the other failed. With consummate skill he managed to glide the heavy machine down to a crash-landing near the village of South Reston, north-west of Skegness. Clambering from his relatively undamaged aircraft, the local Home Guard, rifles and fixed bayonets at the ready, were somewhat puzzled to find Paas was the sole occupant. One of them recalled:

> Charlie Goulsbra and I were members of the Home Guard and involved with fire watching duties practically every night, our base being in an old chicken hut at Authorpe. The Heinkel passed over the hut on a full moon night and we could see both engines were stopped as it glided out of sight. Grabbing our rifles, we donned steel helmets and set off in pursuit on foot across the fields to South Reston where the vicar, another fire-watcher, told us the bomber had only just cleared his roof-top but he had not heard it crash. Accompanied now by the local policeman, we set off again and suddenly came across the plane in a field behind the school. After a conference we very gingerly approached the plane, rifles cocked, bayonets glinting in the moonlight and much to our relief the German airman surrendered. As the prisoner was marched off, one of the rifles was accidentally discharged and although unharmed, I've never seen anyone jump higher than that German did. I was left to guard the plane on my own and I vividly remember how nervous I felt at the time and even more so when, in the early hours of the morning, I heard a shouted order to 'fix bayonets' and a contingent of troops charged across the field towards me. I was only fifteen at the time and I was petrified.

Crash inspectors recorded that painted beneath the cockpit of this Heinkel was a badge consisting of a white flash on a red shield, with a black 'G' in the flash itself.

The subsequent fate of his crew came as a blow to this aircraft captain, who had only the safety of his comrades at heart when he ordered them to bale out as he wrestled with the controls. One by one, Oblt Gunther Trukenbrodt, Uffz Horst Walther, Uffz Paul Weber and Fw Nikolaus Heuser tumbled out of the Heinkel into the inky blackness above The Wash. All four came down in the sea and were drowned. Weber's body was washed up on the Norfolk shore that same day, Walther on the 6th and Trukenbrodt almost a month later, on July 3rd. Now they rest together in a quiet corner of Great Bircham cemetery all, that is, except their compatriot Heuser who is still posted as 'missing'.

Just over a week later, on June 14 1941, Horace Gigney, too, was dead, the victim of another aeroplane accident. The Blenheim he was flying, L6726, suffered flap failure in a turn onto the approach to RAF Wittering, and stalled and spun in near Burghley Park, Stamford.

That same night the experienced team of Sgts Ken Hollowell and Dick

Crossman were back in action again patrolling in a moonlit sky over The Wash. Flying Beaufighter R2154 there were no gun stoppages this time and with just forty-one cannon rounds they made short work of Heinkel He111-H5, wk nr 4027, 1G+FL of I/KG27, which was also on its way to bomb Birmingham. The bomber, piloted by Ofw Alfred Thiede, was hit hard and emitting a trail of sparks it was seen to dive into the sea at the mouth of The Wash. Only one body was recovered from the water. Hollowell was another pilot to complain bitterly of problems with over-keen searchlights when, after losing a second bandit that night, his Beaufighter was held in a searchlight cone near Bircham Newton and he only escaped by continually flashing the code letter of the day.

On July 8 the squadron lost another experienced crew. Dick Crossman teamed up with Tommy Thompson for a training flight involving low-level dummy attacks by several aircraft on army tanks near the boundary of RAF Wittering airfield. Take-off was at noon in Beaufighter T4629. When Fg Off Thompson was called in to attack he dived steeply on the tanks then pulled the nose up sharply, climbing away to port. Suddenly the Beaufighter stalled and with full power on, dived straight into the ground. Thompson died instantly but Crossman was pulled out of the wreckage with severe injuries from which he, too, died later that day. It seems the Beaufighter Mk I, being a relatively heavy aircraft, especially when fully loaded, could not cope with the stress of a quick change of altitude from dive to climb. There was a tendency for it to stall under such conditions and in fact the Air Ministry accident card (Form 1180) for this incident states: "type unsuitable for such an exercise on account of its high wing loading."

Now it was the port of King's Lynn's turn to feel the weight of the Luftwaffe's hand. So far there had been only an occasional single raider to disturb the peace, with little damage, probably due to the existence of a decoy 'town' site just up The Wash coast at Wooton. The town's heaviest raid so far, in property damage and casualty terms, occurred on June 11/12 1941 when Boal Street was wiped out entirely and serious damage caused in neighbouring streets too. Sixteen people were killed. Another year was to pass, almost to the day, before the Luftwaffe exacted its greatest toll from King's Lynn. There were forty-two fatalities when, on the evening of Friday June 12 1942, the Eagle Hotel in Norfolk Street crowded with customers, including many servicemen, took a direct hit.

Meanwhile the cat-and-mouse battle between the Beaufighters of 25 Squadron and Ju88 intruders of NJG2, was rejoined a couple of nights later. At this stage of the proceedings, serviceable aircraft available to this intruder unit seemed to fluctuate between ten and fifteen machines but despite taking losses, it was hunting over England on most nights throughout that summer. RAF Y-Service radio traffic monitoring data suggests the unit flew 315 intruder sorties during June, 270 on twenty-eight nights in July and 260 on twenty-six nights in August.

On June 13/14, controlled by Orby GCI, Squadron Leader Harold

Pleasance with his RO Sgt Bennie Bent, in T4634, intercepted Ju88C-4, wk nr 0550, R4+DM, of II/NJG2 in the Long Sutton area east of Spalding. Directed towards The Wash, in the clear starlit sky Pleasance spotted the bandit 500 yards distant going west at his own altitude of 11,000 feet. Closing to one hundred yards he gave the target a short burst of fire, then reducing the range to seventy-five yards he emptied all four magazines of cannon ammunition at the target. This produced a vivid flash, the Junkers reared up as if mortally hit, then fell into a long diving S-turn streaming white smoke. Sqn Ldr Pleasance kept the E/A in view and saw it pull out of the dive until, completely on fire it finally dived vertically into the ground. However, the Junkers' crew baled out and at 00.30 hours, it crashed at Narford, two miles east of Narborough, near King's Lynn, where some of its 50kg bombs exploded on impact. Pilot Uffz Richard Hoffmann and flight engineer Fw Peter Mayer were captured but the third member of the crew, wireless operator Gefr Johann Reisinger, died.

Crash inspectors from AI1(g) found the armament carried was similar to other examples of Junkers night fighters: one MG FF 20mm cannon and three MG 17 (7.92mm) machine guns clustered in a faired-over nose with two separate MG 15s (7.92mm) in flexible mountings in the crew compartment. It was also noted on this Junkers that the individual aircraft code letter D was black outlined in white, and the fin carried one victory emblem, dated 9/4/41.

Plt Off David Thompson was on patrol in The Wash area with his AI operator, Plt Off Dennis Britain, in Beaufighter R2157 that night too and scored again when he shot down what he thought was a Heinkel He111. His opponent this time was in fact Junkers Ju88C-4 intruder, wk nr 0335, R4+AM, of II/NJG2 which fell onto The Wash mud flats to the south of the Nene river outfall, a couple of miles out from the sea bank. Thompson got a visual on his target but lost it twice before he managed to keep it in view. Making sure this time, he closed the range and let fly with a short but devastating burst from just thirty yards that set the starboard engine on fire and since the Junkers immediately fell into a steep dive, he may have hit the pilot, too. The aeroplane did not recover and disintegrated on impact with the marsh. Six unexploded 50kg bombs were later found lying in the mud and two MG 15s recovered but the marsh is all embracing and apart from these items, little else could be seen of what was once an aircraft. All three crewmen were killed. The graves of Uffz Heinz Schulz (flight engineer) and Uffz Jakob Ried (radio operator) are to be found in Sutton Bridge and Great Bircham cemeteries respectively. Ried's body was washed up on the Norfolk side of the Wash coast some three weeks after the crash. Sadly the body of pilot Uffz Helmut Bahner was never found.

All of the Beaufighters involved with 25 Squadron's combats to date were the early, cannon-only models but the CO David Atcherley commandeered R2251, one of the first of the four cannon and six machine-gun versions to reach the squadron. He put it to good use on June 15/16 when, with just a two-second burst, he and John Hunter-Tod shot down a

Ju88 into the sea off Sheringham, then repeated the dose to another Ju88 on July 4/5 which exploded under the weight of the Beaufighter's heavy punch and fell into the sea twenty-five miles east of Wells-next-the-sea.

Fg Off Herrick's combat on June 22 1941, detailed in Chapter 1, brought to a close what might be regarded as the first – and most intensive – phase of the night battle fought out over the eastern air corridor to the Midlands. Of course there were always the inevitable patrols by defenders who could never relax their vigilance and as the nights increased in length once more, the Luftwaffe returned to attack the larger cities more frequently. It will become apparent that, with steady improvements to the GCI radar system and coverage, such interceptions made by those squadrons under discussion tended to move eastwards, with the fighters getting to grips with the enemy much earlier than a year previously. Furthermore, with the general decline in the Luftwaffe's raids over England since the start of the Russian campaign, those night fighter squadrons not re-designated as intruders themselves, although under less pressure, did not simply sit and wait but utilised the relative inactivity to hone their interception skills even more.

Moreover, this 'lull' allowed night fighter squadrons to provide night cover in directions for which resources were previously short such as, for example, covering the coastal shipping lanes running up the east coast, where convoys were always a target for marauding German bombers day or night. This was in fact one of the reasons for detachments of some of 151 Squadron's experienced Defiant and Hurricane crews during the summer and autumn of 1941 from Wittering to Coltishall, the latter serving as a forward base for such sorties. Among those operating occasionally from Coltishall in 1941 were Hurricane pilot Plt Off Richard Stevens and Defiant pilot Plt Off Ian McRitchie, the latter taking with him Sgt A Beale and Plt Off R Sampson as air gunners on various occasions.

Now flying a cannon-armed Hurricane regularly, Richard Stevens increased his personal tally on July 5/6 while patrolling a convoy off the north Norfolk coast, operating on this occasion directly from Wittering. The convoy was steaming north and Stevens searched ahead and to the east of it at 3,000 feet, trying to keep the ships between himself and the three-quarter moon. It was around 03.00 that he was drawn towards some bomb explosions and AA fire from the ships. An aircraft crossed his track above him and closing on it he identified it as a Ju88. Stevens gave it a one-second burst at 300 yards and saw hits on the fuselage. The bomber dived away, but squeezing off another one-second burst caused a vivid flash near the fighter followed by a large piece of the bomber whizzing past his cockpit. He thought his cannon shells may have hit the bomber's canopy just as it was jettisoned. With flames flickering from it the Junkers did not pull out of the dive and hit the sea in a huge splash. It had taken just twenty-four cannon rounds to despatch this raider, whose watery end was witnessed by the 151 Squadron Defiant crew of Sgts Fielding and Gudgeon, who were also on convoy patrol duty in the same area.

25 Squadron's last brush with the enemy, before it moved from Wittering to Church Fenton, went to Sqn Ldr Harold Pleasance and Fg Off Dennis Britain when they were scrambled at 20.50 hours on October 1. Langtoft GCI sent them after a bandit circling in the vicinity of RAF Upwood and they chased and caught up with it over The Wash at 6,000 feet altitude in bright moonlight. It was a Junkers Ju88 in a shallow dive, going straight and fast, towards home. In X7621, a cannon and machine-gun model, Sqn Ldr Pleasance closed to 250 yards astern, put the gunsight on the target and simply held the firing button down until all his ammunition was exhausted. There were hits on the fuselage and all return fire stopped but the E/A disappeared into cloud in a steep spiral and contact was lost. Sqn Ldr Pleasance finished his patrol stint and returned to Wittering to claim a probable. However he was advised later by Happisburgh CHL station that the E/A was last plotted by them at 3,000 feet, five miles out to sea, flying very slowly and then the plots ceased abruptly. So Harold Pleasance may have traded his 240 shells and 1492 m/g rounds for a kill after all.

Ten months would elapse before 25 Squadron registered another kill.

There is perhaps no better indicator of the reduced activity by the Luftwaffe during that summer than to point out that even Plt Off Richard Stevens was unable to get the enemy in his sights again until October 16. Detached to Coltishall, he was ordered to patrol the outer swept channel where at 19.00 hours his eagle eyes spotted a Ju88, which he attacked and shot down into the sea fifty miles east of Great Yarmouth. He saw more Ju88s but had run out of ammunition so, after trying unsuccessfully to home other 151 Squadron aircraft onto the enemy he had to head back to Wittering where he landed at 19.30 hours.

During a similar patrol in the evening of October 31, Ian McRitchie and air gunner Plt Off Sampson tangled with a gaggle of four Ju88s twenty miles east of Great Yarmouth with similar success. Sampson shot down one bomber into the sea and the others dumped their bombs and beat a hasty retreat. McRitchie caught up with one of these and during some hectic manoeuvring at ranges of between 100 and 150 yards, Sampson scored many hits on it before his guns jammed. Made of sterner stuff and perhaps feeling there was nothing to lose, the pilot of this Junkers now decided to take on McRitchie. Turning on him, the bomber made a head-on pass with all guns blazing at the Defiant, which was flying just 80 feet above the waves. As it passed the fighter – fortunately without scoring any hits on it – Sampson managed to put in another burst from one gun as it headed in the general direction of Holland. McRitchie caught up with it again and Sampson, having cleared his guns, scored more hits with a four-second burst before they all jammed once more. Now, dangerously close to the Dutch coast and with faulty guns McRitchie reluctantly broke off this fifteen-minute running battle and flew back to Wittering to claim one Ju88 destroyed and one damaged.

With the onset of winter weather, enemy air activity slackened off even further. The Coltishall detachment of Alex McRitchie and Albert Beale scored the only success of the month when they destroyed a Ju88 in a head-on clash above a convoy off Great Yarmouth on November 15. Despite this minimal level of enemy air activity, 151 Squadron lost no less than six aircrew in four weeks. Sgt Howard Godsmark died in a flying accident on November 12, Sgts Victor Jee (pilot) and Bill Bainbridge (air gunner) went missing in Defiant AA423 in the North Sea on the 15th, Sgt Lammin was reported missing on the 17th and Sgts Anthony Mills and Royce Gazzard failed to return from a convoy patrol on December 14, all a tragic reminder that night fighting was still a dangerous business.

1941 was the year in which the RAF night air defence organisation established itself as a force to be reckoned with and by the end of that year, its spearhead consisted of nine squadrons operating Beaufighters, six operating Defiants, ten flights of Turbinlite Havocs and one squadron with standard Havocs. RAF Wittering held a pivotal position on the route to the Midlands and 25 and 151 Squadrons policed The Wash corridor, until the former moved out to Ballyhalbert in January 1942. There were, of course, engagements not covered here and others by squadrons covering nearby sectors in a similar way but to all intents and purposes, the Hun had been swept from this part of the sky... for a while.

CHAPTER 7

Mosquitoes Bite and Beaufighters Punch

Almost a year would elapse before the Luftwaffe returned in strength for the next phase of their attacks on the Midlands, this time with Kampfgeschwader 2 (KG2) – the Holzhammer Gruppe – in the van. From April until September/October 1942, Dornier Do217s spearheaded the notorious Baedeker air raids against historical British towns and cities. Mounted in retaliation for the RAF's escalating attacks on the great cities of Germany, these raids were stimulated in particular by those upon the Baltic ports of Lübeck and Rostock in March and April 1942. Dornier Do217s of KG2, together with other units, were heavily involved in the Luftwaffe plan but by the end of that summer would, once again, suffer heavy losses to the RAF's night defences.

Almost coinciding with the beginning of the Baedeker phase, 151 Squadron – still based at Wittering – became only the second squadron to re-equip with the de Havilland Mosquito NF II and made its first Mosquito patrol on April 30. The last of 151's pilots went solo on the Mossie on June 20 and that day its diarist recorded confidently that, "the whole squadron can now be left to its own devices", and in common with other night fighter units, soon got to grips with the enemy once more.

Plt Off Wain in DD608 and Flt Lt Pennington in DD628 reported some AI contacts in their patrols on the night of May 28/29 but it was during enemy mining sorties to The Wash and anti-shipping raids in the Great Yarmouth area on May 29/30 that the squadron's first real engagement occurred with the new fighter. First up from Wittering were Pilot Officer John Wain and Flt Sgt Thomas 'Jock' Grieve in DD608 who tackled a Dornier 217 but could only claim it as damaged. The same night the A Flight commander, Flt Lt Denis Pennington and his RO Flt Sgt David Donnett in DD628, intercepted and fired at what he thought was a Heinkel He111 out over the North Sea but spirited return fire made him break off with an inconclusive result for him, too.

With faster fighters and more effective radar cover, the profile of night air combat was changing distinctly, but because defending fighters were now intercepting more enemy raiders out over the sea, it would also become more difficult to verify some of the results of their combats and subsequent claims.

On Wittering's patch it was the CO of 151 Squadron, New Zealander Wg Cdr Irving Smith, who led the way to success with the new Mosquito. Airborne at 22.45 hours in W4097 for the first patrol of the night of June 24/25, he and his RO Flt Lt Kerr-Sheppard were vectored by Neatishead GCI out to sea from The Wash towards an incoming raid. At 12,000 feet altitude, Kerr-Sheppard soon picked out a contact and guided the wing commander into visual contact at one hundred yards range. It was a Heinkel He111 and in his combat report, he said it looked to be carrying "two torpedoes under the wings." The crew of the Heinkel spotted the incoming Mosquito for it suddenly dived vertically but not before Wg Cdr Smith put a burst of cannon fire into the port engine, which started to blaze and the starboard torpedo – if indeed that's what it was – dropped away. Smith clung to the bomber, firing more short bursts at it from his machine guns as it first dived then pulled up into a stall turn, shedding pieces as the rounds hit home. Now the Heinkel dived again with the Mosquito still on its tail, this time firing another burst of cannon. Diving hard, the two aircraft were enveloped by cloud and although Kerr-Sheppard followed it on the AI set it gradually went out of range. Smith continued to follow the descending track of the Heinkel and at 7,000 feet altitude Kerr-Sheppard regained a contact off to port still losing altitude but again the target disappeared off the display. Wg Cdr Smith claimed a 'probable' for this one and climbed back up to look for more trade. Control put him onto the track of another bandit and at 7,000 feet altitude in bright moonlight he saw the aeroplane two miles distant, in fact just a few seconds before Kerr-Sheppard called out the AI contact. Smith opened up the throttles to close the range and then eased the Mosquito in to 300 yards behind and below another Heinkel He111, also carrying what he also described as "a torpedo under each wing." He just managed to get in a one-second burst of cannon that brought hits on the underside of the wings and fuselage before the Heinkel dived vertically. This time, with its port wing on fire, the enemy bomber continued to dive until it struck the water, where it left a circle of burning wreckage. Claim one He111 destroyed.

The patrol was hotting up indeed and Wg Cdr Smith was directed towards a third bandit on which AI contact was made but then lost at extreme range. Circling at 7,000 feet, control put him onto a fourth bandit, which this time was held on AI right down to visual contact at 300 yards on a Dornier Do217. Smith fired all his remaining cannon ammunition in one long burst at this target, spraying it with hits until wings and fuselage were blazing and parts of the engine cowlings were seen to fall away. The Dornier crew put up a fight, though, and fired back at their tormentor from the dorsal guns but calmly closing the range to a hundred yards, Wg Cdr Smith silenced the return fire with several short bursts from his own machine guns. With the Mosquito windscreen covered in oil from the stricken bomber he was obliged to break off the attack, but by now the Dornier was flying very slowly and losing height rapidly. Wg Cdr Smith drew alongside the bomber and his last view of it was as it flew into cloud, burning fiercely and eerily illuminating the cloud from within. Out of ammunition he headed back to Wittering, landing at 00.52 hours to claim two E/A destroyed and one probable. On the question of the torpedoes under the wings, while it is true that the Heinkel He111 could carry such ordnance, it is possible that on this occasion – and in view of Plt Off Wain's combat report below – Wg Cdr Smith mistook a pair of large calibre bombs loaded on the two bulbous hard points situated at the wing roots, for torpedoes. The He111 had to carry bombs larger than the SC500 externally and two SC1000 or alternatively, two parachute mines – the latter might bear some resemblance to torpedoes when seen in poor light – and these could be what Wg Cdr Smith saw. Furthermore, the squadron diarist didn't do modern researchers any favours when he logged two sorties by Mosquito W4097 at the same time on the night of 23/24 – but flown by two different crews: Plt Off Fisher and Wg Cdr Smith. It seems clear, though, that Wg Cdr Smith's sortie date was flown on that hectic night of 24/25.

Plt Off Wain and Flt Sgt Grieve left Wittering in DD616 shortly after the WingCo. They were handed over to Happisburgh CHL control where trade was still brisk and sent off towards an inbound bandit fifty miles out from The Wash. Wain's combat report was equally brisk, stating:

A visual was obtained against Northern Light at one mile and identified at 600 yards as a Heinkel 111 with two bombs stowed externally. Fire was opened at 250 yards with cannon and machine gun. One long burst caused starboard wing to explode and one third of the wing came off. E/A went into vertical dive leaving a trail of smoke. Time 23.40 hours. An aircraft burning on the sea was seen by Wg Cdr Smith, who was in the vicinity. It is claimed as destroyed.

The night was still young and next off was Sqn Ldr Donald Darling with Plt Off Wright (RO) in DD629 at 00.25. At 01.15 Neatishead GCI put him onto the track of a raider heading south-east at 6,000 feet and shortly afterwards Wright got a blip below and to starboard. Darling got a visual at 700 yards range on a Dornier Do217 but while closing to 200 yards the Mossie was spotted and the bomber dived towards the clouds. Darling put in a short cannon burst as the Dornier entered the cloudbank and with Wright following it on AI he loosed off another burst as they emerged from the cloud. Return fire came from the dorsal turret but this stopped when more bursts of cannon fire from the Mosquito brought hits on the fuselage. Sqn Ldr Darling was unable to stay with the Dornier as it dived hard into the cloud once more so he abandoned the chase and climbed for more trade. After another unproductive chase Plt Off Wright held a new contact, which they turned into a sighting of a Ju88 but once again in the good light conditions the Mosquito was seen and this bomber, too, dived away to sea level where contact was lost. Claim one damaged. Flt Lt Moody flew the last, uneventful, patrol of the night.

Moody was on ops next night when the bright moonlight of June 26/27 brought bombers from Holland in over The Wash in an effort to creep up on Norwich from the least expected direction. A Do217E-4, wk nr 4266, of I/KG2, was lost when Flt Lt Moody and his RO Plt Off Marsh in Mosquito NFII, DD609, caught up with it over The Wash.

Neatishead put Moody on to what turned out to be a friendly then directed him towards a bandit dead ahead. As Marsh was trying to pick out a contact they got quite a fright when a stream of tracer fire zipped past them. Moody dived out of danger and started again. GCI gave him another target at 10,000 feet altitude and Marsh got an AI blip at maximum range. The Mosquito was easily able to overhaul the bandit and in less than a minute Moody had a Dornier 217 in his sight at 800 yards range. He closed in from down-moon and opened fire as the Dornier began a gentle turn to port. Hits on the fuselage were followed by a faint glow and suddenly the bomber blew up, falling into the sea where it exploded again. The aircraft was U5+ML flown by Fw Hans Schrödel, who died with his crew in this engagement.

With the arrival of the Mosquito NFII the science of night fighting had taken great strides since the days of the Blenheim just two years earlier.

During the process of re-equipment, B Flight of 151 Squadron soldiered on with Defiants well into that summer and the tenacity of those Defiant crews – working mainly with the 'eyeball Mk 1' – had fulfilled an important job in plugging gaps in the night defences.

Although by now usually relegated to pottering around on searchlight cooperation sorties, it is interesting to find a few Defiants – described by the squadron itself as "Old Faithfuls" – still around on 151 Squadron in June 1942 – for example AA425, AA436 and AA572 and on the 26th one of these, believed to be AA572, even managed to muscle in and take a slice of the Mossies' action.

Flt Lt Colin Robertson with air gunner Flt Sgt Albert Beale left Wittering at 00.56 hours on the 26th for one of the regular searchlight cooperation sorties with sites around The Wash. They were old hands on the Defiant and when flashes from exploding bombs and fires over in the Norwich direction grabbed Robertson's attention, with the turret fully armed, he could not resist the opportunity to go and investigate. Five miles west of Coltishall Flt Sgt Beale saw a Dornier Do217 coming up behind them at 2,000 feet altitude. Calling for "turn port!" he brought the turret round and opened fire at the bomber from just eighty yards range. Beale saw his fire hit the rear fuselage and this was answered by a stream of tracer from the Dornier's guns as it went into a steep dive under the Defiant, where it was lost to sight.

Turning south-east Robertson saw another Dornier silhouetted against the moon, almost stern on but turning towards them. The Defiant was still only at 1,000 feet altitude when Beale asked for "starboard!" to close the range to 150 yards. Opening fire, he scored hits on the nose and fuselage and stopped return fire from the dorsal gun position. Then Beale's guns chose this moment to jam and the bomber escaped. Landing back at Wittering at 03.14 hours they filed a claim for two Do217s damaged and the Squadron ORB noted: "As Defiants have not been used operationally for some time, this is likely to be the last combat in which this type will engage." Or so they thought.

Always keen to keep his hand in with 'his' squadrons, Wittering station commander Gp Capt Basil Embry borrowed a 151 Mosquito for a dawn patrol to try his luck at catching the 'regular' German PRU Ju88. Much to his disgust he was unsuccessful and since the Luftwaffe looked like staying away for the rest of the month, when the weather clamped in, a squadron party was organised on the 30th to celebrate the month of June successes. But Jerry managed to spoil Robertson and Beale's party by sending a single raider in the wee small hours of June 29/30.

Ground radar tracked an incoming raid across the southern Fens and Flt Lt Robertson with Flt Sgt Beale were scrambled from RAF Wittering. Lashed by rain and hail, their Defiant soon emerged from heavy cloud at 5,000 feet and after twenty minutes, at 03.21 hours, Robertson called "tallyho" on a Ju88. Closing on the Junkers, it was seen flitting in and out of the cloud tops until, when it emerged for a third time, Flt Sgt Beale let go a five-second deflection burst of 200 AP and 200 de Wilde incendiary rounds at the bomber from a range of one hundred down to fifty yards. Later he was of the opinion that the enemy aircraft flew right into his gunfire but it dipped into cloud again and did not re-emerge. The Defiant crew could only claim one Ju88 damaged and a radio fix put them in the vicinity of the town of March in Cambridgeshire.

While much has quite rightly been written about the air war from a pilot's perspective, the achievement of Flt Sgt Albert Beale DFM, in being personally credited with three enemy aircraft destroyed and four damaged while flying in Defiants, is a fine example of the contribution made by air gunners to the night air defence campaign.

151 Squadron continued to make successful interceptions with its new Mosquitoes, even though Luftwaffe incursions were reducing in size and frequency again and thus there were fewer targets to find in the same volume of sky. Apart from the obvious factor of an individual crew's skill in closing a kill, that the squadron could still shoot down the enemy is the most obvious demonstration of the complete effectiveness of the GCI/AI system – it didn't matter how many of them came, radar would find them.

While seeking a target of opportunity along the north Norfolk coast on July 21/22, Ofw Heinrich Wolpers and his crew, including the staffelkapitän Hptmn Frank from I/KG2, ran into a 151 patrol just after midnight. Controlled by Flt Lt Ballantyne of Neatishead GCI, Plt Off G Fisher and Flt Sgt E Godfrey in Mosquito W4090 (AI Mk V) chased the Dornier in and out of cloud cover from The Wash to fifty miles off the Humber estuary, before finally despatching it into the sea. The fight was not all one-sided either. Fisher got in several bursts of cannon and machine-gun fire that eventually put both the ventral and dorsal gunners out of action, but not before their own fire had peppered the Mosquito under the fuselage and engine nacelles and damaged one of the cannon spent-round chutes. Both aircraft were twisting and turning; climbing and diving steeply from 9,000 down to 5,000 feet and back again and it was during one of these dives towards patchy cloud cover that Fisher fired a telling burst and the Dornier's starboard engine caught fire. Going down in an ever steepening dive the flaming engine was suddenly swallowed up by the sea and Fisher who, in all the excitement had not registered his own rapid approach to that same patch of sea, heard Godfrey yelling at him to pull up. He pulled out of the dive at 200 feet – and went home. It had taken twenty-five minutes of hard manoeuvring; 197 rounds of 20mm cannon and 1239 rounds of .303 machine-gun ammunition to despatch Dornier Do217E-4, U5+IH, wk nr 4260.

One particular night in July 1942 can be seen as indicative both of the success of the defensive night fighting force guarding The Wash corridor, of the continuing wide-ranging radius of the sorties and of the recurring problem of confirming combat kills in darkness, often over water. Because of the intensity of air activity over the whole region on this night of July 23 1942, in contrast to the usual rigid censorship and no doubt to bolster civilian morale, the *Lincolnshire Free Press* newspaper was, on the occasion of the night's outstanding events, allowed to print an unusual amount of detail.

For the RAF, while – loosely speaking – Beaufighters of 68 Squadron covered the Norfolk/Suffolk region from RAF Coltishall, 151, having recently completed its conversion from Hurricanes and Defiants to Mosquitoes at RAF Wittering, was assigned The Wash area while the Canadians of 409 Squadron at Coleby Grange (Lincoln), also equipped with Beaufighters, watched over the rest of Lincolnshire towards the Humber. These then were the primary night fighter units in the region in mid 1942. In addition, though, other squadrons added support, so that the umbrella over the approaches to the Midlands by night left few holes for the enemy to pass through unmolested. Not least of the other units were the radar-equipped flying searchlight Turbinlite Havocs of 1453 and 1459 Flights (later 532 and 538 Squadrons) that flew variously from Wittering and Hibaldstow. Until September 1942, when they were re-formed into integrated squadrons, comprising one flight of Havocs and another of Hurricanes, the Havoc flights drew their satellite fighters from Hurricane units with whom they shared a base. In the case of 1453 Flight at Wittering, when 151 re-equipped with Mosquitoes, it called upon the Hurricanes of 486 (NZ) Squadron to make up their Havoc/Hurricane teams. However, in addition to its Turbinlite commitment, 486 Squadron also mounted independent Fighter Night patrols of its own. Generally speaking, though, the twin-engine fighters patrolled about fifty miles out to sea and the singles inland from the coast but inevitably, once the action started, it will be seen there were no rigid areas and overlaps by all units occurred frequently.

Including the two being discussed in detail here, claims for a total of seven enemy aircraft destroyed over East Anglia were submitted for the night of July 23/24 1942. Five of these were made by Beaufighter crews of Wg Cdr Max Aitken's 68 Squadron based at RAF Coltishall, their victims apparently falling either in the sea off the Norfolk coast or in Norfolk itself. Wg Cdr Aitken claimed two, Sgt Truscott one and two Czech crews one each. The other two claims were made by Flt Lt E L (Peter) McMillan of 409 Squadron and Flt Lt Harvey Sweetman of 486 Squadron. Examination of German records in recent years, however, indicates only three enemy aircraft were lost over England that night, while a fourth – almost certainly the result of McMillan's second combat – crashed on landing back at its base. Such is the benefit of hindsight!

With the likelihood of some or all of these defending aircraft chasing around the night sky after declining numbers of enemy aircraft, inevitably duplicate claims were bound to happen. On this night, just such an event occurred.

Oblt Heinrich Wiess of II/KG40 was briefed to attack an aircraft factory in Bedford with four 500kg bombs. With his crew, Fw Karl Gramm, Fw Hermann Frischolz and Ofw Joseph Ulrich, he took off from Soesterberg in Dornier Do217E-4, wk nr 4279, coded F8+CN, just as the moon was beginning to rise. His route from Soesterberg airfield in Holland took him across the North Sea, down the length of The Wash, making landfall over Boston at 10,000 feet before turning south towards the target. It was only five minutes after this point that the Dornier was caught in a searchlight beam and one of the crew saw a single-engine fighter below them about 1,000 yards away to starboard. Oblt Wiess took evasive action by diving the Dornier, first to starboard then curving to port to get back on course. The fighter seemed to have been shaken off but soon another single-engine fighter was spotted below, on the port side this time, flying on a roughly parallel course. After being interrogated later, the transcription of flight engineer Ofw Ulrich's recollection of events went as follows.

> He said he fired a few machine-gun rounds in its direction and the fighter turned in to attack the Dornier from below. The first burst from the fighter set the port wing on fire and the crew baled out. During his parachute descent he saw a twin-engine fighter fly past but he was positive that the aircraft at which he fired and which then shot them down was a single-engine.

Flt Lt Harvey Sweetman, a New Zealander from Auckland, commanded a flight of 486 (NZ) Squadron at RAF Wittering and was a founder member of the squadron in March 1942. The Hurricane IIbs of 486 were usually tied, at night, to the apron strings of the Turbinlite Havocs, but the results of this technique of night interception had been singularly unimpressive so far. On this night, however, it was Harvey's turn to go off chasing the Hun on his own freelance patrol and from his combat report we can piece together his version of events.

Sweetman eased Z3029, SA-R, gently off Wittering runway at a quarter to midnight on July 23 1942. According to his recollections after this sortie, at first he headed north before turning on a reciprocal course that brought him to the vicinity of Spalding. There, outlined against a cloud layer below and to starboard of him, he spotted the menacing shape of a Dornier Do217, flying south. As he closed in, Sweetman's Hurricane was spotted by the Dornier crew and its dorsal turret gunner let fly with a burst of machine-gun fire. The bright red and white tracer rounds were way off target though. Banking to starboard, Sweetman closed to seventy yards, loosing off a deflection burst at the nose of the Dornier from his eight machine guns, but without any visible effect. The Dornier dived rapidly in an effort to escape the line of fire but Sweetman hung on down to 5,000 feet altitude, firing two more bursts as he followed his prey. These seemed to produce an immediate result as "twin streams of thick smoky vapour flowed from the enemy aircraft." Furthermore Sweetman reported that the Dornier "turned right over on its back and dived vertically down out of sight." Although it was bright moonlight, there was some broken cloud around at 3,000 feet and as he orbited the spot, Sweetman saw "the flare of an explosion below", which he took to signal the end of his victim. Calling up Wittering sector operations, his position was fixed to within six miles of the crash site and he set course for base, landing back at 01.00 in an elated mood.

It was established that an enemy aircraft had crashed in a field at Fleet Fen south of Holbeach and according to 58 Maintenance Unit (58 MU) inspectors, it was a Dornier Do217E that was entirely destroyed, with wreckage strewn over twenty acres. It was their task to salvage as much material as possible and gather intelligence about this latest model.

The German crew had baled out and landed in a string between Fleet Fen and Holbeach itself and the occupants on duty in an Observer Corps post just outside the town had quite a shock when a German airman walked in and gave himself up! He was left in the care of two slightly bewildered observers while a colleague, quickly picking up the only rifle in the hut, ran outside and rounded up another of the crew a short distance away. A third German was found hiding in a farmyard and the fourth was apprehended nonchalantly walking down the road in his stockinged feet, having lost his boots when he abandoned the aeroplane.

Flt Lt Sweetman duly submitted a claim for one Dornier 217 destroyed but that signalled the beginning of another battle, this time with one of his own side. When the 486 Squadron Intelligence Officer made enquiries to support Sweetman's claim, the crash having been confirmed by a searchlight battery at Whaplode Drove, he was told that a 409 Squadron Beaufighter crew, Flt Lt E L (Peter) McMillan (pilot) and Sgt Shepherd, had submitted a claim for the same aircraft. It was also verified that there was only one enemy aircraft shot down in that district that night.

In an article written by Bill Norman and published in the December

2000 issue of *FlyPast* magazine former night fighter pilot Peter McMillan recalled his two particular air combats with the enemy in July 1942 and remembered how he had to share his success with another squadron. Flying 409 Squadron Beaufighter VI, X8153, it was the first of his claims that he believed was the Fleet Fen aircraft – the one he, too, claimed as destroyed. Peter claimed only a damaged for his second engagement. From the details contained in McMillan's combat report – just as with Sweetman's – it is impossible to reconstruct clearly his precise location at the time of the Fleet Fen combat. However, a D/F bearing put him in the vicinity of Holbeach, and having fired off 339 rounds of 20mm cannon ammunition, he most certainly had a go at something that night.

McMillan's combat report outlines his version of events. He wrote: "Take-off from RAF Coleby Grange was at 23.05 on the 23rd and after a short while the Beaufighter was handed over to Orby radar station to begin a GCI exercise." This was a quite normal procedure during a patrol so that the night fighter crews could get in as much practice in the air as possible, at the same time as being instantly available if ground control detected a potential target. On this occasion, very soon GCI reported trade and McMillan was vectored northwards. Anticipating imminent action, he told Sgt Shepherd to set the cannon armament to 'fire' which involved Shepherd leaving his seat to go forward to the central weapons bay, between himself and his pilot. While he was doing so his intercom failed owing to a broken headset lead. Fortunately McMillan could still hear Shepherd – vital for the interception – but Shepherd could not hear his pilot's responses. There was a buzzer link between the cockpits, however, and they found by speedy improvisation of a simple code they were able to continue with the interception.

Orby GCI put them onto a vector of 100° and warned McMillan he would have to turn quickly onto the reciprocal of 280°. When the instruction to turn came he brought the Beaufighter hard round and there on Shepherd's display tubes was the blip. But the target was jinking around and the contact was lost just as quickly. The Orby controller gave a quick course correction and Shepherd was back in business and this time he held on to it.

McMillan opened the throttles to 280mph at 9,000 feet altitude and began to close in on the target. At 650 yards range he obtained a visual to port and above and thought it to be a Dornier Do217 that was weaving and varying altitude. Calmly McMillan slid the Beaufighter over to bring his quarry slightly to starboard then closed to 250 yards range to make quite sure it was a hostile.

Confirmation was soon forthcoming because at this point the enemy opened fire, fortunately inaccurately. Slight back pressure on the yoke brought the gunsight on and McMillan let fly with three short bursts of cannon fire of two or three seconds each. After the third burst, a white glow appeared on the port engine and the target began to slow down. This caused the Beaufighter to overshoot its prey but as he passed below the Dornier

McMillan saw the port engine was on fire. He hauled the Beaufighter round in a tight orbit and regained visual contact with the enemy aircraft silhouetted against the moon. He was in time to see two parachutes detach themselves from the aircraft just before it went straight down with the port engine blazing fiercely. He wrote: "My observer saw it explode on the ground and I claim this as destroyed." This is a much more visually positive result than Sweetman was able to offer.

Now 486 Squadron would have nothing to do with this 'sharing' rubbish and the whole squadron closed ranks to validate Sweetman's claim. Sweetman himself, accompanied by Sqn Ldr Clayton from Wittering operations and Plt Off Thomas (the squadron intelligence officer), visited the crash site the next morning where they consulted with Flt Lt Morrison of 58MU from Newark. The latter was responsible for examination and removal of the debris. 486 Squadron documents record that Flt Lt Morrison declared that, despite searching for evidence of cannon strikes, he could find none. It was known of course that Sweetman's Hurricane was armed only with .303 machine guns. However, on this latter point, the recollections of two former 58MU recovery team NCOs, interviewed by Sid Finn for his book *Lincolnshire Air War*, provide a contrary view as they said they worked at the site for many days and found evidence of 20mm cannon strikes on the wreckage.

The New Zealanders did not let it rest there and proceeded to interview the police constable who had arrested the German crew. He stated that one member of the crew said they had been shot down by a Spitfire. This remark was taken to indicate that a single-engine, rather than a twin-engine, aircraft was seen which lent support to Sweetman's claim, it being easy to confuse a Spitfire with a Hurricane in the turmoil of a night battle. In their opinion, a final corroboration of 486's claim came when Captain G A Peacock, a Royal Artillery officer stationed at Wittering, made a formal written declaration, carefully witnessed by an army colleague and Plt Off Thomas. In his statement Capt Peacock wrote:

At about midnight I was walking in the garden of a house at Moulton Chapel, where I was staying on leave. My attention was attracted by the sound of machine-gun fire in the air. I saw two bursts of fire... after which an aeroplane caught fire and dived steeply. It passed across the very bright moon, making the perfect silhouette of a Dornier. The aircraft crashed, a mile from where I stood, in a tremendous explosion... looking up again I plainly saw a Hurricane circling and it was from this aircraft that the gunfire originated. No other aeroplane fired its guns in the vicinity at the time of this action.

The lengths to which 486 Squadron went to back up their claim graphically illustrates the high degree of morale and camaraderie existing in RAF night fighter units at this time. The outcome was that 486 Squadron believed Harvey Sweetman had proved his case conclusively, yet ironically his original combat report does not carry the usual HQ Fighter Command 'claim approved or shared' endorsement. Peter McMillan's report on the other hand is endorsed 'shared $1/2$ with 486 Sqdn'.

What seems clear now is that there were several enemy aircraft and RAF fighters in close proximity that night for, in addition to the Fleet Fen Dornier, at least one more Dornier was lost from each of KG40 and KG2 at unknown locations. The "twin streams of vapour" reported by Flt Lt Sweetman do not necessarily mean the Dornier had been hit, since it was known that aviation fuel had a propensity to produce black exhaust smoke when engine throttles were suddenly rammed open. It might be felt significant that Flt Lt Sweetman also lost sight of his target – last seen in a radical manoeuvre quite in keeping with its design capabilities – at a critical moment, while Flt Lt McMillan recorded that his gunfire set one engine of his target on fire and Sgt Shepherd had it in view down to impact. On the other hand, when questioned by 486 Squadron, the MU officer – without, it has to be said, the benefit of a lengthy inspection – is reported as saying he "found no evidence of cannon strikes", yet his recovery team senior NCO, who spent more than a week at the site, firmly expressed the opposite view. Even one of the German crew admitted seeing a twin-engine aeroplane fly past him as he fell from the bomber.

Well, in the historian's 'paper war', evaluation and accreditation may seem important – and there are certainly puzzles enough in this incident! But in the 'shooting war', while there was clearly a healthy element of unit pride involved, the only important thing in the end is that someone actually shot down a raider when the enemy was at the gate.

This busy night was not yet over for Peter McMillan though, and once again with the advantage of hindsight, the outcome of his second combat was not quite as he thought.

As soon as he had reported the first kill to Orby he was passed to sector control for position fixing and then back to Orby GCI. More trade was reported to the east. McMillan was vectored onto 100° and advised of a target at four miles dead ahead at 8,000 feet altitude. McMillan increased speed to 280mph to close the gap and calmly asked Orby to bring him in on the port side as the moon was to starboard. A stern-chase followed and when he got within one and a half miles range of his quarry Orby GCI advised him they could not help him any more and told him to continue on 110°. After a while Sgt Shepherd picked out and held an AI contact although the target jinked around before settling on a course of 090°. McMillan's vision was hampered by cloud now but Shepherd neatly brought him down to 1,500 yards range and there, off to port and slightly above, was the silhouette of an aircraft. Keeping it in sight he crossed over to approach with it slightly to starboard. With the lighter sky behind him and fearful of being spotted, McMillan swiftly closed to 500 yards, eased up behind it, identified it as a Dornier Do217 and let fly with his cannons, all in a series of smooth, decisive movements. He saw flashes of his fire hitting the enemy aircraft, which immediately did a quarter roll and dived away. McMillan endeavoured to follow but lost sight of the Dornier and it disappeared into the ground returns (electronic 'noise') on Sgt Shepherd's screens. When they reached 4,000 feet with 320mph on the clock he pulled out and returned to base, claiming the Dornier as damaged.

Peter McMillan's second adversary that night was Feldwebel Willi Schludecker, a highly experienced bomber pilot who flew a total of 120 ops, of which thirty-two were made against English targets. Survivor of nine crash-landings due to battle damage, Willi came closest to oblivion the night he ran into Peter McMillan. Willi Schludecker was briefed by KG2 to attack Bedford with a 2,000kg bomb load carried in Dornier Do217, U5+BL, wk nr 4252. Approaching The Wash, Fw Heinrich Buhl, the flight engineer and gunner, had trouble with one of his weapons and let off a burst of tracer into the night sky. Willi thought that may have attracted a night fighter because a little later the crew spotted an aircraft creeping up from astern. This is believed to be McMillan's Beaufighter. Displaying a considerable degree of confidence, Willi decided to hold his course and allow it to come within his own gunners' range. Both aircraft opened fire simultaneously with the greater muzzle flash of the Beaufighter cannons preventing McMillan from seeing return fire and the Dornier crew thinking their own fire had made the Beaufighter explode! When the Dornier made its violent escape manoeuvre – bear in mind it was an aeroplane designed and stressed for dive-bombing – they never saw each other again.

In fact Peter McMillan would have been justified in claiming two Dorniers as destroyed that night because Schludecker's aircraft was so badly damaged in the encounter that he had to jettison the bomb load and head for home. It was with the greatest of difficulty that he made it back to Gilze-Rijen in Holland, where he crash-landed the Dornier at three times the normal landing speed after making three attempts to get the aircraft down. That was Willi's ninth – and last – crash-landing because he spent the next six months in hospital as a result of his injuries and it put an end to his operational flying career.

On March 9 2000 Peter McMillan, Willi Schludecker and Heinrich Buhl came face-to-face for the first time when they met in Hove at a meeting arranged by Bill Norman. This time it was a friendly encounter between men who, in Heinrich Buhl's words, "had been adversaries but never enemies" and who found they had much in common.

Neatishead GCI was involved with so many interceptions at this time, to the extent that occasionally, in its own words, it became "overcrowded". Just such a situation occurred on July 27/28, a night of lively action when Wittering's Mosquitoes claimed two more Do217s off the north Norfolk coast, part of a raid heading for Birmingham. Neatishead GCI took on 151's Sqn Ldr Dennis Pennington and Flt Sgt David Donnett (RO), then handed them back to Coltishall sector control because of too many plots.

Fortunately, while waiting for Coltishall to start the ball rolling Donnett picked out a contact for himself – freelancing, as it was called, which was something all night fighter crews trained to do for these circumstances. They tracked down a Dornier Do217 and although it was hit hard and seen going down, Pennington's night vision was suddenly impaired when an instrument light shield fell off in his cockpit and he lost sight of the target. In action nearby was Mosquito DD629, flown by Plt Off Ernest Fielding and Flt Sgt James Paine (RO) who confirmed they saw an aircraft burning on the sea in Pennington's vicinity. This is believed to be U5+FL from I/KG2 flown by Lt Hans-Joachim Möhring who, with his crew, was lost that night. About the same time, Fielding and Paine, patrolling the swept channel coastal convoy route under the control of Neatishead GCI's Flt Lt Ballantyne, themselves exchanged fire with another Do217, claiming to have hit it hard. The bomber was last seen trailing sparks and flames that disappeared suddenly at sea level east of Cromer, prompting them to claim one Do217 destroyed. Fw Richard Stumpf and his crew from KG2 failed to return that night and it is possible that Fielding was the cause of his demise.

If there needed to be yet further evidence of the high state of morale among RAF night fighter crews at this time, it was emphatically demonstrated yet again on the night of July 30/31 1942, in a war-torn night sky over Peterborough. That night saw a heavy raid on this engineering and railway centre, from which the Luftwaffe did not emerge unscathed, two aircraft falling to the defences, one to AA and another to the RAF.

In the first incident a Junkers Ju88A-4, wk nr 2086, 1T+CR, of III/KG 26 is believed to have been hedge-hopping its way back to a base in Holland (although the unit was actually based at Rennes) when it was hit by anti-aircraft fire over Peterborough. It was seen heading north-east away from the city, at low level and on fire. So low was it that the Junkers collided with overhead electricity cables near the village of Thorney. It staggered and as the pilot fought to keep it airborne, it was hit repeatedly by fire from a .303 machine gun wielded by Sgt Fox, one of the crew of a nearby searchlight post. 1T+CR crashed in Green Drove, Thorney, killing all on board – Ofw V Bechthold, Fw L Drees, Ogfr K Heberling and Gefr H Bredemeier.

That same night a Mosquito crew of 151 Squadron had several lively encounters with enemy raiders, believed to be en route to attack Birmingham, despatching one Dornier Do217 into the cold waters of the North Sea, sixty miles off the north Norfolk coast and another, nearly as far inland, into the depths of the peaty Fenland soil.

It was 22.30 when Fg Off Alex McRitchie, an Australian pilot with 151 Squadron, lifted his Mosquito NFII, DD669, from the runway at RAF Wittering and set course for Cromer in company with his Nav/RO Flight Sergeant E S James. They were briefed to carry out a patrol some sixty miles off the north Norfolk coast. It will be remembered that Alex had cut his teeth flying Fighter Nights on Defiants with the squadron a year earlier and now he had a chance to add to the success that 151 Squadron was enjoying with its new Mosquitoes.

There was just time to get in one practice interception before Neatishead GCI passed McRitchie over to the Chain Home Low (CHL) station at Happisburgh on the north Norfolk coast, which had plotted an incoming raid. After being put onto a chase that turned out to be a false alarm, five bandits were detected heading towards the English coast. McRitchie was vectored onto a course for a stern-chase on one of these incoming aircraft. His target was quickly overhauled and identified as a Dornier Do217 that, after two brief but devastating bursts of cannon and machine-gun fire, caught fire and plunged into The Wash below. Alex McRitchie's victim was Dornier Do217E-4, wk nr 5469, U5+GV flown by Ofw Artur Hartwig of IV/KG2 who, along with his crew, died in the encounter.

At this point McRitchie's radio was playing up and without guidance from ground control it seemed pointless to continue the patrol so he decided to return to Wittering. It seemed he was actually following the raiders since, as he approached the coast, his course was taking him towards some distant AA fire. Almost immediately Flt Sgt James, peering hopefully at his AI Mark V screens, picked out a target at extreme range but lost it equally quickly. Well satisfied with the night's work Fg Off McRitchie turned again for home and was in the Wittering circuit when he noticed yet more AA fire and searchlights probing the sky to the south, over Peterborough. Keen to have another crack at Jerry, he climbed back up to 12,000 feet, and above the prescribed AA level and with the aid of searchlights, worked his way into the vicinity of the raid. This was, to say the least, somewhat hazardous since AA crews were inclined to bang away at anything and ask questions later. Before long Flt Sgt James detected a target, again at maximum range, about three miles away.

This time they hung on to it.

McRitchie sighted his quarry in the flickering light half a mile away and slightly above him. Suddenly a searchlight lit up both the Mosquito and the enemy, moving alternately between them. The alert enemy crew spotted the Mosquito and their aircraft was thrown into a spinning dive down to 6,000 feet. Despite diving after it, with 400mph on the clock, McRitchie could not keep it in sight. Once again this tenacious Mosquito crew climbed back to 12,000 feet to have another try, AA gunners or no. Their persistence paid off, for it was quite a sustained raid on this engineering and rail centre and there was still some trade about.

One of the raiders was caught in a searchlight beam and McRitchie turned towards it. Flt Sgt James was no doubt by now sweating in his helmet and oxygen mask, with his face pressed against the radar display visor, trying to sort out from the clutter of signals anything that looked remotely like a target. Again he found one. It was head on this time and closing fast. McRitchie judged his moment, hauled the Mosquito round in a tight turn and James had it firmly on the tubes. The searchlights chose a good moment to light up the bomber and McRitchie went in for the kill.

Although closing very fast, the searchlights now worked against him, for his aeroplane was spotted again. This time the enemy, identified as a Dornier Do217, corkscrewed violently several times but the Australian clung to its every move. This particular Dornier had been caught before it could deposit its lethal cargo and now, faced with a tenacious adversary, that bomb load was jettisoned almost on top of the Mosquito. At the same time, one alert gunner among the crew drew first blood by directing a burst of machine-gun fire at the Mossie, peppering its starboard wing. McRitchie closed the throttles, dropped astern and let the Dornier feel the weight of his own armament in reply. Cannon strikes rippled along the enemy's starboard wing. Still jinking like a cornered animal the Dornier posed a difficult full deflection target but McRitchie fired again and his cannon shells were taking more effect now, on both the wings and fuselage of the enemy aircraft.

By this time the dogfight had brought both aircraft down to 1,500 feet and McRitchie had great difficulty in keeping the Dornier in sight against the darkness of the ground. Having expended all his ammunition and being very low on fuel, he had no option but to break off and return to Wittering. He had been in the air for four hours; had flown hundreds of miles; fired all his ammunition and had engaged and beaten the enemy at least once. This most eventful patrol illustrates graphically the skill, aggressive spirit and teamwork that were the hallmark of the RAF night fighter crews.

And what of the second Dornier?

At 02.00 on July 31, Dornier Do217E-4, wk nr 5470, U5+ET of III/KG2, with its unfortunate crew, Fws K Laub, K-A Gussefeld, H Werner and Uffz H Hammelmann plunged deep into the peaty fen soil near the village of Conington, five miles south of Peterborough. They now rest together in the tranquillity of the German war cemetery in Cannock Chase.

In 1978 members of the Derbyshire Historic Aviation Society excavated the scene of this ferocious battle. Despite the soft, peaty soil, the speed at which the Dornier impacted, and the subsequent explosion, shattered the aeroplane into many fragments, much of which seems to have been removed at the time. Of the parts recovered in 1978, most recognisable were propeller blades, a crew seat, the tail wheel and some cylinder barrels from a badly smashed engine. The whereabouts of even these few relics is, however, in doubt, as much of the DHAS collection was stolen some years ago.

Although McRitchie and James claimed only a damaged, it is almost certain this was 'their' Dornier, even though its downfall was subsequently credited to the anti-aircraft gun defences.

Shortly afterwards, Kampfgeschwader 2 took quite a mauling on anti-shipping operations during the Dieppe raid in August 1942, losing another quarter of its already depleted strength. This unit was now only capable of mounting sporadic attacks on Britain and a few aeroplanes were being sent out, in ones and twos, on nuisance raids.

Oberleutnant Graf (Count) Romedio Thun-Hohenstein was

staffelkapitän of III/KG2 and it was up to him to try to raise the flagging spirits of his hard-pressed crews. With declining resources, no one was exempt from flying. On the evening of August 7 1942, therefore, Thun-Hohenstein assembled his crew, Fw H Kunze, Uffz H Arnscheid, Uffz P Bremer and took off in Dornier Do217E-4, wk nr 5455, U5+DR, from their base in Holland. It would not be long before U5+DR and its crew joined the growing list of losses sustained by KG2.

At this time RAF Coltishall was home to Wg Cdr Max Aitken's 68 Squadron Beaufighters and six of these were on patrol that night guarding the Norfolk coast, waiting for incoming raiders, some of whom were bound for Cambridge. Although 68 was from a neighbouring sector this combat is mentioned here as it was brought to a conclusion in the middle of Wittering sector.

Around midnight of August 7/8, patience was rewarded as several bandits were called. Among the six Beaufighters was X7553, a Mark I crewed by Plt Off Peter Cleaver and his Nav/RO Flt Sgt Bill Nairn. Originally, this crew was sent off on patrol between Coltishall and The Wash at 22.25 hours but it was recalled and sent out twice more before a raid threatened the sector. At 00.45 hours GCI advised Cleaver of a bandit and vectored him westwards towards it. Then, over The Wash, another better target was offered and Sgt Nairn picked this one up on his AI Mark IV set at 10,000 feet altitude. Plt Off Cleaver obtained visual contact and saw the target was...

jinking violently and it may have spotted our aircraft. We turned to port and closed to 200 yards at which range the bandit was identified as a Dornier. I opened fire and saw strikes on the E/A. It dived with flames coming from the port wing between the engine and fuselage and there was some slight return gunfire. I followed the E/A down through cloud and saw it dive into the ground with a large explosion.

They had caught up with Thun-Hohenstein not far from RAF Coningsby and the Dornier crashed in flames into the middle of Shire Wood, Revesby, in Lincolnshire, but all the crew managed to bale out, even though Arnscheid and Kunze were injured. A gamekeeper, assisted by stalwarts of the local Home Guard, quickly rounded up the Germans. All, that is, except one. He, his identity perhaps fortuitously unknown, reversed that unspoken rule among military captives by actually parachuting into the middle of Moorby prisoner of war camp, whereupon he was pounced on by camp guards, thus no doubt saving everyone a great deal of trouble!

In 1983 that same gamekeeper who, years before, had helped round up the Germans, retold this story to a member of the Lincolnshire Aviation Society. A visit to Shire Wood revealed little sign of the result of this skirmish, beyond some damage to mature trees at the edge of a slight water-filled depression. Closer inspection among the detritus, however, showed the ground to be fairly littered with small fragments of twisted alloy, proving that local reports of a violent explosion were correct.

Further careful searching of the surface produced one or two serial number plates and small identifiable components. Then came the first important find – a crumpled piece of alloy with the all-important aircraft type and wk nr stencilled on it, confirming it as a Dornier Do217E-4 wk nr 5455. Of even more interest was part of a radio tuning dial with not only the werke nummer stamped on it but also the date of manufacture: April 8 1942. Allowing for a short period of time to elapse before this Dornier reached KG2 from the factory, it seems to indicate that it was in Luftwaffe service for only about three months. The RAF was indeed exacting a heavy toll upon this unit.

25 Squadron had moved from Wittering to Ballyhalbert in Northern Ireland in January 1942, then back to England in May of the same year. Fg Off Joseph Singleton, in a Beaufighter IV, X7643 from 25, now based at Church Fenton, caught another of these bandits on the night of August 23/24, about ten miles east of Bourne in Lincolnshire. He and his RO, Plt Off Chris Bradshaw, operating under the control of Neatishead GCI, attacked a Dornier Do217 near the village of Cowbit, a few miles south of Spalding. They found 10/10ths cloud from 800 feet up to 3,000 feet, 5/10ths up to 10,000 feet, then it was clear above that.

The enemy bomber was flying in and out of broken cloud and difficult to track visually. While trying to get within range Fg Off Singleton's fighter was spotted and he was fired upon from both the dorsal and the ventral guns of the bomber as it took violent evasive action. As it dived for thicker cloud cover at 3,000 feet Singleton stayed with the elusive target, firing short bursts at it and getting several back in reply. He lost it for half a minute then saw it well below him and dived into the attack again. The flash of cannon shell strikes could be seen hitting the port wing of the Dornier but the kill was frustrated when his ammunition ran out. The E/A disappeared into thick clouds at 3,000 feet so he had to settle for this one as damaged. It is interesting to note the way that interceptions were being set up now, with for example, this fighter from Yorkshire being guided by a GCI station in mid-Norfolk to a target flying over south Lincolnshire.

There was a cluster of searchlight posts in the vicinity of this combat and speaking in 1990, Joe Singleton recalled that, although they helped at first to indicate the direction of the enemy, they ended up blinding him and illuminating his own fighter. It was at that point, he thought, when Jerry spotted him and began to get nasty. This was his first night engagement and although on this occasion he fired off a lot of ammunition for little result, his future combat record shows he soon mastered his craft. Joe remained with 25 Squadron, subsequently being credited with the destruction of seven enemy aircraft at night and rising to command the squadron after the war, as a Wing Commander with the DSO, DFC and AFC.

Despite the poor weather over 12 Group that night of August 23/24 the

Luftwaffe was still active, putting the Group's night defences under some pressure. In an effort to cope with the situation, 96 (RAF Wrexham) and 256 (RAF Woodvale) Squadrons from 9 Group were ordered to mount patrols towards 12 Group's area, as also was 255 Squadron, from RAF Honiley, in Warwickshire.

255 Squadron put up four aircraft, of which two patrolled locally and two other Beaufighter Mk VIs, X8266 and X7944, were handed over to the control of Digby sector. One of these, X7944 with AI Mk IV, flown by Fg Off Hugh Wyrill with Flt Sgt John Willins as RO, according to the 9 Group diary, "effected no less than six interceptions resulting in one enemy aircraft destroyed and one damaged."

Taking off from Honiley at 22.10 hours, Fg Off Wyrill was ordered to reinforce Digby sector and then passed along the control system to Wittering sector. At 22.45 Langtoft GCI senior controller, Sqn Ldr Grace, instructed him to patrol at 12,000 feet on a north/south line near Wittering. A transcript of his combat report is contained in an intelligence form dated 24/8/42 submitted to HQ Fighter Command. The date of the interception is shown clearly as '23/24/8/42' and Wyrill wrote:

I was given several vectors towards a bandit, finally turning onto 120° at which point Flt Sgt Willins picked up a contact well to starboard at maximum range of 4,000 yards. He held the contact as the bandit did hard turns to port and starboard. At 240mph I closed in and obtained a visual at 1,000 yards range on an aircraft flying at 11,500 feet altitude – slightly above and to starboard of me. I closed to 300 yards to identify but the bandit opened fire, made a vertical bank to port and dived away. It presented a good silhouette against the bright moonlit sky and I identified it as a Dornier Do217. I was south of Peterborough and opened fire with all guns [four 20mm cannon and six .303 machine guns] at 200 yards range and I continued firing as the E/A took extremely violent evasive action, consisting of stall turns and half rolls. At one time I was firing almost vertically downwards. Return fire ceased after my second burst and the Beaufighter sustained no damage. Cannon strikes were seen on the E/A and several good bursts were fired while it was held in sight. After the third burst Flt Sgt Willins saw a large piece of the E/A break away. Visual and AI contact on the bandit were finally lost in haze at 3,000 feet altitude.

This frantic exchange had taken just four short minutes.

Hugh Wyrill's night was far from over, as no sooner had he disengaged from the Peterborough combat than he was directed east to chase the last vestiges of the attacking Luftwaffe force from the mainland. He had another inconclusive encounter with a retreating Dornier Do217 near Ipswich but, like Joe Singleton earlier, exhausted his ammunition – in all 700 x 20mm shells and 2700 x .303 machine-gun rounds – before he could complete a second kill.

Meanwhile, the sequel to this busy night was played out back near The Wash. Mortally wounded, Wyrill's first Dornier staggered towards the coast. No one will know the actual effect of the devastating firepower of the Beaufighter upon the aircraft or its crew, although return fire ceased early in the conflict. Shortly before midnight an explosion lit the sky around East Walton wood, six miles east of King's Lynn. Dornier Do217E-4, wk nr 4267, U5+CK of I/KG2 was totally destroyed and its passing is marked now only by scarred trees and lumps of molten alloy in the soil. The unfortunate crew, all of whom perished, were Ofw R Bodenhagen, Hptmn R Hellmann, (staffelkapitän), Ofw G Ruckstruh and Ofw T Romelt.

In some accounts 'Wyrill's Dornier' is credited to the 25 Squadron Beaufighter team of Sqn Ldr William Alington and Fg Off D Keith but this is believed to be inaccurate since the date of their combat is one day earlier. Furthermore, the Langtoft GCI controller who tracked this interception is quoted thus: "Sqn Ldr Brace [sic] considers this Dornier was the one attacked by Fg Off Wyrill, as it was finally lost by them flying in the direction of King's Lynn at 1,000 feet."

It is perfectly reasonable that Sqn Ldr Alington submitted a claim for the previous night's work but at best he could only claim a damaged – and from the following description it appears he and Keith were lucky to be alive to do even that!

Airborne from Church Fenton on August 22/23 in V8329, Alington and Keith came under Easington CHL control who sent them towards a bandit near The Wash. Initially the controller's instructions made them overshoot without Keith picking up an AI contact. More directions put Alington's Beaufighter on a course to cut across the bandit's track and this time Keith found a blip off to starboard. A tight S-turn brought the AI blip to 1,200 yards in front of the Beaufighter and as Alington closed the range he got a visual of the target 1,000 yards dead ahead and slightly below. Fg Off Keith watched what happened on his Mark IV AI set and described the rest of the interception:

At this point the chase was greatly complicated and nearly terminated by the appearance of another Beaufighter that approached from the left and turned in behind. The blip of this aircraft, which showed IFF, then completely obscured that of the E/A. Pilot got in a one-second burst on the E/A and saw strikes on fuselage and wings, E/A turned very steeply to port and dived straight into cloud. Immediately the third aircraft opened fire on us from point blank range behind but his shooting fortunately was of the same standard as his recognition [!] When the blips separated, instructions were given to us at first to chase the wrong one, by which time E/A was behind, on left and below and too far round to pick up again satisfactorily.

CO of 25 Squadron, Wg Cdr Harold Pleasance, with Flt Lt Dennis Britain (RO), was also airborne on the night of 23/24 and he, too, submitted a claim – dated one day later than that of Sqn Ldr Alington – for a Dornier Do217 destroyed twenty miles east of Mablethorpe. He saw one of the Dornier's crew exit the blazing aircraft and a parachute open, then the bomber exploded and dived into the sea.

Some of the most significant factors to emerge from the events of both these nights are the quantity of night fighter squadrons at Fighter Command's disposal to cope with Luftwaffe incursions at this stage of the war, and the scale and flexibility of organisational control. This latter was clearly able to move aircraft around the country, like chessmen to relieve pressure, reminiscent of the Battle of Britain days. Concentrating so many night fighters into the blackness of a relatively small aerial arena, each picking up and losing both radar and visual contacts, inevitably led to multiple claims – even to accusations of 'poaching' or attack from one's own side. In view of the relatively small numbers of enemy aircraft involved at this stage of the war, this scenario does not of course compare with the scale of the Luftwaffe's own night defence of the Reich later on, but it is a far cry from the lone Blenheims and Fighter Night aircraft stumbling about the sky in 1940 and a portent of what destruction could be wrought on a bomber force by organised defenders with the right equipment.

Towns around The Wash, however, had still remained subject to sporadic air attacks since the middle of 1942, with Stamford being hit on June 13, Skegness (six killed) and Boston in the daylight of July 27. Spalding was relaxing on August 2, the Bank Holiday Sunday, when around tea-time a lone bomber – a Dornier 217 according to reliable eye-witnesses – popped out of low cloud and laid a stick of HEs along the High Street, Church Street and into Ayscoughfee Hall public gardens, causing considerable property damage but fortunately few casualties – except in the case of the public gardens, where a bomb annihilated the entire population of the bird-house! Those same eyewitnesses cheered out loud when the sound of gunfire was heard and the unmistakable shape of a Beaufighter could be seen dipping in and out of the cloud in hot pursuit of the enemy bomber. The accuracy of this tale was confirmed years later by reference to the 68 Squadron ORB. Examination of the records of all twin-engine fighter units in or near the region showed 68 Squadron as the only unit in eastern England to have scrambled an aircraft that day. It was quite usual to have radar-equipped night fighters on standby during daytime bad-weather conditions as, naturally, their interceptions were unaffected by thick cloud. The incident is described thus:

2 August 1942. 68 Sqn, Coltishall. Beaufighter R2248.
Pilot: Plt Off D P Paton. Nav/RO: Plt Off G E Bennett.
Airborne 15.05. Landed 17.50.

Scrambled, very cloudy. After lunch an E/A approached off sector in 10/10 cloud conditions. P/O Paton had four visuals during a chase of over 300 miles in and out of the cloud but the enemy bomber managed to escape.

Eleven HE bombs caused four deaths in yet another raid on Boston during the night of August 22/23, but these raids finally petered out in the Fenland region after brave little Skegness was hit yet again on the nights of September 15/16 and October 24/25. Three people were killed in the first of these attacks and fourteen in the second.

With little enemy air activity over the UK during the previous ten days, night fighter Mosquito NFIIs of 151 Squadron, Wittering, at last found some trade during the late evening of September 17, in what appears to have been a final fling by the Luftwaffe – at least for a while. KG2, for example, had taken quite a beating during the past six months and needed time to draw breath and rebuild. On some occasions the teamwork of RAF night fighters and GCI stations could be almost clinical in its effectiveness as a killing machine and is well illustrated by an incident on this date.

With just scattered light clouds, a half-moon promised good visibility as Flt Lt Henry Bodien and Sgt George Brooker (RO) eased off Wittering's runway at 21.43 hours. Flt Lt Bodien's name will be remembered from 151's early Defiant days. He had come a long way since then, rising through the ranks and earning an enviable reputation on the way and certainly with a more potent weapon in his hands now.

Flying Mosquito NFII, DD610, they were taken over by Sqn Ldr Grace, CO and senior controller at the nearby Langtoft GCI station, who guided them to the vicinity of nine raiders coming in over The Wash, heading for King's Lynn. Brooker, head down under the visor of the latest AI Mk V set, got a momentary contact to port then lost it, but despite there being a lot of interference on the set, picked out another target slightly to starboard. It was 1,000 yards ahead, level with them at 7,000 feet altitude and going in the same direction. In a classic interception, Henry Bodien obtained a visual when the enemy's outline took shape as it turned to port in front of him. It was a Dornier Do217, one of the enemy aircraft attacking King's Lynn and it had just released part of its bomb load. Bodien eased closer from astern and slightly below. From the way the Dornier began to make diving turns to right and left, losing height to 4,000 feet, the German crew may have spotted the Mosquito but there was no defensive fire during the engagement. Bodien came in from slightly below and let fly with several short bursts of cannon from 200 to 300 yards range as the target jinked in and out of his gunsight, first hitting the port wing then the engine, which caught fire. His cannon fire now raked the Dornier's fuselage as it darted from side to side trying to escape the hail of shells that sprayed into the starboard engine. The port engine blew up and now going down with both motors on fire, pilot Fw Franz Elias jettisoned the remaining bombs and ordered his crew, Gefrs G Buchner and W Berg and Uffz F Leibrecht, to bale out. The stricken bomber, U5+UR, wk nr 4265 of III/KG2, plunged to earth between the villages of Fring and Shernborne about ten miles east of King's Lynn and the crew were all taken prisoner. Local inhabitants' memory of this incident has faded now and few realise why the final resting place of this Dornier was known locally as 'the aeroplane field'.

By September 1942 KG2 had lost so many crews that it was reduced to twenty-three out of its original complement of ninety and the remainder of the year was spent in mounting occasional nuisance raids. Once again RAF night fighters had given the Luftwaffe enough of a bloody nose to make it necessary for it to withdraw and regroup its resources. But it was not through yet.

CHAPTER 8

Steinbock, Gisela and Buzz-bombs

Having rebuilt its strength by February 1943, KG2 was back in the front line again and in addition to the build up of fresh crews it was also re-equipped with the latest Dornier Do217K- and M- sub-types. With reorganisation and re-equipment being prevalent in the second half of 1942, the RAF had not stood still either and thus the stage was set for another clash in the night sky around The Wash. By the end of that spring of 1943, though, KG2's casualties began to mount once again, peaking in March with the loss of twenty-six crews.

In May of 1942, 25 Squadron relocated from Ballyhalbert to RAF Church Fenton and later that year began re-equipment with the Mosquito. The quantity of defensive night fighter units was decreasing by this time and from its base in Yorkshire, the squadron would be called upon to provide cover to a wide area, involving them in sorties as far south as The Wash and north Norfolk coast and well out into the North Sea. By the start of 1943 the Turbinlite Havocs of 532 Squadron (formerly 1453 Flight) and the other similarly equipped squadrons, were disbanded and their crews were dispersed among other night fighter and intruder units. For example, Fg Off Jack Cheney and his RO, Plt Off Mike Mycock, already mentioned earlier, were posted to 25 Squadron in January 1943.

151 Squadron, having finally seen its Defiants and Hurricanes replaced by the Mosquito NFII, had a fairly thin time during the summer of 1942. Many nights went by without a sniff of the Luftwaffe and when it did venture over it was often just an odd aircraft or two with no discernable purpose other than of a nuisance value.

As was mentioned in Chapter 1, from the beginning of 1942 cooperation between night fighters and searchlights was reorganised into a tactical 'box' system with boxes, forty-four miles wide by fourteen miles long, within which a night fighter circled a stationary vertical beam [the 'beacon'] to maintain station. When an enemy aircraft entered the box, other searchlights converged to indicate the location of the raider as it approached the central 'killer' zone. Evidence of this box structure lying across the route to the Midlands can be gleaned from some 151 Squadron interceptions during that summer, each one occurring during the periods of no moon, when searchlights would be at their most effective.

On the night of August 11/12, for example, Plt Off E Rayner and Flt Sgt

V Brown (RO) intercepted and damaged a Ju88 at 01.30 hours near Grantham while patrolling searchlight box 14 under Digby sector control. Rayner was probably deprived of a kill because his firing buttons had accidentally been wired in reverse and for his crucial first burst the machine guns fired when he thought he was firing the cannon. Just before 23.00 hours on September 8/9 two 151 Mosquitoes were sent off to patrol boxes 15 and 20 and showed just how effective the current tactics could be – AI Mk V not withstanding. Flt Lt Henry Bodien with Sgt George Brooker as RO, were first up:

> ... with orders to man S/L box 15 under Wittering sector control. After orbiting beacon they were given 'smack'. This proved fruitless but as they returned to the orbit a contact at 15,000 feet altitude, maximum range was obtained, followed by a visual of exhausts at 650 yards range slightly above and to starboard, heading SE at about 230mph. Pilot was told to investigate with extreme caution as it was probably friendly but owing to the darkness of the night, definite identification was difficult. The aircraft was chased from NW Bedford to Clacton and down to 10,000 feet and it was just on midnight when searchlights illuminated both aircraft. From sixty yards range it became possible to identify it as a Do217 with black crosses and a number visible on the green camouflaged underside of wings. Bandit made a diving turn across the nose of Mosquito and received a burst of cannon fire outside its port engine. It then straightened up and a second burst from 150 yards astern hit port wing behind the engine. Visual was then lost through searchlight dazzle at 6,000 feet altitude and the AI became unserviceable as a result of vibration from the cannon fire. Landed back at Wittering at 00.57 and this Do217 is claimed as damaged.

There was a rather intriguing comment on Bodien's combat report to the effect that his Mosquito was: "camouflaged in a special manner as devised by 151 Squadron", but this was not explained further. The term 'smack' is the order for the fighter to leave the beacon and head in the direction given towards a possible target, usually indicated by searchlight activity.

Three minutes later Fg Off Alex McRitchie and Flt Sgt E James (RO) followed Bodien down Wittering's runway to man S/L box 20 under Duxford sector control. This is their account of the sortie.

> Pilot orbited beacon at 12,000 feet. Given 'smack' and saw S/L beams fifteen miles away, which doused as Mosquito approached. Then proceeded in direction of more beams to the south and saw a flare dropped. Duxford control ordered pilot to return to beacon but he obtained permission to continue as he felt sure hostile aircraft were near. He was then warned of presence of a bogey. A blip was obtained at 10,000 feet altitude at maximum range. The blip spread

and pilot assumed this indicated bombs dropping. Several other blips followed which came down to 650 yards range and spread as in the first case but contact was lost again. Bombs were seen exploding and RO was warned by control of possibilities of a contact. A few seconds later an AI blip was obtained at maximum range and a visual of exhausts was obtained when it was at 500 yards range. Mosquito was at 7,000 feet altitude with the E/A, confirmed through binoculars by the RO as a Dornier Do217, jinking violently at 200mph, 500 feet above and in front, heading north. Opened fire from astern at 300 yards with a four-second burst that hit the fuselage and a fire broke out. E/A began diving turns and fired back ineffectually but failed to avoid a three-second burst that set the port engine on fire. Another three-second burst from 300 yards hit the wings and the bomber dived into the ground, exploding in a vivid white flash.

The Dornier F8+AP from II/KG40 crashed at 23.35 hours at Rectory Farm, Orwell near Cambridge and its crew of Fw A Witting, Ofw F Heusser, Ogefr A Hoppe and Uffz A Eysoldt all died in the engagement. This was McRitchie's last combat victory and promoted to Flt Lt, he was posted away on non-operational duties in April 1943. His name returned to prominence with a bang though in February 1944 when he took part in the Mosquito raid on Amiens prison, during which he was shot down and made POW.

In April 1943, 151 Squadron would leave Wittering for Colerne in the West Country from where it began intruder operations. From the beginning of that year, 151 Squadron's preparations for its transition from a defensive to an offensive role became evident from the increase in cross-country training flights and regular classroom sessions on navigation for the observers (RO), who would themselves become part of the navigator fraternity with the option of wearing the N brevet.

Other subtle improvements were filtering through 151 Squadron in January 1943, such as one or two Mosquitoes having their four Browning machine guns removed to make way for a new mark of AI equipment in the nose that it was believed would give better results.

This is a reference to the Mk VII version of AI, which had a small, moving dish scanner, mounted behind the nose cone of the aircraft, instead of the external arrowhead, fixed dipole antennae associated with the Mk IV and Mk V. Maximum range was now about seven miles and this apparatus represented a considerable improvement over previous versions, including allowing radar-guided interceptions to be made at altitudes below about two thousand feet, something earlier AI sets could not cope with. Sqn Ldr Lewis Brandon explains:

The performance of AI Mk IV depended largely on the altitude at which the fighter flew. The range in feet was roughly equivalent to the altitude at which the aircraft was being flown. The return echo from the ground was of course much stronger than from an aircraft. The lower the fighter flew, the further down the azimuth and elevation display tubes the ground return came... so that eventually at about 1,000 feet [altitude] it would blot out any other echoes.

AI Mk VII worked on the same principle as the Mk IV but the main difference was a more powerful, beamed transmission, which gave a greater maximum range and to a large extent eliminated or reduced the ground returns, thus improving interception of low-flying enemy aircraft such as mine-layers. So far as the RO was concerned the Mk VII was also easier to operate, as there was only one display tube for him to look at.

There was also a version in between these two: the Mark V, which has been mentioned in several of the preceding incidents. It had the same external antenna system as the Mk IV but with a different display tube arrangement – including one mounted on the top of the instrument panel for the pilot to view. Some were of the opinion that it only served to ruin his night vision, even if he had time to use it! The Mk V seems to have become generally disliked but was factory-installed in the first batches of Mosquitoes to be issued to squadrons, so 151 Squadron was among the first to experience this version. Lewis Brandon was involved with the testing of AI Mk VII at RAF Ford and then went on to serve with 157 Squadron, the first unit to receive the Mosquito NFII, and his opinion of the interim Mk V was quite scathing.

Fighter Command perpetrated a blunder almost as bad as the Turbinlite fiasco. They decided to install in our beautiful Mossies a wretched new Mark V AI that had all the faults of the Mk IV plus many of its own. It was a retrograde step even when compared to the Mk IV but compared to the Mk VII it was like going back to a divining-rod. There were times when I thought that if I took a hazel twig, persuaded a dachshund to lift a leg against it and then took it into the Mossie with me, it would lead me to a German more readily than would AI Mk V.

GCI radar was undergoing its own changes, too, with the rolling out of the permanent 'Final AMES' version to, among others, Langtoft and Neatishead. These installations became irreverently known to their staff as 'Happidrome', being named after the popular 1941 radio programme about an imaginary variety theatre where everything went wrong and nobody seemed to know what was going on. It was not long before those in the know about radar realised the similarities between the radio programme and the new Final GCI installations and thus the new brick and concrete operations buildings were dubbed accordingly. The development of the radar also allowed each GCI station to handle several interceptions simultaneously and four 151 Squadron Mosquitoes were sent off on the

23rd to test the system with Neatishead.

While it had become patently obvious, in view of the demise of the Turbinlite Havoc squadrons, that the Turbinlite concept was a dead duck, someone had conjured up the bright (!) idea of grafting a Turbinlite onto a Mosquito and wanted to try it out. 151 Squadron became involved with this venture when Flt Lt Henry Bodien and Fg Off Yeats flew down to Heston aerodrome on January 8 1943 to collect the prototype Turbinlite Mosquito W4087. That turned out to be a wasted journey because the aeroplane wasn't even ready when they arrived. Next day Bodien and Fg Off Rayner went down again and this time Bodien was able to fly the Turbinlite back to Wittering. Rayner should have brought back their NFII but had to wait for it to be repaired after a Polish airman very prettily taxied a Tiger Moth into it.

Temporarily, Sqn Ldr Stewart, OC 532 (Turbinlite) Squadron – mentioned in Chapter 5 and still clearing up at Hibaldstow – was sent down to Wittering where he and one of the remaining 532 Squadron ROs, Fg Off Andy Cunningham, were to put the Turbinlite Mosquito through its paces. This took them all of a day and then they were ferried back to Hibaldstow. The result of the test is unclear but W4087, which was officially on charge to 1422 Flight at Heston, was ordered to remain at Wittering. It does seem a terrible waste of the Mosquito's true potential to encumber it with all that gear but as there were no more Mosquito conversions, fortunately a veil seems to have been drawn quickly over the experiment.

There was little enemy activity in the sector until in the clear moonlight of January 15/16 the Luftwaffe attacked Lincoln with about twelve bombers. Four Mosquitoes were launched from Wittering but the only confirmed kill fell to Canadian new boy, Sgt Earl 'Tex' Knight and his RO Sgt Bill Roberts, who were on their first operational sortie.

Airborne at 20.25, twenty minutes later they came under Patrington GCI controller Sqn Ldr Donaldson who put them onto a bandit coming in over the Lincolnshire coast at 10,000 feet. Roberts lost his first contact on the AI Mk V set but the controller helped him to pick out another one at maximum range, and he brought Knight into visual range of a Dornier Do217 at 1,000 yards. Closing to 150 yards Sgt Knight fired a two-second cannon burst into the port engine just as the Dornier dived hard down to 4,000 feet, jinking right and left and even making complete circles in the process. As machine-gun fire from the Dornier's dorsal turret zipped over the Mosquito's wing tip, Knight's second burst hit the starboard engine and a third burst from a hundred yards range riddled the bomber's fuselage. Shedding debris and with both engines on fire it dived into the ground, exploding near Boothby Graffoe, ten miles north of Sleaford. The Dornier Do217E was wk nr 4308, U5+KR of II/KG2 and its crew, Lt Wolff, Ogefr Krusewitz and Uffzs Knorr and Semlitschka, all died.

This was the last combat of any significance by 151 Squadron before it moved out of Wittering to Colerne in April 1943. In its place, 141 Squadron was due to move into Wittering with Beaufighters but, although it would be available for defensive night fighting if called upon, its role was principally that of offensive intruder and bomber support duties.

So, although fighters from other sectors could be involved from time to time, now the defensive night fighter force policing not only The Wash corridor but also the rest of the East Midlands was concentrated at RAF Coleby Grange, the grass airfield a few miles south of Lincoln. We have seen from Peter McMillan's earlier combat the other Canadian night fighter unit, 409 Squadron under Wg Cdr Paul Davoud, had two spells at Coleby Grange, separated by 410 Squadron, with Mosquito NFIIs for its home defence work, between February and October 1943. It is also worth commenting that since night fighter cover was actually pretty thinly spread over this part of the country at this point in time, it was just as well that the Luftwaffe either did not seem to have worked that out or, more likely, was simply unable to exploit it.

During their respective spells at Coleby Grange there was little trade and both 409 and 410 Squadrons lost more aircraft in accidents than they had combats with the enemy. For example Sqn Ldr Bruce Hanbury and two airmen died when Beaufighter II, T3142, crashed at Leverton (Lincs) on March 27 1942 while Hanbury was demonstrating its stalling characteristics to a new 409 pilot. On January 13 1944, in their second spell, Beaufighter VI, MM918, suffered instrument failure during a night standing patrol and spun in at Wisbech, with the loss of its navigator Fg Off Harry Kirton. Even without the presence of the Luftwaffe, night fighter crews practiced constantly to improve their skills. Trying hard to keep on the tail of a colleague during a cine-gun exercise cost 410 Squadron and Flt Sgt William Cheropita and his RO, WO Neil Dalton, their lives when Mosquito NFII, DZ305, crashed near Sutton Bridge on August 27 1943.

It was from Coleby Grange that the 410 Squadron crew of Fg Off D Williams and his RO, Plt Off P Dalton, took off late on March 18 1943 to patrol the south of the county.

At about the same time, in bright moonlight, twenty-four enemy bombers were crossing the Norfolk coast at various points between Great Yarmouth and The Wash. They were a mixed force of Dornier 217s and Junkers 88s from Fliegercorps IX, including aircraft from KG2 and KG6. Their main targets were Norwich, Lowestoft and Great Yarmouth and night fighters operating from RAF Coltishall would be in action against these, too. But one or more of their number may have been seeking to disturb the sleeping outpost of the Central Gunnery School at RAF Sutton Bridge, or possibly RAF Wittering itself.

Another favourite target in that area was the decoy Q-site at Terrington Marsh, which was very successful in protecting RAF Sutton Bridge from receiving too much attention from enemy air attacks. Much to the chagrin of the villagers of Terrington St Clements – perhaps not unreasonably given that it was only 300 yards from the outskirts – it attracted an estimated 142 HE, 750 incendiaries and one oil bomb during the course of the war.

At 23.00 that night the air was rent by the thunderous 'crump' of two aerial mines and a phosphor bomb exploding near Sutton Bridge. Flashes lit up the dark landscape and a ground crew airman from CGS, LAC Douglas Broome, returning to camp after a night out, recalled how these were visible from many miles away across the flat Fens. As Fg Off Williams eased Mosquito NFII, HJ936, off Coleby's grassy acres, the Canadian had no inkling he would become involved in an unusual combat. Digby sector control instructed him to climb to 10,000 feet, steer south and then handed him over to Flt Lt Tuttle at Orby GCI. Almost immediately he was advised of a target at three miles range. The Mosquito easily had the acceleration to close in on the enemy and Dalton picked out a tell-tale blip on the AI Mk V set at two miles range. No sooner had he begun to give his pilot an interception course when another, closer, contact was discerned on the display.

This new target, at 1,000 yards range, slightly below and to port, was in a much better position for an attack. Williams nudged down the nose of HJ936 and the sinister shape of a Dornier Do217 floated into view, about 700 yards dead ahead.

The crew of the Dornier Do217, an E-4 wk nr 5523, U5+AH of I/KG2 – Uffzs Horst Toifel, Ludwig Petzold, Heinrich Peter and Ofw Georg Riedel, were clearly on the alert, for in the comparatively bright conditions they were quick to spot the danger stalking them. Before Williams could get close enough to put in a burst, the Dornier was thrown into a half-roll and tried to dive away from the Mosquito. Fg Off Williams slammed open the throttles and followed the Dornier down in its plummet towards the sanctuary of darkness 8,000 feet below where, no doubt, the pilot hoped the clutter from ground returns would hide the bomber from the Mosquito's prying radar eye.

Fg Off Williams could not close on the fleeing Dornier and with speed building up and the controls becoming heavy, he hauled back on the stick, pulling it out of the dive at 1,800 feet. But the Dornier continued to dive and with the pilot Toifel probably unable to regain control of his machine, it plunged into the ground to be consumed with the crew in a huge ball of fire. Williams obtained a fix from Orby GCI that put him in the vicinity of King's Lynn and was then recalled to base.

Fg Off Williams said in his combat report that at no time did he fire his guns and neither anti-aircraft fire nor searchlights were seen in the area of the engagement. The Observer Corps found wreckage and a parachute from a Do217 that had crashed near Ongar Hill, a few miles north of King's Lynn at the time of Williams' engagement. RAF intelligence officers found the main wreckage on sandbanks at the mouth of the Ouse river nearby. It would seem from the description of the combat that the enemy pilot lost control of the Dornier in a dive while trying to out-manoeuvre Williams' Mosquito. In another somewhat harsh judgement his claim for one E/A destroyed was amended to a half Do217 destroyed, shared with AA.

This encounter marked the beginning of the end of the Luftwaffe's offensive on the Midlands and East Anglia and there are, for example, no significant air attacks recorded against towns around The Wash during 1943. Furthermore apart from a few hit and run raids during 1944 that were mounted as part of the overall Operation Steinbock offensive, the Luftwaffe Kampfgruppen were a spent force over the region.

It has been seen that a significant role was played by GCI stations in bringing the night bomber menace under control and Orby GCI station near Skegness was typical of these installations. One night's action during the Steinbock period will give an idea of how what should rightly be viewed as a 'system' functioned when things hotted up. It will also be noted that the night fighter squadrons operating from Coleby Grange had been reorganised yet again, and after the departure of 409 in February, the Polish 307 Squadron was now in residence, flying Mosquitoes with the very latest radar equipment.

Operation Steinbock, sometimes referred to in Britain as the 'Baby Blitz', was Hitler's retaliation to heavy RAF raids on the German heartlands and was to be a concerted effort against London and other important British cities and ports. The raids, in which the Heinkel He177 aircraft – the Luftwaffe's only viable heavy bomber – featured prominently, began on January 21 1944 and continued on and off until May of that year. The Luftwaffe took a leaf out of the RAF's book and used pathfinder techniques and concealment behind anti-radar screens of air-dropped tin-foil strips – called 'düppel' by the Luftwaffe and 'window' by the RAF – during approaches to the British coast.

RAF Orby was now equipped with permanent AMES Mark VII GCI apparatus, with a rotating antenna producing a 360° representation on a cathode ray screen called a plan position indicator. Orby was one of the 'Happidrome' stations and could handle more than one interception simultaneously. Targets were usually picked up initially by coastal Chain Home or Chain Home Low radar stations and passed to filter rooms where a raid identity was allocated. If there was no IFF radio signal from the contact the target would be classified as hostile and passed to a GCI station into whose coverage the hostile was headed. The GCI station control staff would then direct one or more night fighters – most likely already on standing patrol and held ready, orbiting a beacon – to intercept it. Reinforcements could be called up as the tactical situation required.

After a series of eleven raids on London since the start of Steinbock, the Luftwaffe turned its attention to Hull. On the evening of March 19 1944 operations at Orby Happidrome began to heat up around 20.30 hours when enemy air activity seemed imminent. Controllers on duty that night were Fg Off Shimeld and Fg Off Board, working under the general control of Sqn Ldr Clark. Assistant controllers were Sgt Barratt and Cpl Tricker and the duty shift ran 17.30 on 19th to 08.30 on 20th. Weather conditions were good, with some cloud between 2,500 and 3,500 feet. The sun had set at 19.13 while the moon was in its last quarter and was due to rise at 04.23 next morning.

Shortly before 21.00 the Orby scanner picked up indications of a düppel screen being sown parallel to the coast about ninety miles east of Skegness and past experience had showed this was normally a prelude to a German air attack. Digby sector operations had already taken the decision to launch two Mosquito night fighters from the Polish 307 (Lwowski) Squadron at RAF Coleby Grange. Patiently orbiting beacon K at 15,000 feet altitude were 'Duckpond 18' a Mosquito XII, HK119, fitted with AI Mk VII, flown by Fg Off Jerzy Brochocki with Fg Off Henryk Ziolkowski as AI operator and 'Duckpond 31', a Mosquito XIII, HK522, flown by Fg Off Jerzy Pelka with Plt Off Gamsecki as AI operator. Once enemy activity was confirmed, Fg Off Dean at sector ops handed over control of both Mosquitoes to Orby GCI.

Now Orby controllers directed the fighters east towards the jamming screen while two more Mosquitoes ('Luncheons 42 and 48') were scrambled in support. Fg Off Shimeld took control of Duckpond 31 while Fg Off Board, operating from a separate interception room, controlled Duckpond 18. Interception tracking began at 21.10 at the forward edge of the düppel screen when it was about sixty miles off Skegness. Because of the problems posed by the düppel, all the interceptions were made head-on, i.e. from the west with the targets coming from the east, so as to keep the first two Mosquitoes to the west, and clear of the jamming screen.

The control situation was made more difficult because, in addition to the spurious düppel echoes and hostile aircraft, a variety of friendlies were also approaching the coast. Earlier this night, Mosquitoes had been sent to bomb Berlin, Düsseldorf and Aachen, while Stirlings had sown mines off the Dutch coast. Furthermore three 'Serrate' Mosquitoes were in action and four RCM and six OCU sorties had been flown or were in progress. It was going to be a busy night.

As the düppel screen moved nearer the English coast, Luncheons 42 and 48, themselves supported by another fighter, Luncheon 55, were brought back inland to orbit beacons in anticipation of the penetration by hostile aircraft. Duckpond 31 was now vectored towards a number of potential targets by GCI, six of which were acquired successfully by the Mosquito's radar operator. But there was no joy as one turned out to be friendly and the remainder were found to be düppel echoes. Simultaneously, Fg Off Board was attempting to guide Duckpond 18 to a series of interceptions. Henryk Ziolkowski actually picked out eight separate radar contacts over an area between the coast and sixty miles out. He homed in on three of these one after the other but he, too, was frustrated when Fg Off Brochocki visually identified each of them as friendlies. It is to be wondered what the crews of these RAF targets would have thought if they had known just how close they had come to the business end of a deadly night fighter.

Fg Off Brochocki's luck changed with the next contact. His radar operator picked up a solid return, at four miles range, from an aircraft inbound at 16,000 feet altitude about fifteen miles east of Skegness. Ziolkowski made a perfect approach to visual range and this target was unmistakeably a Heinkel He177 on a course of 290°. Brochocki wasted not a second more and opened fire, shells from his four 20mm cannon (no machine guns on this model) scoring hits on the underside of the fuselage. His second burst set the port engine on fire and the Heinkel was last seen diving vertically before the Poles lost sight of it. There was no time to waste in searching further as Board gave them yet more vectors – unfortunately all of which turned out to be either spurious or friendly contacts. All was not lost, though, because the Mosquito's gunfire had in fact been very effective. GCI logged the interception of the Heinkel at 21.46, in grid square G3887. Observer Corps post 'How 1' at Skegness recorded an aircraft crashing into the sea at 21.48 in a position estimated as grid square G38 and this sighting was taken as confirmation of the destruction of the Heinkel He177. Brochocki used 240 rounds of 20mm ammunition to despatch this big bomber.

Although the düppel screen, measuring some seventy miles long and fifty miles wide, eventually penetrated ten to twelve miles inland, there were no further interceptions coordinated by Orby GCI that night. By 22.50 hours all enemy activity in the area had ceased and the two active Mosquitoes were handed back to sector control. The Luftwaffe flew 131 sorties that night, of which about fifty are believed to have crossed the coasts of Lincolnshire and Norfolk. Most of the bombs intended for Hull seemed to fall in rural areas due, it is thought, to incorrect estimation of the wind strength, causing pathfinder flares to fall well to the south of the intended target. During the period covering the interceptions mentioned above, for example, over one hundred HE and an estimated 40,000 incendiary bombs were dropped in the Louth and Spilsby rural districts in Lincolnshire, causing little damage in the process.

Once again post-war research enables Brochocki and Ziolkowski's Heinkel to be identified as He177A-3, 6N+OK, of I/KG100, which failed to return having set out as part of the raid on Hull on March 19/20 1944. Its crew was Hptmn Muller, Ogefr Kuchler, Uffzs Gundner, Hockauff and Rodenstein and Ofw Utikal, all of whom were reported as missing in action.

That night, British night fighter defences shot down nine German aircraft, including the above Heinkel, and one other raider was brought down in Lincolnshire. This was Dornier Do217 M-1, U5+RL of I/KG2 shot down at Legbourne near Louth. The kill was achieved by Fg Off R L J Barbour in a Mosquito of 264 Squadron based at Church Fenton and controlled by Patrington GCI. It also proved to be a particularly memorable night for one 25 Squadron Mosquito crew, controlled by Happisburgh CHL and Neatishead GCI. Flt Lt Joe Singleton and his RO Fg Off Geoff Haslam shot down three Ju88s from KG30 during a devastating thirteen-minute period sixty miles out over the North Sea, NNE of Cromer on the Norfolk coast. The remaining four kills are believed to have been another Dornier Do217, two more Ju88s and a Ju188.

All in all it was a successful night for the defences since the Luftwaffe, with its diminishing numbers of bombers, could not sustain a loss rate of 7% like this for very long. To put this latter figure into some sort of context, RAF bomber loss rate, while averaging between 4% and 5% between January 1942 and August 1944, suffered peaks of 5.5% in June 1942, 6.3% in January 1944 and 6.5% in June 1944 before falling away to between 1% and 2% thereafter. Indeed the Steinbock raids petered out during May as the Luftwaffe cut its losses and saved its energy and resources for the expected invasion of France.

If the Luftwaffe's bombers were being contained, the same could not be said about the Fernnachtjäger – the intruders. It is well known that the Luftwaffe night fighter force was playing havoc with RAF Bomber Command operations over continental Europe and its thoughts turned once more to that other of its effective but underplayed tactics – the intruder.

Airfields in eastern England were, once again, about to feel the effect of this dangerous foe and the Fenland region would be littered with the evidence of success, even though it would be shortlived. After a gap of two years, RAF losses to intruders over England began to mount again. Luftwaffe success increased from August 1943 when even the Mosquito was vulnerable to attack in its take-off and landing phases, as Fg Off W Foster of 410 Squadron was to find out in the early hours of September 1. Fg Off Foster and Plt Off J Grantham were scrambled from Coleby Grange at 03.07 hours and while taking off had the fright of their lives as streams of red and silver flashes took them by surprise. Just east of Navenby, at 400 feet with only 150mph on the clock and navigation lights lit, the Mosquito was suddenly enveloped by a long burst – they thought it must have been almost twenty seconds – of firing. Foster doused the navigation lights but at that speed could take no evasive action. Either the enemy aircraft overshot or ran out of ammunition but the Mosquito, hit in the wings, rear fuselage and tailplane and with a shell through the main fuel tank, managed to keep flying. The elevators were damaged so Foster climbed gently to 10,000 feet, tested controls and hydraulics and with great relief all round was able to land back at Coleby Grange without further mishap. Later the same month a 57 Squadron Lancaster was shot down near Spilsby and another from 101 Squadron near Wickenby.

It was during the period April to June 1944 that Me410s of V/KG2 and II/KG51 really made their presence felt. Forty RAF and USAAF aircraft were shot down, with April bringing the highest loss of twenty-nine Allied aircraft. Patrolling in the vicinity of airfields was always likely to be the most effective method but not all victims fell within airfield boundaries, as the following incidents will show.

Tasked to attack a range of French communications targets in the run up to D-Day, on the night of April 18/19, RAF Bomber Command sent 273 Lancasters, including twenty-six aircraft from 115 Squadron, to bomb railway marshalling yards at Rouen. None were lost over the target but Me410s cruising East Anglian skies lay in wait for the returning force.

Lancaster LL667, KO-R, was caught as twenty-year-old Plt Off John

Birnie arrived in the vicinity of RAF Witchford. His aircraft was shot down at Coveney Fen north of Ely with the loss of all seven crew members. Shortly afterwards New Zealander Flt Lt Charlie Eddy MBE, circling the same area in LL867, A4-J, was shot down almost certainly by the same intruder. This Lancaster crashed north of Witchford, also with the loss of all seven airmen on board. Meanwhile, a little further west, having successfully attacked railway targets at Juvisy, Plt Off A E O'Beary and his Australian crew were heading home to RAF East Kirkby in Lancaster ND475. This 57 Squadron crew was shot down by an intruder two miles south-east of Whittlesey, killing all eight airmen on board.

It was not just the operational bombers that were caught either. On the night of the 14th a Stirling from 1654 CU was shot down during a practice sortie over the Bassingham bombing range west of Sleaford, while a pre-dawn local flying practice sortie on April 21/22 turned nasty for Plt Off James Banister, a pupil with 7 (P)AFU at RAF Peterborough. No doubt concentrating on his final approach to the airfield he was easy meat for an enemy fighter and his bullet-riddled Miles Master crashed into marshy ground just short of the airfield boundary. When removed to the nearby crematorium Banister himself was found to have sustained bullet wounds which were almost certainly fatal. Some thirty years later the remains of his aircraft were brought to the surface by an excavator working on a massive housing and industrial development project in the area, known as north Bretton, that was eventually to extend into the Westwood area, engulfing the whole of the former airfield. That same night, intruder activity by II/KG51 severely disrupted the American 2nd Air Division returning to its bases in Norfolk and Suffolk when at least fifteen bombers were brought down.

Intruders came back again on April 24/25 to harass RAF bombers returning from a raid on Karlsruhe. Making the long trek northwards from the English Channel to 76 Squadron's base at Holme-on-Spalding-Moor in Yorkshire, Plt Off Douglas Dibbins and his comrades in Halifax LK789 were picked off over Welney Wash near Ely. Plt Off Dibbins failed in his attempt to crash-land the Halifax and only the rear gunner, Flt Sgt Anderson, escaped alive.

A seven-day snapshot of the ORB for RAF Ashbourne and Darley Moor in Derbyshire, paints a picture of a well-ordered atmosphere at 42 Operational Training Unit. Weather and daylight permitting, day flying training was usually carried out between 07.00 and anywhere up to 20.00, then night flying from dusk to dawn, on a regular basis. The unit was equipped with the Armstrong Whitworth Albemarle twin-engine bomber. As might be expected at a training station, various inspections by Group staff are liberally sprinkled among the entries, for example: AVM Hollingsworth visited from 38 Group HQ for the purpose of interviewing officers desirous of permanent commissions. But the really big event, and the most detailed entry, came when an Air Ministry officer opened the brand new station cinema with the screening of the film *The Life and Death of Colonel Blimp*.

All-in-all this was pretty mundane stuff. But tucked away midst all this dull routine is an entry dated April 22, 1944.

> During night flying exercise [on 22/23] Albemarle V1610 was shot down by enemy aircraft. Three members of crew were killed. A court of inquiry was held on April 27 attended by the two survivors of the incident, which happened over south Lincolnshire.

The fate of Albemarle V1610 was attributed to it being shot down by an enemy intruder aircraft at 04.00 hours on April 23 1944 with the loss of three of its five crew. This was the only aircraft based at RAF Ashbourne to be lost to enemy action in WW2 and the following is a summary of the events of that terrible night, recalled by one of the survivors, Sgt J Davis, and published in the book *RAF Ashbourne*.

> The schedule for the night flying programme on April 22 was not a heavy one and flying did not actually begin until well after midnight. Albemarle V1610 was the second aircraft away at 02.30 hours. The outward leg of their journey began uneventfully enough and the crew settled down to carry out their individual duties. Sgt John Hutchinson, pilot, set a course that took it north to Yorkshire then south across Lincolnshire at an altitude of 2,500 feet. It was a routine low-level cross-country flight to allow the crew to become accustomed to low flying at night. Back in the navigator's seat Sgt Kenneth Rusby was checking the aeroplane's position and noted it was near one of the many bomber bases in Lincolnshire, which is believed to have been a reference to RAF Coningsby. Bomb aimer, Sgt Anthony Whittome, had his attention focused on the radar set while air gunner, Sgt Thorogood, sat in his turret scanning the night sky.
>   Around 04.00 Sgt Davis, the wireless operator, switched his set to 'radio only', thus isolating himself from the rest of the crew, as he knew it was about time for broadcast messages to be received in Morse code. Suddenly there was an almighty explosion in the port wing and the Albemarle rolled to starboard. Sgt Davis was thrown from his seat and sent sprawling to the floor. Recovering his senses, he regained his seat and plugged in his intercom cord to find out what had happened but by this time he could see the port wing was on fire. Then the pilot told them they had been hit and to abandon the aircraft.
>   Quickly removing his flying helmet, Davis clipped on his parachute and climbed up to the escape hatch just above his position. At first the hatch refused to budge and he struggled to free it with some degree of panic. Suddenly it came free, so he climbed out onto the starboard wing whereupon he was literally blown away and sent hurtling through the air, managing to pull the ripcord of his parachute

...er 23/24 minor damage was caused when a flying bomb exploded
...s Ferry near March. Eric Cox was a schoolboy back in those days
...years on, he recalled:

...ard this one fly over Wisbech when I was inside the Empire
...ma. The pulsating sound of its engine was loud and
...istakable and I hoped it would just keep going! It did, thank
...dness. Next day my pal Tom Mills told me he was just coming
...of the Hippodrome cinema when the air raid siren sounded and
...actually saw the exhaust flame go over the town, heading south-
...st. The flying bomb crashed south-west of March, in the area
...own as Botany Bay, between Bordinghouse and Bradley Farms.

...e night of October 13 1944 the engine of another V-1 cut out to the
...of Spalding but beyond rattling windows in the surrounding area, it
...ded harmlessly in Mathy Wood between Bourne and Thurlby. From
...osition of eye-witnesses (including this writer's father) the progress
...s V-1 could be charted by watching its fiery tail. It came in along the
...side of The Wash then inland, passing over Moulton village, across
...ling at about 500 feet, on towards the village of West Pinchbeck then
...ver the featureless fens to the west, before making its final plunge to
...on rising ground west of Bourne. There is some evidence that a
...nd V-1, the only one to have come down in Rutland, followed a similar
...k and exploded near Stocken Hall. Christmas Eve saw the unexpected
...al of an air-launched V-1 at Woodford, near Kettering, fortunately
...out causing casualties. One flying bomb carved out a crater adjacent
...astor and Ailsworth railway station (demolished in the late 1950s), on
...Nene Valley line to the west of Peterborough, on January 3 1945 but
...sed little damage and no casualties, while the final buzz-bomb incident
...he region is believed to have occurred at Irthlingborough, also near
...ttering, on January 13, 1945. If anything, these latter incidents suggest
...intended target might might have been Birmingham rather than the north of
...gland.

...Due to the presence of radar-assisted night fighter patrols and the
...erent practical difficulties of the air-launch technique, for both the
...dland region and the potential targets up north, the air-launched
...odlebug menace was thankfully ineffectual and short-lived. It was over
...the second week of January 1945, by which time about 1,200 V-1s had
...en air launched at England but with only about half that number being
...corded as crossing the coast between the Thames and Bridlington,
...orkshire. Over the whole air-launch campaign the Luftwaffe is said to
...ave lost, to all causes, a total of seventy-seven carriers out of an
...perational establishment of 101 aeroplanes. This is an extremely high rate
...f attrition but it should be weighed against the massive diversion of air and
...round resources and vast amount of work it took to reorganise the AA gun
...efences along the east coast.

at the same time. Descending in pitch darkness, without seeing
another parachute, he landed in a ploughed field 'somewhere in
Lincolnshire'.

The Albemarle had crashed in Kirton Fen, an arable farming area
between Boston and Coningsby. As he wrapped up the parachute his
eyes became accustomed to the inky blackness and he discerned
some shapes in the distance. Walking towards them, they turned out
to be cottages so he knocked on the door of one of them. It took some
time to reassure the occupants he was a British airman before they let
him inside where he was told the village was nearby. Setting out to
walk to it he met the local Home Guard patrol, which informed him
there was another airman in the village pub. This turned out to be Sgt
Thorogood. Both men were taken by ambulance to RAF Coningsby
where arrangements were made with RAF Ashbourne to collect them
in a Whitley aircraft. Later the airmen learned they were the only
survivors. Being hit so suddenly and at such a low altitude would
have given Sgt Hutchinson little time to do more than keep the
rolling aircraft on an even keel long enough for the rest of his crew
to try to bale out.

There is actually no conclusive evidence for a night fighter action in this
case although it is a commonly held view that V1610 fell victim to an
Me410 from KG51, a Luftwaffe intruder unit based at Évreux in France
that had been plaguing this area for some time.

In the late 1980s a recovery dig at the crash site by the Lincolnshire
Aircraft Recovery Group brought to a conclusion many years of
painstaking searching for this relatively unusual aircraft. Almost from the
date of the group's formation in the Boston area, members had been aware
of rumours that an aircraft had crashed in Kirton Fen during the war. One
local resident, the late Bernard Mastin, even described it as "an Albemarle
from Derby" and quoted the name "Tom Whittome" as a member of its
crew.

Other contacts guided LARG to the general area of the crash site and
metal detector searches confirmed the presence of metallic remains. Now
came the most difficult part: to obtain a licence from the Ministry of
Defence to excavate the site. In order to get permission it was necessary to
provide the MOD with the identity of the aeroplane so that appropriate
checks could be carried out, not least of which was to establish if the
presence of human remains or ordnance was likely to be involved. The
actual aircraft serial eluded the group for many a year until the local
resident's mention of a Derbyshire-based unit was linked with an incident
recorded in the book *Intruders Over Britain*. In the latter, V1610 was said
to have been shot down near Lowestoft, more than a hundred miles away.
Although this subsequently proved to be incorrect, armed with both this
valuable clue and the name of a possible crew member, the results of a
search in RAF Ashbourne ORB and a recent book about the station's

wartime history by Malcolm Giddings, finally allowed LARG to submit a successful request for a licence.

Excavated in August 1988, the site proved in the final analysis not to be amongst LARG's most rewarding of digs. Some of the propeller blades, one prop boss and several shattered engine cylinders and hydraulic components were the most substantial finds along with a tangle of pipes, cables, some metal skinning and a pile of generally unrecognisable wreckage. One of the most valuable lessons learned by LARG from this dig was that no matter how much research and paperwork is done, nothing can substitute for the vital item of local knowledge emerging at the right time.

There is, however, another school of thought that suggests the demise of the Albemarle may have been due to friendly fire. Bernard Mastin recounted tales circulating on the grapevine in those far off days of the aircraft being brought down, either as a result of a hit by an anti-aircraft shell fired from RAF Coningsby defences when the wrong colours of the day were fired, or by an RAF night fighter. A single explosion, such as described by the survivors, might lend weight to the AA shell theory, whereas gunfire from a night fighter might have had a more prolonged effect over a greater area of the aircraft structure and be recognisable as such by the crew. Even to this very day friendly fire incidents are emotive issues that officialdom tries to keep out of the limelight for as long as modern journalism allows.

The disruptive power of Luftwaffe intruders hit RAF and USAAF operational and training programmes alike, its psychological effect being of a much higher value to the Germans than the actual losses of aircraft – on either side – implies. Like the intruder campaign of 1940/41 though, just as its impact was really biting, the Luftwaffe was ordered to curtail II/KG51's activity so that it could be flung against the Allied invasion forces. Nine more months would elapse before the next and final, concerted intruder effort over England and whatever the outcome, it would be too little, too late.

Before the Luftwaffe's final fling in this region there was a period when it made an ingenious attempt to thwart defending night fighters and ground defences by air-launching Fieseler Fi 103 flying bombs, more commonly known as V-1 or doodlebug or even buzz-bomb, in the general direction of northern cities. The use of ground-launched V-1s began in July 1944 but it was not until later in the year that air-launched V-1s – perhaps the world's first 'stand-off' bomb – ostensibly aimed at Manchester, began to fall in the counties of Lancashire, Yorkshire and Cheshire during this new mode of attack on England. Twenty-five landed in the aforesaid counties, while many others landed ineffectually along the route to the north, in Lincolnshire, Nottinghamshire, Derbyshire and even one reported in County Durham. A few others fell haphazardly in the east Midlands including one of the very first of the air-launched variety at Creaton, a village between Kettering and Rugby, on July 22.

Heinkel He111-Hs were modified with [...] shackle at the wing root of the main spar and [...] V-1 was slung beneath the starboard wing, betw[...] the wing root, with stabilisers resting on the V-[...] Interrogation of crew members revealed that w[...] by, for example, removal of internal bomb stov[...] tank, the carriage of a V-1 caused no stability p[...] speeds by about 10mph. An electrical conne[...] fuselage, just above the wing root, to energise t[...] flying bomb.

Operational launch procedure was for the He1[...] in the general direction of the Lincolnshire and N[...] height, to evade detection by radar. To reach a l[...] Heinkel, climbing at about 110mph to 2,000 [...] vulnerable. Once launch altitude and bearing was r[...] dive brought the Heinkel's speed up to the 150mp[...] fly, the motor was ignited and when running, the[...] carrier then turning and diving for a low-level run b[...]

Although by intercepting radio messages the Briti[...] able to provide the RAF with advance warning of [...] since the launch sequence itself took only ten minu[...] there was very little time to effect a night fighter int[...] the carrier unit, III/KG3 (re-designated I/KG53 at [...] 1944), is reported to have lost only sixteen aircraft to n[...] September 1944 when the main air-launch phase beg[...] January 1945. Another account suggests that, durin[...] KG53 lost twenty-nine more aeroplanes to other cau[...] that failed to separate from their charges at the crucial [...] that probably flew into the sea during the wave-hugging[...]

Flying from RAF Church Fenton, 25 Squadron,[...] Mosquito Mk XVII then the Mk XXX, provides an exan[...] rate against this new night menace. This squadron cla[...] flying bombs between July and November 1944 and sev[...] most of the interceptions taking place well out into the [...] Lincolnshire and Norfolk coasts.

The east Midlands area, however, did not entirely esca[...] of this noisy raider. The actual number of V-1s flying over[...] seven are recorded as falling in the region itself, although [...] it is difficult to be sure of their intended targets.

First of these was seen to cross the coast at Skegne[...] September 19 1944. Observers plotted its fiery progress unt[...] a potato field at Tanvats, Metheringham Fen. Breaking a [...] windows, it blew a crater twenty-five feet in diameter and si[...] the target of 'strategic importance' destroyed amounted t[...] potatoes! From Observer Corps times of sightings and impac[...] this V-1 was calculated as 260mph. A few days later, on[...]

at the same time. Descending in pitch darkness, without seeing another parachute, he landed in a ploughed field 'somewhere in Lincolnshire'.

The Albemarle had crashed in Kirton Fen, an arable farming area between Boston and Coningsby. As he wrapped up the parachute his eyes became accustomed to the inky blackness and he discerned some shapes in the distance. Walking towards them, they turned out to be cottages so he knocked on the door of one of them. It took some time to reassure the occupants he was a British airman before they let him inside where he was told the village was nearby. Setting out to walk to it he met the local Home Guard patrol, which informed him there was another airman in the village pub. This turned out to be Sgt Thorogood. Both men were taken by ambulance to RAF Coningsby where arrangements were made with RAF Ashbourne to collect them in a Whitley aircraft. Later the airmen learned they were the only survivors. Being hit so suddenly and at such a low altitude would have given Sgt Hutchinson little time to do more than keep the rolling aircraft on an even keel long enough for the rest of his crew to try to bale out.

There is actually no conclusive evidence for a night fighter action in this case although it is a commonly held view that V1610 fell victim to an Me410 from KG51, a Luftwaffe intruder unit based at Évreux in France that had been plaguing this area for some time.

In the late 1980s a recovery dig at the crash site by the Lincolnshire Aircraft Recovery Group brought to a conclusion many years of painstaking searching for this relatively unusual aircraft. Almost from the date of the group's formation in the Boston area, members had been aware of rumours that an aircraft had crashed in Kirton Fen during the war. One local resident, the late Bernard Mastin, even described it as "an Albemarle from Derby" and quoted the name "Tom Whittome" as a member of its crew.

Other contacts guided LARG to the general area of the crash site and metal detector searches confirmed the presence of metallic remains. Now came the most difficult part: to obtain a licence from the Ministry of Defence to excavate the site. In order to get permission it was necessary to provide the MOD with the identity of the aeroplane so that appropriate checks could be carried out, not least of which was to establish if the presence of human remains or ordnance was likely to be involved. The actual aircraft serial eluded the group for many a year until the local resident's mention of a Derbyshire-based unit was linked with an incident recorded in the book *Intruders Over Britain*. In the latter, V1610 was said to have been shot down near Lowestoft, more than a hundred miles away. Although this subsequently proved to be incorrect, armed with both this valuable clue and the name of a possible crew member, the results of a search in RAF Ashbourne ORB and a recent book about the station's wartime history by Malcolm Giddings, finally allowed LARG to submit a successful request for a licence.

Excavated in August 1988, the site proved in the final analysis not to be amongst LARG's most rewarding of digs. Some of the propeller blades, one prop boss and several shattered engine cylinders and hydraulic components were the most substantial finds along with a tangle of pipes, cables, some metal skinning and a pile of generally unrecognisable wreckage. One of the most valuable lessons learned by LARG from this dig was that no matter how much research and paperwork is done, nothing can substitute for the vital item of local knowledge emerging at the right time.

There is, however, another school of thought that suggests the demise of the Albemarle may have been due to friendly fire. Bernard Mastin recounted tales circulating on the grapevine in those far off days of the aircraft being brought down, either as a result of a hit by an anti-aircraft shell fired from RAF Coningsby defences when the wrong colours of the day were fired, or by an RAF night fighter. A single explosion, such as described by the survivors, might lend weight to the AA shell theory, whereas gunfire from a night fighter might have had a more prolonged effect over a greater area of the aircraft structure and be recognisable as such by the crew. Even to this very day friendly fire incidents are emotive issues that officialdom tries to keep out of the limelight for as long as modern journalism allows.

The disruptive power of Luftwaffe intruders hit RAF and USAAF operational and training programmes alike, its psychological effect being of a much higher value to the Germans than the actual losses of aircraft – on either side – implies. Like the intruder campaign of 1940/41 though, just as its impact was really biting, the Luftwaffe was ordered to curtail II/KG51's activity so that it could be flung against the Allied invasion forces. Nine more months would elapse before the next and final, concerted intruder effort over England and whatever the outcome, it would be too little, too late.

Before the Luftwaffe's final fling in this region there was a period when it made an ingenious attempt to thwart defending night fighters and ground defences by air-launching Fieseler Fi 103 flying bombs, more commonly known as V-1 or doodlebug or even buzz-bomb, in the general direction of northern cities. The use of ground-launched V-1s began in July 1944 but it was not until later in the year that air-launched V-1s – perhaps the world's first 'stand-off' bomb – ostensibly aimed at Manchester, began to fall in the counties of Lancashire, Yorkshire and Cheshire during this new mode of attack on England. Twenty-five landed in the aforesaid counties, while many others landed ineffectually along the route to the north, in Lincolnshire, Nottinghamshire, Derbyshire and even one reported in County Durham. A few others fell haphazardly in the east Midlands including one of the very first of the air-launched variety at Creaton, a village between Kettering and Rugby, on July 22.

Heinkel He111-Hs were modified with strengthening plates and a shackle at the wing root of the main spar and for operational launches, the V-1 was slung beneath the starboard wing, between the engine nacelle and the wing root, with stabilisers resting on the V-1 wings to stop it wobbling. Interrogation of crew members revealed that with the aeroplane lightened by, for example, removal of internal bomb stowage and the fuselage fuel tank, the carriage of a V-1 caused no stability problems and only reduced speeds by about 10mph. An electrical connecting lead ran from the fuselage, just above the wing root, to energise the pulse jet motor of the flying bomb.

Operational launch procedure was for the He111 to cross the North Sea in the general direction of the Lincolnshire and Norfolk coasts at wave-top height, to evade detection by radar. To reach a launch point, though, the Heinkel, climbing at about 110mph to 2,000 feet, was at its most vulnerable. Once launch altitude and bearing was reached a further shallow dive brought the Heinkel's speed up to the 150mph needed for the V-1 to fly, the motor was ignited and when running, the V-1 was released, its carrier then turning and diving for a low-level run back to base.

Although by intercepting radio messages the British Y-service was often able to provide the RAF with advance warning of V-1 carrier operations, since the launch sequence itself took only ten minutes or so to complete, there was very little time to effect a night fighter interception. As a result, the carrier unit, III/KG3 (re-designated I/KG53 at the end of October 1944), is reported to have lost only sixteen aircraft to night fighters between September 1944 when the main air-launch phase began, and its close in January 1945. Another account suggests that, during the same period, KG53 lost twenty-nine more aeroplanes to other causes, including some that failed to separate from their charges at the crucial moment and others that probably flew into the sea during the wave-hugging phase.

Flying from RAF Church Fenton, 25 Squadron, at first with the Mosquito Mk XVII then the Mk XXX, provides an example of the success rate against this new night menace. This squadron claimed twenty-four flying bombs between July and November 1944 and seven launch aircraft, most of the interceptions taking place well out into the North Sea off the Lincolnshire and Norfolk coasts.

The east Midlands area, however, did not entirely escape the attentions of this noisy raider. The actual number of V-1s flying over is unknown but seven are recorded as falling in the region itself, although from their tracks it is difficult to be sure of their intended targets.

First of these was seen to cross the coast at Skegness at 04.15 on September 19 1944. Observers plotted its fiery progress until it exploded in a potato field at Tanvats, Metheringham Fen. Breaking a few farmhouse windows, it blew a crater twenty-five feet in diameter and six feet deep and the target of 'strategic importance' destroyed amounted to one acre of potatoes! From Observer Corps times of sightings and impact, the speed of this V-1 was calculated as 260mph. A few days later, on the night of

September 23/24 minor damage was caused when a flying bomb exploded at Floods Ferry near March. Eric Cox was a schoolboy back in those days but sixty years on, he recalled:

> I heard this one fly over Wisbech when I was inside the Empire cinema. The pulsating sound of its engine was loud and unmistakable and I hoped it would just keep going! It did, thank goodness. Next day my pal Tom Mills told me he was just coming out of the Hippodrome cinema when the air raid siren sounded and he actually saw the exhaust flame go over the town, heading south-west. The flying bomb crashed south-west of March, in the area known as Botany Bay, between Bordinghouse and Bradley Farms.

On the night of October 13 1944 the engine of another V-1 cut out to the west of Spalding but beyond rattling windows in the surrounding area, it exploded harmlessly in Mathy Wood between Bourne and Thurlby. From the position of eye-witnesses (including this writer's father) the progress of this V-1 could be charted by watching its fiery tail. It came in along the east side of The Wash then inland, passing over Moulton village, across Spalding at about 500 feet, on towards the village of West Pinchbeck then out over the featureless fens to the west, before making its final plunge to earth on rising ground west of Bourne. There is some evidence that a second V-1, the only one to have come down in Rutland, followed a similar track and exploded near Stocken Hall. Christmas Eve saw the unexpected arrival of an air-launched V-1 at Woodford, near Kettering, fortunately without causing casualties. One flying bomb carved out a crater adjacent to Castor and Ailsworth railway station (demolished in the late 1950s), on the Nene Valley line to the west of Peterborough, on January 3 1945 but caused little damage and no casualties, while the final buzz-bomb incident in the region is believed to have occurred at Irthlingborough, also near Kettering, on January 13, 1945. If anything, these latter incidents suggest the intended target might have been Birmingham rather than the north of England.

Due to the presence of radar-assisted night fighter patrols and the inherent practical difficulties of the air-launch technique, for both the Midland region and the potential targets up north, the air-launched doodlebug menace was thankfully ineffectual and short-lived. It was over by the second week of January 1945, by which time about 1,200 V-1s had been air launched at England but with only about half that number being recorded as crossing the coast between the Thames and Bridlington, Yorkshire. Over the whole air-launch campaign the Luftwaffe is said to have lost, to all causes, a total of seventy-seven carriers out of an operational establishment of 101 aeroplanes. This is an extremely high rate of attrition but it should be weighed against the massive diversion of air and ground resources and vast amount of work it took to reorganise the AA gun defences along the east coast.

Now the stage was set for the final act of the night air war.

Operation Gisela was to be a concerted mission over England by some 140 intruders drawn from NJGs 2, 3, 4 and 5. Planned at length but mounted at short notice, Gisela was launched on the night of March 3/4 1945. As Geoffrey Jones put it:

> On this date was the final fling of the Nachtjagd. As allied bombers withdrew after attacking Kamen and Ladbergen... more than one hundred German night fighters took to the air in pursuit. Two waves of Ju88s and He219s headed for targets in Norfolk, Suffolk, Lincolnshire and Yorkshire, with a full moon to help them.

Due to its location amid this aerial battlefield, Fenland night skies would resound once more to the noise of gunfire and the anguish of screaming, crashing aircraft. Even towns and villages came in for attention from the raiders; houses in Spalding and Holbeach (Lincs), being strafed by Ju88s that evening.

Among the luckier ones were two Halifaxes of 158 Squadron returning to RAF Lissett from Kamen. Both were attacked by enemy intruders over The Wash and although damaged they managed to evade their attackers and make it back to base. Meanwhile, a 214 Squadron electronic countermeasures (ECM) B-17 Fortress III, HB802, also survived an attack near Peterborough whereupon receiving radio orders not to land back at its base at RAF Oulton, the pilot followed pre-determined instructions for just such a situation and beat a hasty retreat to safer climes – way out west at RAF Brawdy.

Also returning from the Kamen raid Halifax NR229 of 466 Squadron (RAF Elvington) was mortally hit near Lincoln. Plt Off A E Schrank and his crew of six baled out over RAF Waddington while NR229 sailed majestically on to crash at Friskney Church End near Skegness but with unhappy consequences, as the local newspaper described.

> Tragedy came to the village of Friskney in the early hours of Sunday, when an aeroplane crashed on a cottage and reduced it to rubble. The roof was carried several yards away. The cottage was occupied at the time by George Severs aged seventy-two, his wife Mehetabel Severs aged fifty and their daughter Ruth aged fifteen. They were asleep at the time of the crash and both mother and daughter lost their lives. The husband, however, although injured was found alive and taken to hospital.

The other Free French bomber unit based at Elvington was 347 Squadron, which also lost a Halifax to the intruders that night when NA680 was set on fire over Sleaford and crashed at Anwick Grange. Five French airmen managed to bale out successfully: 2/Lt Giroud (bomb aimer), Aspirant L

Viel (navigator), Sgt C Pochont (WOp), Sgt P Charrière (MUG) and Sgt Hemery (RG), but the pilot Capitaine Laucou and his flight engineer, Sgt LeMasson, went down with the aeroplane.

Accounts vary as to how many enemy aircraft were committed to Gisela – estimates ranging from 100 to 200 – and what were the material losses on that eventful night. Between midnight and 04.00 on the 4th it is believed that as many as forty-eight bombers may have been attacked by enemy intruders, with at least twenty RAF aeroplanes being destroyed – eight of these in Lincolnshire – and fourteen damaged. The Luftwaffe is known to have lost three aircraft over England but records indicate a further nineteen were missing or destroyed and twelve damaged while returning to bases on the continent.

In the region covered by this story it was the Luftwaffe that drew final blood in the battle. On the night of March 20/21 1945, Halifax 'U-Uncle' from 1665 Heavy Conversion Unit at RAF Tilstock, was shot down between Wittering and Peterborough by an intruder while the pilot, Fg Off Peter Nettlefield, was on a cross-country training flight. Nettlefield, his flight engineer and an air gunner died, but six other airmen on board escaped unhurt.

With the cessation of hostilities just a couple of months later, the night sky around The Wash became eerily quiet. No more distant thunder of bombers setting out or returning. No more staccato bursts of gunfire flashing in a moonlit sky. No more fiery trails across the night sky. The bombers and night fighters were silent.

It would be difficult – if not pointless – to attempt to quantify the night-time conflict described in this story in terms of numbers in order to determine, in some simplistic way, who appeared to win or lose. What emerges beyond any doubt is the vital role of teamwork among the aircrews themselves – pilots, air gunners and AI operators – and as time progressed, controllers manning the radar stations on the ground. This is not to forget, of course, the role played by searchlights, AA and the Observer Corps. However, when night combat is brought into cold focus it comes down to a 'one against one' duel and we have seen how that produced a winner and a loser – usually. But what has also been shown of course is that such an outcome applied equally to the RAF and the Luftwaffe – because in a wartime night sky there was no place for chivalry.

APPENDIX 1

Imperial German Naval Zeppelin incursions over the Midlands region in WW1

Raid date	Airship	Commander
19/20 Jan 1915	L4	Kptlt Magnus von Platen-Hallermund
8/9 Sep 1915	L13	Kptlt Heinrich Mathy
31 Jan/1 Feb 1916	L11	Kptlt Horst Freiherr Treusch von Buttlar-Brandenfels
	L13	Kptlt Heinrich Mathy
	L14	Kptlt Alois Böcker
	L15	Kptlt Joachim Breithaupt
	L19	Kptlt Odo Loewe
	L20	Kptlt Franz Stabbert
	L21	Kptlt Max Dietrich
31 Jul/1 Aug 1916	L14	Hptmn Kuno Manger (army officer seconded to navy)
	L16	Kptlt Erich Summerfeldt
2/3 Sep 1916	L14	Hptmn Kuno Manger
23/24 Sep 1916	L13	Kptlt Franz Georg Eichler
1/2 Oct 1916	L14	Hptmn Kuno Manger
	L21	Oblt-z-S Kurt Frankenberg
	L34	Kptlt (Reserve) Max Dietrich
27/28 Nov 1916	L21	Oblt-z-S Kurt Frankenberg
19/20 Oct 1917	L41	Hptmn Kuno Manger
	L44	Kptlt Franz Stabbert
	L45	Kptlt Waldemar Kolle
	L47	Kptlt Max von Freudenreich
	L52	Oblt-z-S Kurt Friemel
	L55	Kptlt Hans-Kurt Flemming
12/13 Apr 1918	L62	Hptmn Kuno Manger
5/6 Aug 1918	L70	Kptlt Johannes von Lossnitzer (with Fregattenkapitän Peter Strasser aboard)

Raid Summary	1915	1916	1917	1918	Total Raids	Sorties
Midland Region	2	6	1	2	11	25
England	20	23	7	4	54	202

Note: On several of the above dates other naval Zeppelins flew sorties over the UK that are not included in the table because their flight profiles are not relevant to the area covered by the narrative.

Map showing the tracks of German Naval Zeppelins during the first airship raid on Britain on the night of January 19/20 1915

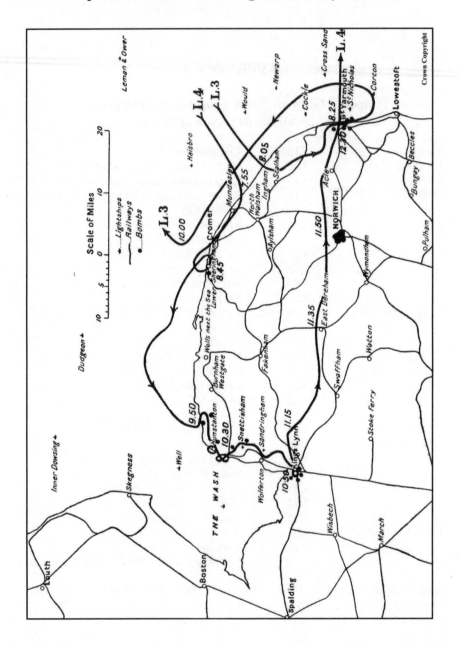

Map showing the tracks of German Naval Zeppelins inbound over Lincolnshire and Norfolk during the Silent Raid on the night of October 19/20 1917

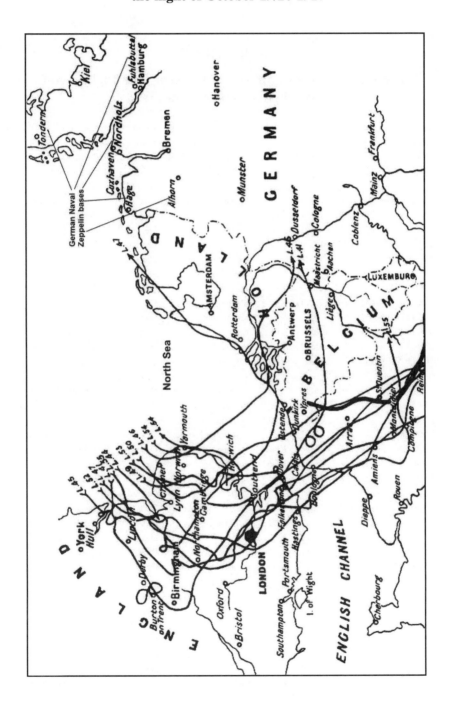

APPENDIX 2

Interceptions made by aircraft of Wittering and Digby sector night fighter squadrons in WW2

Date	Sqn	A/c	E/A	Unit	Night fighter crew	Claim	Location
18/19 Jun 40	23	Bl	He111		Close/Karasek	Dam	Near King's Lynn
18/19 Jun 40	23	Bl	He111	KG4	Duke-Woolley/Bell	Des	Blakeney
18/19 Jun 40	23	Bl	He111	KG4	O'Brien/Little	Des (shared 19)	Fleam Dyke (Cambs)
17/18 Aug 40	29	Bl	He111		Rhodes/Gregory	Des	Sea, Cromer Knoll
24/25 Aug 40	29	Bl	He111	KG55	Braham/Wilsden	Des	Humber
2 Oct 40	151	H	He111	KG53	I Smith	Des	Chapel St Leonards
13/14 Oct 40	29	Bl	u/i		Roberts/Mallett	Dam	Grantham
7 Nov 40	151	H	Do17		Blair and Copeland	Dam	Skegness
14/15 Nov 40	29	Bl	u/i		Kells/Lilley	Dam	Swaffham
15/16 Jan 41	151	H	Do17	KG3	Stevens	Des	Brentwood
15/16 Jan 41	151	H	He111	KG53	Stevens	Des	Canvey Island
15/16 Jan 41	151	H	Ju88		McMullen	Dam	Cromer
15/16 Jan 41	151	H	Ju88		Blair	Dam	Spalding
4 Feb 41	151	D	Do17	KG2	Bodien/Jonas	Des	Weldon (Northants)
9/10 Feb 41	151	H	Ju88	KG1	Wagner	Des (shared AA)	Mildenhall
12/13 Mar 41	151	H	Ju88		Stevens	Dam	Orfordness
13/14 Mar 41	29	B	Do17	KG2	Braham/Ross	Des	Sea off Wells (Norf)
13/14 Mar 41	29	B	Ju88	NJG2	Widdows/Ryall	Des	Louth
14/15 Mar 41	29	B	He111	KG1	Gibson/James	Des	Sea off Skegness
8/9 Apr 41	151	H	He111	KG27	Stevens	Des	Wellesbourne
8/9 Apr 41	151	H	He111	KG55	Stevens	Des	Desford
8/9 Apr 41	151	D	He111	KG55	McMullen/Fairweather	Des (shared AA)	Windsor
8/9 Apr 41 (2)	151	D	He111		Wagner/Sidenberg	Dam (2)	Coventry
9/10 Apr 41	25	B	Ju88	NJG2	Bennett/Curtis	Des	Langham (Rutland)
9/10 Apr 41	151	D	He111	KG27	Bodien/Jonas	Des	Birmingham
9/10 Apr 41	151	D	He111		Staples/Parkin	Prob	Birmingham
9/10 Apr 41	151	D	Ju88	KG77	McMullen/Fairweather	Des	Bramcote (Warks)
9/10 Apr 41	151	D	Ju88	KG1	Darling/Davidson	Des (shared AA)	Whitwell (Herts)
10/11 Apr 41	151	H	He111	KG55	Stevens	Des	Kettering
10/11 Apr 41	151	H	Ju88	KG1	Stevens	Des	Murcott (Oxon)
20 Apr 41	151	H	He111	KG4	Stevens	Des	Chatham
23/24 Apr 41	29	B	Do215		Gibson/James	Dam	Boston
2/3 May 41	151	D	Ju88	KG30	Edmiston/Beale	Des	Weybourne (Norf)

Date	Sqn		Type	Unit	Crew	Result	Location
3/4 May 41	25	B	He111	KG53	Hill/Hollis	Des	Sharrington (Norf)
3/4 May 41	151	D	He111		Bodien/Wrampling	Des	Sea off N Norfolk
4/5 May 41	25	B	Ju88	KG1	Atcherley/ Hunter-Tod	Des	Bourne (Lincs)
4/5 May 41	25	B	Ju88		Hollowell/Crossman	Prob	N of The Wash
4/5 May 41	25	B	Ju88		Hollowell/Crossman	Dam	The Wash
4/5 May 41	25	B	u/i		Pleasance/Bent	Dam	Aldeburgh (Suffolk)
5/6 May 41	25	B	Ju88		Holloway/Pound	Prob	Near Watton (Norf)
7/8 May 41	25	B	Do17	NJG2	Thompson/Britain	Des	N of Boston
7/8 May 41	25	B	He111		Pleasance/Bent	Dam	Near Skegness
7/8 May 41	25	B	Ju88		Hill/Hollis	Dam	Holt (Norf)
7/8 May 41	25	B	Ju88		Herrick/Lewis	Prob	S of Hull
7/8 May 41	151	H	He111	KG4	Stevens	Des	Hull
7/8 May 41	151	H	He111	KG55	Stevens	Des	Hull
8/9 May 41	25	B	Do17		Hollowell/Crossman	Dam	SW of Hull
8/9 May 41	25	B	Do17		Pleasance/Bent	Prob*	Sea off Wells (Norf)
8/9 May 41	25	B	He111		Thompson/Britain	Dam	N Norfolk coast
8/9 May 41	25	B	Ju88		Holloway/Pound	Dam	Grantham
9/10 May 41	25	B	Fw200		Picknett/Sellick	Dam*	The Wash
10/11 May 41	25	B	He111		Pleasance/Bent	Dam	Sea off Wells (Norf)
10/11 May 41	25	B	He111		Thompson/Britain	Dam	Skegness
10/11 May 41	151	H	He111	KG28	Stevens	Des	London
10/11 May 41	151	H	He111		Stevens	Prob	London
10/11 May 41	151	D	He111	KG53	Copeland/Sampson	Des	Gravesend
10/11 May 41	151	D	He111	KG55	McMullen/ Fairweather	Des	Withyham (Sussex)
10/11 May 41	151	H	He111		I Smith	Dam	Southend
16/17 May 41	25	B	He111		Hollowell/Crossman	Des	Cromer
16/17 May 41	151	D	Do17Z		Edmiston/Beale	Dam	Melton Mowbray
16/17 May 41	151	D	He111		Edmiston/Beale	Dam	SE of Derby
16/17 May 41	151	D	He111		Edmiston/Beale	No claim	E of Coventry
4/5 Jun 41	25	B	He111	KG4	Gigney/Charnock	Des	South Reston (Lincs)
4/5 Jun 41	25	B	He111	KG27	Hollowell/Crossman	Des	The Wash
13/14 Jun 41	25	B	Ju88	NJG2	Pleasance/Bent	Des	Narford (Norf)
13/14 Jun 41	25	B	Ju88	NJG2	Thompson/Britain	Des	The Wash
13/14 Jun 41	151	H	He111		Stevens	Des	Royston (Cambs)
16/17 Jun 41	25	B	u/i		Atcherley/Hunter-Tod	Des	Sea off Sheringham
21/22 Jun 41	25	B	Ju88	NJG2	Herrick/Yeomans	Des	Deeping St James
21/22 Jun 41	151	D	Ju88		Edmiston/Beale	Des**	Sea 5m E of Cromer
4/5 Jul 41	25	B	Ju88		Atcherley/ Hunter-Tod	Des	Sea off Wells (Norf)
4/5 Jul 41	151	D	He111		Edmiston/Beale	Prob	Leicester/ Leamington
5/6 Jul 41	151	H	Ju88		Stevens	Des	Sea off Happisburgh
11/12 Sep 41	151	D	Do215		Haviland/Stolz-Page	Dam	Luffenham
1/2 Oct 41	25	B	Ju88		Pleasance/Britain	Prob	Off Wells (Norf)
16/17 Oct 41	151	H	Ju88		Stevens	Des	Sea off Gt Yarmouth
22/23 Oct 41	151	H	Ju88	I/606	Stevens	Des (shared 256)	Mkt Drayton (Salop)

Date	Sqn	A/c	E/A	Unit	Crew	Result	Location
31 Oct 41	151	D	Ju88		McRitchie/Sampson	Des	Sea off Gt Yarmouth
31 Oct 41	151	D	Ju88		McRitchie/Sampson	Dam	Off Gt Yarmouth
1/2 Nov 41	409	B	Do217		Davoud/Carpenter	Des	Sea off Skegness
15/16 Nov 41	151	D	Ju88	1/106	McRitchie/Beale	Des	Sea off Gt Yarmouth
29/30 May 42	151	M	Do217		Wain/Grieve	Dam	The Wash
29/30 May 42	151	M	He111		Pennington/Donnett	Dam	Nth Sea off Lincs/Norf
24/25 Jun 42	151	M	Do217		I Smith/Kerr-Sheppard	Dam	Nth Sea off Lincs/Norf
24/25 Jun 42	151	M	Do217		Darling/Wright	Dam	Nth Sea off Lincs/Norf
24/25 Jun 42	151	M	He111		I Smith/Kerr-Sheppard	Des	Nth Sea off Lincs/Norf
24/25 Jun 42	151	M	He111		I Smith/Kerr-Sheppard	Prob	Nth Sea off Lincs/Norf
24/25 Jun 42	151	M	He111		Wain/Grieve	Des	Nth Sea off Lincs/Norf
25/26 Jun 42(2)	151	D	Do217		Robertson/Beale	Dam (2)	Near Coltishall
26/27 Jun 42	151	M	Do217	KG2	Moody/Marsh	Des	The Wash
29/30 Jun 42	151	D	Ju88		Robertson/Beale	Dam	March (Cambs)
21/22 Jul 42	151	M	Do217	KG2	Fisher/Godfrey	Des	Sea off Humber
23/24 Jul 42	486	H	Do217		Sweetman	Des (shared 409)	Fleet Fen
23/24 Jul 42	409	B	Do217	KG40	McMillan/Shepherd	Des (shared 486)	Fleet Fen (Lincs)
23/24 Jul 42	409	B	Do217	KG2	McMillan/Shepherd	Des	Crashed at Dutch base
27/28 Jul 42	151	M	Do217	KG2	Pennington/Donnett	Des	Off N Norfolk coast
27/28 Jul 42	151	M	Do217	KG2	Fielding/Paine	Prob	Off N Norfolk coast
30/31 Jul 42	151	M	Do217	KG2	McRitchie/James	Des	Nth Sea off The Wash
30/31 Jul 42	151	M	Do217	KG2	McRitchie/James	Des	Holme, Peterborough
17/18 Sep 42	151	M	Do217	KG2	Bodien/Brooker	Des	Fring, Norfolk
15/16 Jan 43	151	M	Do217	KG2	Knight/Roberts	Des	Boothby Graffoe (Lincs)
18/19 Mar 43	410	M	Do217	KG2	Williams/Dalton	Des (shared AA)	In Wash off K Lynn
12/13 Jul 43	410	M	Do217		Lawrence/Wilmer	Des	10m E of Humber
19/20 Mar 44	307	M	He177	KG100	Brochocki/Ziolkowski	Des	Sea off Skegness

Notes: A/c: Bl = Blenheim, D = Defiant, H = Hurricane, B = Beaufighter, M = Mosquito

* Claimed as destroyed, but not seen to crash
** Up and down at Coltishall

The following sorties were made by aircraft from squadrons based at: (a) Kirton in Lindsey, (b) Coltishall, (c) Church Fenton, (d) Honiley, but the victims fell within the sectors covered by this book.

2/3 Jul 42	303(a)	Ju88	2/106	Wunsche and Popek	Des	Near Spilsby (Lincs)
2/3 Jul 42	303(a)	Ju88	2/106	Kolecki and Rokitnicki	Des	Near Spilsby (Lincs)
7/8 Aug 42	68(b)	Do217	KG2	Cleaver/Nairn	Des	Revesby (Lincs)
22/23 Aug 42	25(c)	u/i		Alington/Keith	Dam	The Wash
23/24 Aug 42	25(c)	Do217		Singleton/Bradshaw	Dam	S of Spalding
23/24 Aug 42	25(c)	Do217		Pleasance/Britain	Des	Sea off Skegness
23/24 Aug 42	255(d)	Do217	KG2	Wyrill/Willins	Des	E of King's Lynn

APPENDIX 3

Explanatory notes and diagram for AI Mk IV

(reproduced by kind permission of Airlife Publishing Limited)

AI Mk IV was the first mass-produced airborne radar set and was relatively unsophisticated. The operating frequency was 190 to 195 MHz with a wavelength of 1.5 metres. The on-board equipment comprised a receiver, transmitter, control panel, modulator, indicator unit and a system of fixed dipole aerials. On the Beaufighter, the latter consisted of a 'double arrowhead' shaped transmit aerial on the nose of the aircraft, a pair of azimuth aerials protruding above and below the leading edge of each wing between the machine guns and the wingtip and a pair of elevation aerials above and below the wing surface near the roundel on the starboard side.

The indicator (display) unit at the RO's position consisted of two cathode ray tubes (CRT) displaying elevation and azimuth bearings respectively (see diagram). The three items on the diagram are the transmitter pulse (the root of the 'Christmas tree'), the target blip somewhere on the time trace (the trunk of the tree) and the ground return (the branches of the tree).

It is evident from the diagram that a target could not be detected at any range beyond the ground returns. The detection range was related to the altitude of the aircraft. Thus at 20,000 feet altitude the range would be just under four miles, which was also about the limiting range of the set. The minimum range at which the AI operator could see a target blip on the time trace was about 400 feet. At ranges closer than this the target merged with the transmission pulse at the 'root' of the tree. Furthermore, at altitudes below 1,000 feet the ground return would swamp the tubes.

It should be noted that the two small CRTs of the AI Mk IV had no scales or calibration marks printed on them to help the operator. His directions and running commentary of what was happening in the night sky were based entirely on his estimate of where the target was in relation to his own aircraft – in a constantly changing situation. It was guesswork, based on experience, as to how many degrees the target was to port or starboard in the azimuth plane or how many feet the target was above or below the night fighter in the elevation plane and how many feet it was in front of them. In the air defence role the night fighter crew would rely on GCI to get them within AI range of the target.

The diagrams of a typical interception are simplistic representations of what the AI operator would see. In reality, the picture would be confused by spurious echoes and interference and would actually present a shimmering, pulsating mass of green lines and signals, from which he would have to identify the one that mattered. An AI operator might spend up to four hours peering at this display. If he took a break he might miss the one and only contact of the sortie. That is a measure of what it took to be a successful AI operator.

Respresentation of the display screens of A1 Mk IV

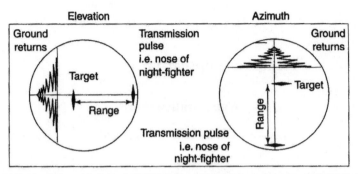

1. Night-fighter flying at height of 20,000 ft. Target blip ahead at range of 18,000 ft, 20 degrees to starboard and 20 degrees below. (The 'minimum range' diamond at the root of the 'Christmas tree' may be taken to represent the nose of the night-fighter).

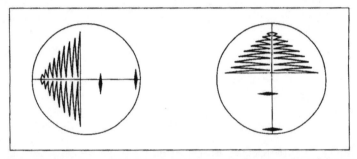

2. The night-fighter has now lost height down to 13,000 ft. The target is still ahead, but the range has decreased to 8,000 ft. The target is now 20 degrees on the port side, and 10 degrees below.

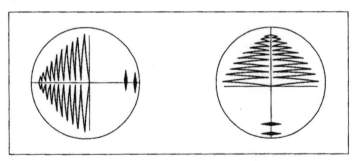

3. The night-fighter has now come down to a height of 11,000 ft – the target's range is 1,000 ft, dead ahead and 15 degrees above the night-fighter . . . closing slowly, the pilot should soon obtain 'a visual' as the blip disappears into the 'minimum range' diamond at the 'root' of the 'Christmas tree'.

APPENDIX 4

Comparative ranks

RAF	Luftwaffe	Army	Royal Navy	German Navy
Group Captain	Oberst	Colonel	Captain	Kapitän-zur-See
Wing Commander	Oberstleutnant	Lieutenant Colonel	Commander	Fregattenkapitän
Squadron Leader	Major	Major	Lt Commander	Korvettankapitän
Flight Lieutenant	Hauptmann	Captain	Lieutenant	Kapitänleutnant
Flying Officer	Oberleutnant	Lieutenant	Sub-Lieutenant	Oberleutnant-zur-See
Pilot Officer	Leutnant	2nd Lieutenant	Acting Sub-Lt	Leutnant-zur-See
Warrant Officer	Hauptfeldwebel	Warrant Officer 1		
Flight Sergeant	Oberfeldwebel	Staff Sergeant		
Sergeant	Feldwebel	Sergeant		
Senior Aircraftman	Unteroffizier	Corporal		
Leading Aircraftman	Obergefreiter	Lance Corporal		
Aircraftman 1st Class	Gefreiter	Private		
Aircraftman 2nd Class	Flieger	Private		

APPENDIX 5

Maps showing Group and Sector boundaries in WW2

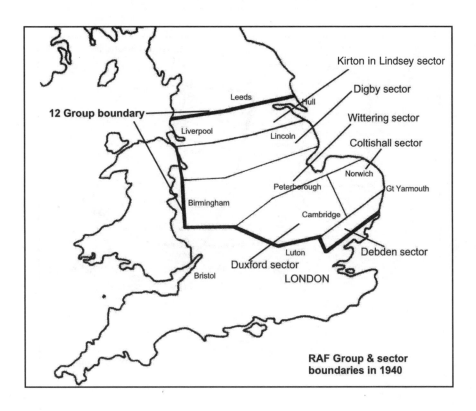

Kirton in Lindsey sector

Digby sector

12 Group boundary

Leeds

Hull

Wittering sector

Liverpool

Lincoln

Coltishall sector

Norwich

Peterborough

Gt Yarmouth

Birmingham

Cambridge

Luton

Debden sector

Duxford sector

Bristol

LONDON

RAF Group & sector boundaries in 1940

APPENDIX 6

Map showing locations of Fg Off R P Stevens' air victories

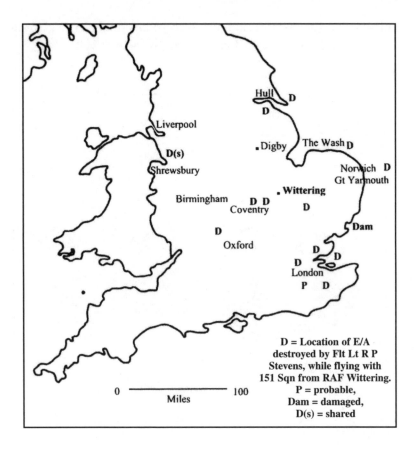

D = Location of E/A
destroyed by Flt Lt R P
Stevens, while flying with
151 Sqn from RAF Wittering.
P = probable,
Dam = damaged,
D(s) = shared

APPENDIX 7

Map showing the distribution of interceptions made by Digby and Wittering night fighter squadrons in WW2

APPENDIX 8

Abbreviations used in text

1/Lt	First Lieutenant
2/Lt	Second Lieutenant
AA	Anti-aircraft gun(fire)
AC	Aircraftman
AC1	Aircraftman First Class
ACM	Air Chief Marshal
AG	Air Gunner
AHB	Air Historical Branch (of MOD)
AI	Airborne Interception (radar)
Air Cdre	Air Commodore
AM	Air Marshal
AMES	Air Ministry Experimental Station (radar)
AOC	Air Officer Commanding
Aus	Australia(n)
AVM	Air Vice-Marshal
BAT	Beam Approach Training
BG	Bombardment (Bomb) Group (US)
Can	Canada(ian)
Capt	Captain
CBE	Commander of the Order of the British Empire
CGS	Central Gunnery School
C-in-C	Commander-in-Chief
CO	Commanding Officer
Cpl	Corporal
CU	Conversion Unit
DH	de Havilland
E/A	Enemy aircraft
Fg Off	Flying Officer
Flt	Flight
Flt Lt	Flight Lieutenant
Flt Sgt	Flight Sergeant
Fr	France (French)
FRS	Fellow of the Royal Society
FTS	Flying Training School
Fw	Feldwebel

GCI	Ground Controlled Interception
Gp Capt	Group Captain
HCU	Heavy Conversion Unit
HD	Home defence
HE	High explosive
Hptmn	Hauptmann
Kptlt	Kapitänleutnant
KG	Kampfgeschwader (Bomber Wing)
LAC	Leading Aircraftman
Lt	Lieutenant or Leutnant
Lt-z-S	Leutnant-zur-See
Maj	Major
Mk	Mark
MOD	Ministry of Defence
MU	Maintenance Unit
n/a	not applicable
n/k	not known
Nav/Rad	Navigator (Radio), navigator/airborne radar operator
NF	Night fighter
NFT	Night flying test
NJG	Nachtjagdgeschwader (Night Fighter Wing)
NZ	New Zealand(er)
Oblt-z-S	Oberleutnant-zur-See
Ofw	Oberfeldwebel
Ogefr	Obergefreiter
ORB	Operational Record Book
(P)AFU	(Pilot) Advanced Flying Unit
Plt Off	Pilot Officer
PPI	Plan Position Indicator
PRU	Photographic Reconnaissance Unit
Q-site	Decoy airfield lighting installation
R/T	Radio Telephony
RCM	Radio countermeasures
RFC	Royal Flying Corps
RLG	Relief landing ground
RNAS	Royal Naval Air Service
RO	Observer (Radio), (airborne radar operator)
RR	Rolls-Royce
S/Lt	Sous Lieutenant (Fr)
S/M	Sous Matelot (Fr)
Sgt	Sergeant

S/L	Searchlight
Sqn	Squadron
Sqn Ldr	Squadron Leader
Sub Lt	Sub-Lieutenant
u/i	unidentified
Uffz	Unteroffizier
wk nr	werke nummer (production number)
W/T	Wireless Telegraphy
Wg Cdr	Wing Commander
WingCo	,, ,,
WIDU	Wireless Intelligence Development Unit
WO	Warrant Officer
WOp/AG	Wireless Operator/Air Gunner

BIBLIOGRAPHY

Allen, Michael. (1999) *Pursuit Through Darkened Skies*: Airlife Publishing Ltd
Bates, H E. (1952) *The Stories Of Flying Officer 'X'*: Jonathan Cape
Beckett, Constance Mary. (1995) *The Sky Sweepers*: Regal Life Ltd
Bevis, Trevor. (1978) *From Out Of The Sky – March and WW2*: Westrygate Press
Blackamore, Ian. (2002) *Metal Birds, Vols 1 to 3*: Blackamore.
Bowen, E G. (1987) *Radar Days*: Adam Hilger
Bowman, Martin W. (1995) *The Men Who Flew The Mosquito*: Patrick Stephens Ltd
Bowyer, Chaz. (1980) *Fighter Command 1936-1968*: J M Dent & Sons Ltd
Bowyer, Michael J F. (1986) *Air Raid!*: Patrick Stephens Ltd
Braham, J R D. (1985) *Scramble!*: Wm Kimber & Co Ltd
Brandon, Lewis. (1992) *Night Flyer*: Goodall Publications
Chisholm, Roderick. (1953) *Cover Of Darkness*: Chatto & Windus
Clayton, Aileen. (1993) *The Enemy Is Listening – Story Of 'Y' Service*: Crécy Books Ltd
Cole, Christopher & Cheesman, E F. (1984) *The Air Defence Of Britain 1914-1918*: Putnam
Douglas, Sholto. (1966) *Years of Command*: Collins
Ege, Lennart. (1973) *Balloons and Airships*: Blandford Press
Falconer, Jonathan. (1993) *RAF Fighter Airfields Of World War Two*: Ian Allan Ltd
Finn, Sid. (1973) *Lincolnshire Air War 1939-1945*: Aero Litho Co
Finn, Sid. (1983) *Lincolnshire Air War 1939–1945 Book Two:* Control Column Publications
Foreman, John. (1985) article 'German Night Intruders': *FlyPast*, Key Publishing Ltd
Foreman, John. (1994) *Air War 1941. The Turning Point. Part 2*: Air Research Publications
Gibson, Michael L. (1980) *Aviation In Northamptonshire*: Northamptonshire Library
Giddings, Malcolm. *RAF Ashbourne*
Goodrum, Alastair. (1997) *Combat Ready!*: GMS Enterprises
Goss, Chris. (1995) article 'Victory Through Air Power': *FlyPast* Special; Key Publishing Ltd

Goss, Chris. (2000) *The Luftwaffe Bombers' Battle Of Britain*: Crécy
Grove, Trevor. (2000) 'Forgotten Heroes, The Boys Who Fell To Earth',
    article 13/3/00: *Daily Mail*
Halley, James J. (1980) *The Squadrons Of The Royal Air Force*: Air Britain
Hancock, Terry. (2004) *Bomber County*: Midland Publishing
Harris, Richard. (1994) *Guy Gibson*: Vickery
Hough, Richard & Richards, Denis. (1989) *The Battle Of Britain*: Hodder
    & Stoughton
Jackson, Robert. (2000) *Air War At Night*: Airlife
Johnson, David. (1981) *V For Vengeance*: Wm Kimber & Co Ltd
Jones, Geoffrey. (1981) *Night Flight*: Wm Kimber & Co Ltd
Latham, Colin & Stobbs, Anne. *Radar, A Wartime Miracle*: Alan Sutton
    Publishing
Longmate, Norman. (1981) *The Doodlebugs*: Hutchinson
Mason, Francis K. (2001) *Hawks Rising, The Story Of 25 Squadron*:
    Air-Britain (Historians) Ltd
Morris, Capt Joseph. (1969) *The German Air Raids On Great Britain 1914-
    1918*: Pordes
Montgomery, Peter. (1969) 'Fighter Command's Air Gunners': *Aircraft
    Illustrated* June 1969
Nowarra, Heinz. (1980) *Heinkel He111, A Documentary History*: Jane's
    Publishing Co Ltd
Parry, Simon. (1987) *Intruders Over Britain*: Air Research
Poolman, Kenneth. (1960) *Zeppelins Over England*: Evans Brothers Ltd
Price, Alfred. (1974) *Aircraft Profile No.261 Do217 Variants*: Profile
    Publications
Price, Alfred. (1991) *Pictorial History Of The Luftwaffe*: Airlife
Pritchard, David. (1989) *The Radar War. Germany's Pioneering
    Achievement 1904-1945*: Patrick Stephens
Ramsey, Winston G, Editor. (1980) *The Battle Of Britain Then And Now*:
    Battle Of Britain Prints International Ltd
Ramsey, Winston G, Editor. (1987) *The Blitz Then And Now Vols 1-3*: After
    The Battle.
Robertson, Bruce. (1987) *British Military Aircraft Serials*: Midland
    Counties Publications
Shaw, Michael. (1986) *No.1 Squadron*: Ian Allan Ltd
Shores, Christopher & Williams, Clive. (1994) *Aces High*: Grub Street
Shores, Christopher. (2004) *Those Other Eagles*: Grub Street
Smith, Peter J C. (2004) *Flying Bombs Over The Pennines*: Smith
Storey, Neil R. (2001) *The North Norfolk Coast*: Sutton Publishing Ltd
Terraine, John. (1997) *The Right Of The Line*: Wordsworth Editions
Thetford, Owen. (1957) *Aircraft Of The Royal Air Force Since 1918*:
    Putnam
Whitehouse, Arch. (1978) *The Zeppelin Fighters*: New English Library
Wynn, Kenneth G. (1989) *Men Of The Battle Of Britain*: Gliddon Books

Various issues of:
Air Link: Journal Of The Lincolnshire Aviation Society
Flypast (by kind permission of the editor and Key Publishing Ltd)
Lincolnshire Free Press
Lincolnshire Standard
Lynn News & Advertiser
Peterborough Advertiser
Skegness Standard
Spalding Guardian

Records, including the following, held by the National Archives (PRO), Kew and MOD (Air Historical Branch) London have been consulted:

Accident record cards (Forms AM1180)
AIR class 22 for crashed E/A intelligence reports (AIR22/266)
AIR class 27 for Squadron Operations Record Books (RAF Form 540)
e.g. 29 Squadron ORB Form 540 (AIR27/341)
AIR class 28 for Station Operations Record Books e.g. Wittering
    (AIR28/950)
AIR class 50 for Combat Records. e.g. 25 Squadron (AIR50/13)
AI 1(g) and AI 1(k) air intelligence reports from various classes e.g. AIR
    2/8735; AIR 22/266; AIR40/2429.

Index

NAMES
Adams, Flt Lt Jack 68-9
Adams, Sqn Ldr 47
AEG-Mayer 109
Aikens, Sqn Ldr 84
Aitken, Wg Cdr Max 130
Alington, Sqn Ldr William 142-3
Allan, 2/Lt D 36
Allen, Michael 86
Altmeyer, Fw 57
Amberger, Fw Karl 13
Anderson, Flt Sgt 157
Anderson, Plt Off Donald 71
Arnim, Oblt Joachim von 15-6
Arnscheid, Uffz H 139
Ashworth, Sgt Jack 71
Atcherley, Gp Capt Richard 84
Atcherley, Wg Cdr David 106-7, 120
Auer, Uffz L 80

Bachfelden, Lt Alfred von 58
Bahner, Uffz Helmut 120
Bahr, Fw 48
Bainbridge, Sgt Bill 123
Ballantyne, Flt Lt 128, 136
Ballas-Andersen, Fg Off Konstantine 18
Banister, Fg Off James 157
Barbour, Fg Off R L J 155
Barnett, Plt Off S S 81
Barratt, Sgt 153
Barritt, Plt Off Roy 16
Beale, Sgt Albert 57, 121, 123, 127-8
Bechgaard, Plt Off Ole 90
Bechthold, Ofw V 136
Becker, Uffz Adam 106
Beetz, Obgefr Wilhelm 104
Behnke, Admiral von 28
Bell, AC2 Derek 12-3
Bell, Fg Off Charles 65
Bell, Sgt 82
Bennett, Plt Off G E 143
Bennett, Sgt N O 81
Bennett, Sgt S 104
Bent, Sgt Benjamin 107, 116, 120
Berg, Gefr W 145
Bergemann, Hptmn Hans 92-4
Beul, Uffz Heinrich 8, 20-4
Bevis, Ivan 108
Bichard, Sgt Frederick 17
Birley, Capt G 35-6
Birnie, Plt Off John 157
Blair, Flt Lt Kenneth 43, 45-7, 87, 91, 95, 99

Blucke, Sqn Ldr R 8
Board, Fg Off 153, 155
Böcker, Kptlt Alois 29, 31
Bodenhagen, Ofw R 142
Bodien, Sgt Henry 47-8, 54-5, 57-8, 105-6, 144, 147, 150
Böttner, Uffz Englebert 51-2
Bowen, Dr E G 'Taffy' 10, 41, 103
Bradshaw, Plt Off Chris 140
Braham, Plt Off J R D 'Bob' 66-8, 73, 75-9
Bramley, Sgt T C 'Tosh' 83, 85
Brandon, Sqn Ldr Lewis 11, 148-9
Bredemeier, Gefr H 136
Breithaupt, Kptlt Joachim 31
Bremer, Uffz P 139
Britain, Plt Off Dennis 109, 111, 116, 120, 122, 143
Brochocki, Fg Off Jerzy 154-5
Brooker, Sgt George 144, 147
Broome, LAC Douglas 152
Brotz, Gefr Franz 104
Brown, Flt Sgt V 147
Brown, Lt W 39
Buchanan, Plt Off Jack 71
Buchner, Gefr G 145
Bufton, Fg Off John 17-8
Bufton, Flt Lt Hal 9
Buhl, Fw Heinrich 135
Buttlar-Brandenfels, Kptlt Horst von 27, 30
Byng-Hall, Plt Off Percy 71

Cadbury, Flt Lt Egbert 36, 39
Campbell, Flt Lt Alex 68-9, 75
Capewell, Sgt Samuel 90
Cardnell, Plt Off Charles 17
Carter, Sgt 97
Chard, Sgt H Y 81
Charnock, Sgt Gerard 117
Charrière, Sgt P 164
Cheney, Fg Off Jack 83, 88, 94, 96, 99, 100, 146
Cheropita, Flt Sgt William 151
Cherwell, Lord 41
Chrystall, LAC 16
Clark, Sqn Ldr 153
Clarke, Sgt Nobby 94
Clayton, Aileen 75
Clayton, Sqn Ldr 133
Cleaver, Plt Off Peter 139
Close, Sgt Alan 12
Clymer, Sgt Jerry 94
Cooper, Minnie 107

Copeland, Sgt Percy 43, 50, 59-60
Cox, Eric 162
Cronika, Gefr Rudolf 104
Crossman, Sgt Richard 107, 117, 119
Cunningham, Sgt Andy 90, 150
Curtis, Sgt Frank 104
Cutts, PC 110

Dachschel, Gefr Rudolf 106
Dalton, Plt Off P 151-2
Dalton, WO Neil 151
Darling, Sqn Ldr Donald 55-6, 126
Darycott, Plt Off Frank 90
Davidson, Plt Off J 55-6
Davies, Mr (AID Inspector) 99
Davies, Plt Off Roy 70
Davis, Sgt J 158
Davoud, Wg Cdr Paul 151
Dean, Fg Off 154
Deansley, Flt Lt 55
Denison, Flt Lt Bill 52
Dibbins, Plt Off Douglas 157
Dietrich, Kptlt Max 31, 35
Dixon, Capt Aubrey (de Wilde) 62
Donaldson, Sqn Ldr 150
Donnett, Flt Sgt David 124, 135-6
Douglas, AM Sholto 41, 69
Dowding, ACM Hugh 41-2, 70
Drees, Fw L 136
Drummond, Lt 39
Duke-Woolley, Flt Lt R M 12-6

Eddy, Flt Lt Charlie 157
Edmiston, Plt Off Guy 57
Eichler, Kptlt Franz 34
Elias, Fw Franz 144
Embrey, Gp Capt Basil 91, 128
Everitt, Sgt Geoffrey 72
Eysoldt, Uffz A 148

Fairweather, Sgt Sam 20, 53-4, 60
Fielding, Plt Off Ernest 136
Fielding, Sgt 121
Finn, Sid 133
Fisher, Plt Off G 126, 128-9
Fizel, AC1 Joseph 74
Flemming, Kptlt Hans-Kurt 37
Focke, Gefr Karl 106
Foreman, John 67
Foster, Fg Off W 156
Foulsham, Pte Albert 35
Fox, Sgt 136
Fradley, Sgt William 88
France, AC2 Benjamin 16
Frank, Hptmn 128
Frankenberg, Oblt-s-See Kurt 35
Fraser, Sgt 72
French, Sgt Thomas 76
Freudenreich, Kptlt Max von 37
Friemel, Oblt-s-See Kurt 37
Frischolz, Fw Hermann 130
Fritze, Kptlt Johann 27

Gallagher, Plt Off 90
Gamsecki, Plt Off 154
Gaynor, Lt 36

Gayzler, Plt Off 61
Gazely, Mrs Alice 28
Gazzard, Sgt Royce 123
Geiger, Fw 57
General Airwork Trading 99
General Electric Co (GEC) 86, 89
Genahr, Fw 79
Gersch, Fw Paul 15
Gesshardt, Uffz Willi 79
Gibbens, Lt Heinz 49-50
Gibson, Flt Lt Guy Penrose 74, 76-80, 82
Giddings, Malcolm 160
Gigney, Sgt Horace 117-8
Gilyeat, AC2 Harold 72
Gipson, Mr D 108
Giroud, 2/Lt 163
Glen, Sgt Dave 91
Goate, Percy 28
Godfrey, Flt Sgt E 128-9
Godsmark, Sgt Howard 123
Goodrum, George 114
Gordon-Dean, Fg Off Peter 50
Gorlt, Uffz Erich 104
Gouldstone, Sgt Ronald 69
Goulsbra, Charlie 118
Grace, Sqn Ldr 141, 142, 144
Gramm, Fw Karl 130
Grantham, Plt Off J 156
Green, Sgt Jimmy 97
Gregory, Sgt William 66-7
Grieve, Flt Sgt Thomas 'Jock' 124, 126
Grove, Trevor 14
Gudgeon, Sgt 121
Gunnill, Sgt Joe 90, 96-7
Gundner, Uffz 155
Gussefeld, Fw K-A 138

Hahn, Fw Hans 81
Hamilton, Sgt 'Hammy' 83
Hammelmann, Uffz H 138
Hanbury, Sqn Ldr Bruce 151
Harding, Fg Off Nelson 12
Haresign, Cecil 34
Harman, Air Mech A 39
Harrison, Lt 38
Hartwig, Ofw Artur 137
Haslam, Fg Off Geoff 155
Hauck, Fw Karl 15
Haviland, Plt Off John 62
Heberling, Ogefr K 136
Hellmann, Hptmn R 142
Helmore, Wg Cdr W 85
Hemery, Sgt 164
Herden, Uffz Georg 110-1
Herrmann, Oblt Kurt 51-2
Herrick, Fg Off Michael 21-23, 113, 121
Heuser, Fw Nikolaus 118
Heusser, Ofw F 148
Hewitson, Sgt F 81
Hill, Sgt Arnold 105-6
Hockauff, Uffz 155
Hoffman, Uffz Richard 120
Holborrow, Sgt 81
Hollingsworth, AVM 157
Hollis, Sgt Ernest 105
Hollowell, Sgt Kenneth 107, 117-9

Holt, Sgt S J 81
Hopewell, Sgt James 50
Hoppe, Ogefr A 148
Horrell, Plt Off Jacques 90
Howard, Sgt Arthur 83-4
Hucks, B C 26
Humphries, Plt Off Jack 74, 78
Hunter-Tod, Flt Lt John 106-7, 120
Hutchinson, Sgt John 158-9

Inkster, Flt Lt J 103
Isherwood, Sgt Donald 71-3

Jackson, AC2 Arthur 71, 74
Jackson, Flt Lt Derek 95
Jackson, Violet 107
Jacobson, AC2 Norman 67-9
James, Flt Sgt E S 136-8, 147
James, Sgt Richard 77-80, 82
James, Sgt W P 81
Jee, Sgt Victor 123
Johnson, Sgt Charles 103
Jonas, Sgt D E O 47-8, 54-5
Jones, Geoffrey 163
Jones, Sgt Edwin 70
Jordan, Oblt Ulrich 16

Karasek, LAC Lawrence 12, 16
Kauhardt, Gefr B 58
Keetley, Sgt E 81
Keiser, Oblt H von 79
Keith, Fg Off D 142
Kells, Fg Off Lionel 75
Kerr-Sheppard, Flt Lt 125
Keys, Lt R 39
King-Clarke, Plt Off C 11
Kirton, Fg Off Harry 151
Kitzelmann, Gefr Reinhold 106
Kliem, Uffz 48
Knight, Flt Lt Roland 12
Knight, Sgt Earl 'Tex' 150
Knorr, Uffz 150
Kolecki, Plt Off 94
Kolle, Kptlt Waldemar 38
Körner, Gefr Hans 79
Kreuzer, Uffz A 43
Krisch, Oblt H 48
Krusewitz, Ogefr 150
Kuchler, Ogefr 155
Kunze, Fw H 139

Lammin, Sgt Joseph 123
Lane, Flt Lt Brian 16
Lappage, Charles 107
Laser, Fw 57
Laub, Fw K 138
Laucou, Capt 164
Leckie, Capt Robert 39
Leibrecht, Uffz F 145
Leimer, Ofw Max 13
Lemasson, Sgt 164
Lettenmeir, Fw Wilhelm 109-10
Lilley, Sgt Robert 75, 78
Limbert, Fg Off Johnny 99
Lindner, Uffz Willi 104
Little, Cpl David 11, 15

Loewe, Kptlt Odo 31
Lossnitzer, Kptlt Johannes von 39
Lovell, Plt Off Victor 77-8
Lowndes, Sgt 97
Lynas, Sgt 50

Mackey, Cpl Dennis 9
Maier, Fw Willi 15
Majer, Fw 94
Mallett, Sgt Ronald 73
Mandel, Gefr Hermann 20, 23
Manger, Hptmn Kuno 33, 38-9
Marsh, Plt Off 127
Massenbach, Maj Dietrich von 13
Mastin, Bernard 159-60
Mathy, Kptlt Heinrich 29-31, 35
Mawdesley, Sqn Ldr 94
Maxwell, Sgt Harold 104
Mayer, Fw Peter 120
McAdam, Cpl William 12
McMillan, Flt Lt E L 'Peter' 130-5, 151
McMullen, Flt Lt Desmond 20, 45-7, 53-4,
  59-60
McRitchie, Plt Off Alex 61, 63, 87, 121-3,
  136-8, 147-8
Menage, Sgt Thomas 72
Meyer, Lt B 79
Mills, Sgt Anthony 123
Mills, Tom 162
Mittag, Gefr Johann 104
Montgomery, Peter 48-9
Moody, Flt Lt 126-7
Möring, Lt Hans-Joachim 136
Morrison, Flt Lt 133
Muller, Hptmn 155
Munn, Flt Sgt Wellesley 68, 71-2, 77-8
Mycock, Plt Off James 'Mike' 84, 96, 99-100,
  146

Nairn, Flt Sgt Bill 139
Nettlefield, Fg Off Peter 164
Noble-Campbell, Lt 39
Norman, Bill 131, 135
Nowarra, Heinz 113

O'Beary, Plt Off A E 157
O'Brien, Sqn Ldr J 11, 13-6
Ostaszewski, Flt Lt 94

Paas, Oblt Hans 118
Paine, Flt Sgt James 136
Parker, Flt Lt E 77-8
Parkin, Sgt K 55
Parr, Sgt Douglas 74
Parry, Simon 67
Paton, Plt Off D P 143-4
Pattinson, Plt Off Aberconway 12
Pauer, Uffz H 80
Peacock, Capt G A 133
Pelka, Fg Off Jerzy 154
Pennington, Flt Lt Denis 124, 135-6
Peter, Uffz Heinrich 152
Peterson, Oblt-s-See W 31
Petre, Fg Off G W 'John' 15
Petzold, Uffz Ludwig 152
Pfeiffer, Lt 81

Pfleger, Plt Off 61
Picknett, Plt Off Alan 112-3
Pix, Gefr Helmut 108
Platen-Hallermund, Kptlt Magnus von 27
Pleasance, Sqn Ldr Harold 107, 116, 120, 122, 143
Pochont, Sgt C 164
Podlesch, Uffz Friedrich 108
Popek, Flt Sgt 94
Preston, Sgt 95
Price, Alfred 74
Pulling, Flt Sub-Lt Edward 36

Rayner, Plt Off E 146-7, 150
Reed, Sgt Andrew 64
Reichel, Mons Frantz 28
Reisinger, Gefr Johann 120
Reynat, Gefr B 58
Rhodes, Plt Off Richard 65-9
Richter, Uffz W 58
Ried, Uffz Jakob 120
Riedel, Ofw Georg 152
Roberts, Flt Sgt D 104
Roberts, Sgt Alan 78
Roberts, Sgt Arthur 73-4
Roberts, Sgt Bill 150
Robertson, Flt Lt Colin 127-8
Robertson, Sgt Bob 18
Robinson, Lt Leefe 33
Rodenstein, Uffz 155
Rokitnicki, Sgt 94
Romelt, Ofw T 142
Ross, Sgt 77-9
Roth, Gefr Hans 67
Rucker, Fw 79
Ruckstruh, Ofw G 142
Rüppel, Fw Wilhelm 51
Rusby, Sgt Kenneth 158
Russell, Sgt 81
Ryall, Sgt Derek 79

Sampson, Sgt R 60, 63, 121-2
Sanders, Flt Lt 68
Schludecker, Fw Willi 135
Schramm, Fw Gustav 67
Schrank, Plt Off A E 163
Schrödel, Fw Hans 127
Schulz, Uffz Heinz 120
Seeburg, Maj W 57
Seidel, Oblt H 43
Seidel, Uffz H 80
Sellick, Plt Off G F 112-3
Semlitschka, Uffz 150
Sergeant, Lt F 38
Service, Sgt 65
Severs, George 163
Severs, Mehetabel 163
Severs, Ruth 163
Shepherd, Sgt 131-2, 134-5
Sherman, Sgt J S C 81
Shimeld, Fg Off 153
Sidenberg, Sgt 53
Siegmann, Uffz Rudolf 108
Singleton, Wg Cdr Joseph 102, 140-1, 155
Sisman, Plt Off Peter 64

Skillen, Sgt Victor 68, 72-3
Sly, Sgt Oliver 74
Smith, Flt Lt Roddick 42
Smith, Wg Cdr Irving 42, 45, 59-61, 125-6
Smith, Sgt Jimmy 83
Sommer, Ofw 81
Spangenberg, Gefr Karl-Heinz 79
Stabbert, Kptlt Franz 31, 37
Staples, Sgt Lionel 55
Steele, Plt Off 73
Stevens, Plt Off Richard 18-20, 45, 47, 53, 56-61, 87-8, 121-2
Stevens, Sgt Cyril 17
Stevens, Sgt E C 81
Stevens, Sgt Robert 74
Stewart, Flt Lt C L W 95, 150
Stokoe, Sgt Sydney 72, 76
Stolz-Page, Sgt R G 62
Strasser, Korvettenkapitän Peter 30, 36, 38-9
Stugg, Lt G 79
Stumpf, Fw Richard 136
Sudders, Sgt James 88
Summerfeldt, Kptlt Erich 33
Sweetman, Flt Lt Harvey 130-4

Taylor, Sgt Ken 76
Tempest, 2/Lt W J 35
Thiede, Ofw Alfred 119
Thomas, Plt Off 133
Thomas, Sgt R R 81
Thomas, Uffz Herbert 109-11
Thompson, Fg Off David 109, 112, 116, 119-20
Thompson, Sgt C M 81
Thorogood, Sgt 158
Thun-Hohenstein, Oblt Romedio 138-9
Toifel, Uffz Horst 152
Tricker, Cpl 153
Trukenbrodt, Oblt Gunther 118
Truscott, Sgt 130
Turner, Flt Lt George 89
Tuttle, Flt Lt 152

Uehlemann, Fw 48
Ulrich, Ofw Joseph 130
Usborne, Wg Cdr N F 26
Utikal, Ofw 155

Viel, Aspirant L 164
Völker, Lt Heinz 17-8

Wagner, Sgt Alan 49-50, 53
Wain, Plt Off John 124, 126
Walker, Flt Lt Percy 16
Wallace, Sgt Jack 50
Walther, Uffz Horst 118
Watson, Plt Off Lionel 68, 70
Weber, Uffz Paul 118
Weidner, Ofw V 43
Weise, Ofw Otto 20-1, 23
Welch, Sgt Eric 88
Werner, Fw H 138
Whittome, Sgt Anthony 158-9
Whitty, Flt Lt Bill 18
Widdows, Sqn Ldr Charles 64-5, 70-1, 74-80

Wiess, Oblt Heinrich 130
Wilhelm, Kaiser 25
Willans, Plt Off Derek 12
Williams, Fg Off D 151-2
Willins, Flt Sgt John 76, 141
Wilsden, Sgt Albert 68, 72
Wilson, AC2 Bill 65
Wilson, Cpl Ronald 16
Wilson, Plt Off Len 75-6
Wingfield, Sgt Victor 71, 78
Winlaw, Sqn Ldr R de W K 84
Winn, Flt Lt Charles 75
Witting, Fw A 148
Wolff, Lt 150
Wolpers, Ofw Heinrich 128
Wood, Sgt 85
Woodward, Mr (AID Inspector) 99
Wooton, Fg Off Jimmy 99
Worledge, Sgt George 50
Wrampling, Sgt 57-8
Wreschnick, Lt Joachim 107-8
Wright, Plt Off 126
Wunsche, Flt Sgt 94
Wyrill, Fg Off Hugh 141-2

Yeats, Fg Off 150
Yeomans, Plt Off 8, 21-3

Zenkel, Ofw Fritz 67
Zeppelin, Count Ferdinand von 25
Zickler, Ofw W 43
Ziller, Ofw K 43
Ziolkowski, Fg Off Henryk 154-5
Zumbach, Sqn Ldr Jan 92

PLACE NAMES
Aachen 154
Adderley 88
Ailsworth 162
Aire, Point of 73-4
Aldeburgh 107-8
Aldwincle St Peter 90
Amiens (prison) 148
Amsterdam/Schipol 67, 93
Anwick Grange 163
Ashbourne and Darley Moor   157-9
Auckland 130
Authorpe 118

Bacton 27
Ballyhalbert 91, 123, 140
Banbury 56
Barkston Towers 84
Barrow in Furness 57
Bassingbourn 18
Bassingham (bombing range)   157
Beck Row 81
Bedford 37, 65, 135, 147
Beeston (Notts) 9
Belfast 57, 106
Berlin 30, 154
Bicester 56
Bircham Newton 73, 119
Bircham, Great 118, 120
Birmingham 9, 31, 35, 38, 48-50, 52, 54-6, 73,

104, 117, 119, 135-6, 162
Biscay, Bay of 100
Black Buoy Sand 81
Blakeney Creek 13, 16, 58
Boothby Graffoe 150
Boston 31, 37, 57, 82, 111, 114-5, 130, 143-4,
    159
Botany Bay (Cambs) 162
Bourne (Lincs) 81, 106, 114, 140, 162
Bramcote (Warks) 44, 54
Brawdy 163
Bredstedt 9
Brentwood 47
Bremen 81
Brest 81, 93, 100
Bridlington 162
Buckminster 30, 32, 35, 38
Burghley (Park) 104, 118
Burton on Trent 31
Buxton 31

Cambridge 15-6, 37, 139
Cannock Chase 138
Canvey Island 47
Carrington (Lincs) 111
Castor 162
Catterick 84
Chapel St Leonards 42
Chatham 57
Chester 66-7
Chichester 105
Church Fenton 65, 83-5, 88, 91, 97, 99, 122,
    140, 142, 146, 155, 161
Clacton 147
Coleby Grange 97, 103, 129, 132, 151-4, 156
Colerne 148, 150
Collyweston 9, 11, 90, 103
Coltishall 58, 61, 66, 95, 98, 121-3, 127, 129-
    30, 135-6, 139, 143, 151
Coningsby 139, 158-60
Conington 138
Corby 35, 48
Cottesmore 81
Coveney Fen 157
Coventry 19-20, 38-9, 52-3, 56, 73-5, 89
Cowbit 140
Cranfield 89-90
Cranwell 32, 38, 70
Creaton (Northants) 160
Cromer 27, 29, 31, 35, 45-6, 65, 67, 117, 136,
    155
Crowland 88
Cuffley 33
Cuxhafen 27

Debden 17, 64, 103
Deeping St James 22, 24
Derby 9, 31, 43, 48, 105-6, 159
Desford 19
Dieppe (raid) 138
Digby 8, 10, 16, 18, 42, 50, 58, 64-6, 68, 70-2,
    74-8, 80, 82, 101, 103, 108-9, 116, 141,
    147, 152, 154
Dinard/Pleurtuit 92-3
Donna Nook 78
Downham Market 31, 33

Dowsby 34
Dowsing, Inner light 69
Dungeness 37
Düsseldorf 154
Duxford 16, 59, 147

Easington (CHL) 142
East Kirkby 111, 157
East Walton Wood 142
Elvington 163
Ely 29, 31, 115, 157
Everingham 85
Évreaux 159

Fakenham 58
Filton 103
Fleam Dyke 15-6
Fleet Fen 131-2, 134
Floods Ferry 162
Folkestone 37
Ford 71, 149
Forest Farm LG 84
Fosdyke 113
Fowlmere 59
Freiston 38
Fring 145
Friskney Church End 163
Fuhlsbuttel 27-8

Gainsborough 16
Gat Sand 113
Gedney Hill 104
Gibraltar Point 69
Gillingham 60
Gilze-Rijen 20, 43, 104, 109, 135
Glasgow 79
Goole 96
Gosberton (Fen) 30, 34
Grantham 31, 46, 58, 73, 75-6, 108, 147
Gravesend 60
Great Yarmouth 28-30, 32, 36, 39, 46, 63, 115, 122-4, 151
Grimsby 27, 31, 68, 77, 115
Grimsthorpe (Park) 81
Grimston 27

Hamburg 27
Happisburgh (CHL) 31, 122, 126, 137, 155
Harling Road (Norfolk) 32
Harwich 37
Hastings 37, 68
Heacham 27
Helpston 16
Henlow 24
Heston 150
Hibaldstow 92, 94-5, 97-9, 129, 150
Holbeach (Marsh) 32, 37, 131-2, 163
Holbeach St Mark's 81
Holme next the Sea 37
Holme-on-Spalding-Moor 157
Holt 58, 105-6
Holywell 81
Honiley 141
Honington 11
Horncastle 92
Horwich (Lancs) 92-3

Hoylake 70-1
Hull 58-9, 78, 94, 108, 153, 155
Hunsdon 61, 87
Hunstanton 27, 29, 31, 33, 40

Ipswich 37, 52, 141
Irthlingborough 162

Juvisy 157

Kamen 163
Karlsruhe 157
Kettering 56-7, 160, 162
Ketton 50
Kidderminster 31
Kidlington 83, 91
King's Lynn 12, 27-9, 31, 33, 51, 81, 107, 115, 119-20, 142, 144-5, 152
King's Norton 54
Kirton Fen 159
Kirton in Lindsey 44, 65, 78, 92, 94-5
Kleves 9
Knutsford 111

Ladbergen 163
Land's End 93
Langham (Norfolk) 117
Langham (Rutland) 104
Langtoft GCI 62, 101-2, 106, 108, 112, 122, 141-2, 144, 149
Lanveoc/Poulmic 93
Leadenham 32, 35-6
Leeds 35
Leeming 78
Leeuwarden 117
Legbourne 155
Leicester 38, 75-6, 115
Leverton 151
Lille-Roubaix 11
Lincoln 31, 94, 103, 112, 114-5, 129, 150-1, 163
Lissett 163
Little Bytham 81
Liverpool 30, 32, 57-9, 70, 73, 78, 88, 107
London 25, 27-30, 32-5, 37-8, 47, 51, 57, 59-60, 82, 113, 153
Long Sutton 120
Lorient 17
Loughborough 99
Louth 79, 155
Lowestoft 31, 151, 159
Lübeck 124
Luffenham 62

Mablethorpe 17, 77-8, 97, 143
Man, Isle of 93
Manchester 18, 32, 51, 82, 160
Mannheim 81
March 33, 108, 128, 162
Marham 11, 32, 36, 38, 81
Market Deeping 21, 88
Market Drayton 88
Mathy Wood 162
Mattishall 32, 39
Melton Mowbray 30
Merville 11

Metheringham Fen 161
Middle Wallop 77
Middlesborough 30
Mildenhall 11, 49, 81
Moorby (POW camp) 139
Moulton (Lincs) 162
Moulton Chapel (Lincs) 133
Mundesley 33
Murcott 56

Narborough (Norfolk) 32, 120
Narford 120
Navenby 156
Neatishead GCI 101, 125, 127, 135-7, 140,
    149-50, 155
Nene Valley 162
Newark 33, 65
Newcastle 29
Newmarket 14-5, 29
Newton 107
Nordholz 27, 35, 39
Northampton 37-8
Northborough 23
Northolt 9
North Weald 103
Norwich 28, 30-1, 101, 115, 127, 151
Nottingham 32, 35, 62

Ongar Hill 152
Orby GCI 21, 78, 101, 103, 107-8, 116-7, 119,
    132, 134, 152-5
Orfordness 52
Orwell (Cambs) 147
Oulton 163
Oundle 35
Oxford 56, 83

Paris 28
Patrington GCI 150, 155
Pembrey 52
Pembroke Dock 52
Peterborough 17, 35, 37, 39, 61, 114-5, 136-8,
    141, 157, 162-4
Pinchbeck, West 162
Plymouth 51
Potters Bar 35

Ramsey 37
Rauceby 73, 76
Redhill 71
Rennes 136
Revesby 139
Rivington 93
Rostock 124
Rothwell Lodge 57
Rouen 156
Royston 61
Rugby 160

Sandringham 27-8
Scampton 17
Scunthorpe 31, 92
Sharrington 58, 105-6
Shawbury 74
Sheffield 32, 35, 79
Sheringham 46, 121

Shernborne 145
Shrewsbury 31
Six Mile Bottom 15
Skegness 17, 22, 31, 33, 37, 39-40, 42, 69, 71-
    2, 77-8, 80, 101, 116, 118, 143-4, 153-5,
    161, 163
Sleaford 31-2, 35, 73, 76, 103, 150, 157, 163
Smethwick 55
Snettisham 27
Soesterberg 130
Southend 61
South Reston 118
Spalding 8-9, 30-1, 34, 36-7, 46, 73, 83, 85,
    89, 104, 112-7, 120, 131, 140, 143, 162-3
Spilsby 92, 155-6
Spurn Point 66
St Athan 71, 74-5
St David's Head 93
Stamford 31-2, 35, 37-9, 47, 50, 89, 91, 118,
    143
Stavanger 21
Stiffkey 117
Stocken Hall (Rutland) 162
Stoke on Trent 31
Stowgate 88
Surfleet (Fen) 30, 34
Sutton Bridge 12-3, 18, 31, 46, 78, 112, 116-
    7, 120, 151-2
Sutton on Sea 37
Swaffham 75
Swanton Morley 90-1

Tangmere 105
Tathwell 79
Ternhill 65-7, 69-72, 74
Terrington Marsh (Q-site) 151
Terrington St Clement 12-3, 51, 81, 112, 151
Thetford 32
Thorney (Cambs) 136
Thrapston 56
Thurlby 162
Tilstock 164
Tunbridge Wells 60
Tydd St Mary 32, 38

Ufford 91
Upwood 33, 122

Waddington 45, 79, 97, 163
Wainfleet 69
Warwick 75
Waterbeach 81
Watton 50
Weldon 48
Wellesbourne 19
Wellingore (Hall) 42, 44, 64-5, 68, 73, 76-7
Wells-next-the-Sea 29, 31, 33, 39, 79, 116,
    121
Welney Wash 107, 157
West Malling 82, 89
West Raynham 116
Weybourne 57
Whaplode Drove 131
Whitewater Lake 89, 95
Whittlesey 157
Whitwell (Herts) 56

Wickenby 156
Wight, Isle of 68
Wilhemshaven 29
Windsor Great Park 20, 56
Winterton 45-6
Wisbech 31, 37, 117, 151, 162
Witchford 157
Withyham 60
Wittering 8-9, 12-4, 16-24, 32, 42, 44-50, 52-
    63, 65, 69-73, 75, 83, 85-8, 90-2, 95-9,
    101, 103-4, 106, 109, 112-3, 116, 121-31,
    133, 135-41, 144, 147-8, 150-1, 164
Wolverhampton 31
Woodford (Kettering) 162
Woodvale 141
Woolwich Arsenal 62
Wooton 119
Wrexham 88, 141
Wyton 8

York 9

Zuider Zee 8

UNITS
1 Sqn 61
1 School of Army Co-op 62
6 OTU 18, 62
7 SFTS 83
9 Group 141
11 Group 86
11 OTU 18
12 Group 9, 77, 86, 94, 97-8, 140-1
14 OTU 81
19 Sqn 11, 16
23 Sqn 9-11, 16-7, 71, 113
25 Sqn 17, 21, 23, 82, 91, 99, 102-3, 105-9,
    112-3, 116-7, 119-20, 122-3, 140, 142-3,
    146, 155, 161
29 Sqn 11, 64, 67, 69-71, 74-5, 77-8, 82, 103
38 Sqn 30, 32, 34-5, 38
38 Group HQ 157
42 OTU 157
44 Sqn 97
49 Sqn 17
51 Sqn 32, 35-6, 38-9
51 OTU 89, 95
54 OTU 78, 83, 99, 102
56 OTU 116
57 Sqn 156-7
58 MU 131, 133
66 Sqn 11
68 Sqn 98, 129-30, 139, 143
71 Sqn 44
74 Sqn 11
76 Sqn 157
79 Sqn 52
85 Sqn 87
90 Sqn 30
96 Sqn 141
99 Sqn 81
101 Sqn 156
115 Sqn 81, 156
141 Sqn 150
149 Sqn 81
151 Sqn 18-20, 42-5, 47, 49-51, 53, 56-9, 61,
    62-3, 87, 89-90, 103-5, 113, 121-5, 127-9,
    136, 144, 146-50
157 Sqn 149
158 Sqn 163
214 Sqn 163
229 Sqn 16, 64
234 Sqn 16
253 Sqn 88, 92
255 Sqn 141
256 Sqn 55, 88, 141
264 Sqn 155
266 Sqn 57
302 Sqn 24
303 Sqn 92, 94
307 Sqn 153-4
312 Sqn 74
347 Sqn 163
409 Sqn 103, 129, 131-2, 151, 153
410 Sqn 151, 156
466 Sqn 163
486 Sqn 90-1, 95, 129-31, 133-4
532 Sqn 95, 98-9, 129, 146, 150
538 Sqn 97-8, 129
600 Sqn 71
604 Sqn 11
615 Sqn 68
616 Sqn 91
1422 Flight 150
1451 Flight 86
1453 Flight 61, 85-7, 89, 92, 95, 129, 146
1459 Flight 92, 129
1529 BAT Flight 90
1654 CU 157
1665 HCU 164
Central Gunnery School 151-2
Fliegercorp IX 151
KG1 49, 56, 79, 106
KG2 48, 79, 124, 127-8, 134-40, 142, 144-6,
    150-2, 155-6
KG3 47, 161
KG4 11, 57, 117
KG6 151
KG26 136
KG27 11, 55, 119
KG28 59
KG30 20, 57, 155
KG40 130, 134, 148
KG51 156-7, 159
KG53 43, 47, 58, 60, 161
KG55 56-7, 59-60, 67-8
KG77 54, 107
KG100 155
KuFlGr106 92
KuFlGr606 88
KuFlGr806 106
NJG1 67
NJG2 8, 17, 20, 51, 67, 79, 81-2, 104, 108,
    119-20, 163
NJG3 163
NJG4 163
NJG5 163
USAAF, 2nd Air Div 157
WIDU 8-9

Ro